The Reading Portfolio

The Reading Portfolio

Diane Perotti Bosco

Suffolk County Community College

Janice Anselmo Buchner

Suffolk County Community College

Houghton Mifflin Company   Boston   New York

Senior Sponsoring Editor: Mary Jo Southern
Associate Editor: Kellie Cardone
Senior Development Editor: Martha Bustin
Senior Project Editor: Fred Burns
Senior Production/Design Coordinator: Carol Merrigan
Manufacturing Manager: Florence Cadran
Senior Marketing Manager: Nancy Lyman

Cover design and image: Dutton & Sherman

Acknowledgments for reprinted material appear starting on page 319.

Printed in the U.S.A.

Library of Congress Catalog Number: 00-133843

Student Edition ISBN: 0-395-96703-1

Instructor's Edition ISBN: 0-395-96704-X

1 2 3 4 5 6 7 8 9—QUF—04 03 02 01 00

Brief Contents

Contents

Preface

The Reading Portfolio was written to address the needs of the first-level college reading student. Central to the approach of this text are our beliefs that

1. Literacy instruction should exist within meaningful context; and
2. Meaning is constructed by the reader.

Building from these ideas, *The Reading Portfolio* places concise reading instruction within the context of interesting and timely thematic units. The exercises and reading selections within each chapter explore a real life issue of interest to students. The chapters on unstated main ideas and chronological pattern of organization, for example, consider risk-taking behavior and career choices, respectively.

In addition, *The Reading Portfolio* offers a variety of activities that encourage students to extend their writing and critical thinking skills—that is, to see meaning as something which they themselves actively construct. Throughout the text, portfolio activities in particular allow students to show their effort, progress, and achievement and to make connections as they learn. All of the activities in *The Reading Portfolio* may be assessed by either traditional means, by the use of a portfolio approach, or by a combination of these methods. While its primary focus is reading, this text recognizes, through the range of its activities, the interrelation of reading, writing, speaking, and listening skills. It encourages students to pursue development of these interrelated skills. In this way, students can truly enhance their literacy skills and become lifelong readers, instead of reluctant readers.

Text Features

- **Thematic organization and holistic approach to reading.** Each of the book's five units—The Reading Process, Vocabulary Strategies, Main Ideas, Patterns of Organization, and Reading Critically—explores a theme throughout its chapters' exercises and readings. The unit themes are relationships, heroism, fear, social issues, and the search for truth. These themes make the skills-building activities and reading selections coherent and relevant for the student. Students expand their knowledge and develop their reading skills in context.
- **Current, high-interest readings.** Interesting, relevant, and readable selections have been chosen from a wide variety of contemporary sources, including the Internet. Selections include, "Joe Foss" by Tom Brokaw; "Gift

of Fear" by Gavin DeBecker; "Making a Job Search Plan" by Bob Adams; and "Downsize Your Debt" by Glinda Bridgeforth.

- **Focus on the reading process.** Reading is presented as a process in which the student actively participates. *Before, during,* and *after* reading strategies encourage students to activate their background knowledge, create a purpose for reading, and monitor their understanding of a selection. The chapters of *The Reading Portfolio* are organized to model the reading process using the *before, during,* and *after* reading strategies.
- **Application of strategies.** Reading skills and strategies such as finding the main idea, identifying supporting details, understanding text patterns, and defining vocabulary in context are developed and reinforced throughout the text.
- **Vocabulary concepts.** Vocabulary is presented before reading with the "Words to Preview" feature and after reading through the "Word Connections" feature. Students are asked to go beyond a word's definition to complete word maps and concept of definition maps, to use word parts, or to explain a concept.
- **Critical thinking connections through portfolio opportunities.** In each chapter, portfolio activities guide students in applying critical thinking skills and integrating ideas in writing and in class discussions.
- **Collaborative work.** Each chapter contains a collaborative activity that allows students to explore the theme of the chapter and work on developing skills together.
- **Graphic organizers.** Each chapter and unit ends with a summary in the form of a graphic organizer, giving students a visual representation of the skills and strategies presented.
- **Appendix.** Forms or charts used by the student are provided in the appendix to minimize duplication needs.
- **Limited answer key.** Students have a limited answer key so that they may self-assess their responses.

Organization

All units and chapters of *The Reading Portfolio* are organized using a clear, easy-to-follow pattern.

Unit structure: The five units are organized as follows. Units begin with

1. **Unit Introduction:** A quotation and several paragraphs that establish the unit's theme.
2. **Unit Overview:** A brief description of the reading skills and strategies to be covered.
3. **Unit Objectives:** A list of the strategies that students will learn by completion of the unit.

Units end with

4. **Unit Review:** A summary of the reading strategies that have been presented within the unit.

5. **Unit Summary Graphic Organizer:** A visual representation of how the reading strategies covered in the unit relate to one another.

6. **Unit Portfolio Suggestion:** An additional activity for the student's portfolio.

Chapter structure: The fourteen chapters of *The Reading Portfolio* are organized as follows:

1. **Chapter introduction:** A quotation and several paragraphs introduce the chapter's theme. The chapter theme is related to the unit theme. Students are encouraged to activate their background knowledge about the theme.

2. **Chapter objectives and a "Focus On" section:** Chapter objectives state the particular strategies that students will learn by the completion of each chapter. "Focus On" sections provide a clear and concise explanation of each reading strategy and skill, modeled for better understanding.

3. **Short exercises:** These activities provide students an opportunity to practice and evaluate their understanding of the strategy.

4. **Reading selections:** This section gives students an opportunity to apply the reading strategies they have learned to three authentic, thematically linked selections. These readings may be in the form of a short essay, an article, a poem, or an excerpt from a book. Related exercises and support apparatus include:

   - **Before Reading** (strengthens the practice of previewing a selection);
   - **Words to Preview** (provides the definition and part of speech of unfamiliar words);
   - **During Reading** (a consistent reminder to readers to predict, visualize, and monitor comprehension as they read);
   - **After Reading** (provides the reader with an opportunity to evaluate and recall and review the selection);
   - **Word Connections** (vocabulary questions pertaining to words found in the selection; students may be required to complete a word map, fill in a concept of definition map, or explain the concept of a word); and
   - **Connecting Meaning** (asks questions to help the student evaluate his or her understanding of the selection; the questions also help to review and recall important information).

5. **Portfolio Activities:** A variety of engaging activities promote critical thinking skills:

   - **Integrating Ideas** (allows students to connect new concepts to those they already know);

- **Extending Concepts** (provides an opportunity to integrate reading and writing);
- **Collaborative Activity** (affords an opportunity for students to work with peers); and
- **Additional Portfolio Suggestion** (furnishes a chance for students to be creative in their class work).

6. **Chapter Summary Graphic Organizer.** This feature gives students a visual representation of the strategies covered and establishes a model for a student's own use of graphic organizers.

Ancillary Materials

- **Instructor's Annotated Edition** The annotated instructor's edition is identical to the student text, but includes all answers printed directly on the pages where questions occur.
- **Instructor's Manual** An instructor's manual provides additional hints for teaching each chapter, and is bound into the back of the Instructor's Annotated Edition.
- **Test Bank** This supplement features a multiple-choice quiz on the reading strategies presented in each chapter. Each unit has an additional reading not printed in the student text to use for assessment purposes.

Acknowledgments

We wish first to thank our students—they are at the heart of this book and are a constant source of inspiration.

We are also grateful to those who reviewed our manuscript. Their many excellent ideas, comments, and suggestions have made this a better book. We gratefully acknowledge:

Bill Morris, *College of the Redwoods*

Judith Olson-Fallon, *Case Western Reserve University*

Candace R. Ready, *Piedmont Technical College*

Pat Rottmund, *Harrisburg Area Community College*

Nancy E. Smith, *Florida Community College at Jacksonville*

Jane Weber, *Camden County College*

Paul Wolford, *Walters State Community College*

Donna Wood, *State Technical Institute at Memphis*

We are especially indebted to our sponsoring editor, Mary Jo Southern, for her enthusiastic support of this project; to Martha Bustin, our development editor, for her valuable editorial insights; to our marketing manager Nancy Lyman, for her expertise and creativity, and to Fred Burns, Carol Merrigan, and Florence Cadran, who have helped bring this text successfully through the production and manufacturing process.

Finally, we are grateful to our families for their unending encouragement and support. Thank you Vinny, Christina, and Daniel. Without you, none of this would be possible. Thank you Rich, Eric, Mom, Dad, and Diana for your inspiration and heartfelt support.

Diane Perotti Bosco

Janice Anselmo Buchner

■ ■ ■ ■ To the Student

What is a Portfolio?

A portfolio is a collection of pieces that showcases your work. Many instructors will ask you to collect your course work in a portfolio that will show your effort, progress, and achievement. Throughout this text, you will find suggestions of items that you may include in your portfolio. These recommendations will relate the theme and strategies presented in each unit.

In most cases, choosing what goes into your portfolio is an individual decision. One student may place several reading journal entries, a reading log, a literacy autobiography, and a special report in the portfolio. Another student may choose to include test scores, comprehension strategies, self-assessment notes, and a tape of an oral reading. Though some items may be included at the request of the instructor, most will reflect your own choices.

Choosing what to include gives you an opportunity to evaluate your growth as a reader and writer. You create a window into your learning and make connections across reading, writing, and thinking. The ongoing process of assembling your portfolio is at least as important as the finished product.

The Reading Process

Theme of Readings: *Relationships*

No man is an island.

JOHN DONNE

■ ■ ■ ■ ■ Relationships

In *Reaching Out*, David Johnson states, "From the moment we are born to the moment we die, relationships are the core of our existence. We are conceived with relationships, are born into relationships, and live our lives within relationships." We have no choice: we depend on others for food, shelter, education, love, fun, and identity. Life becomes a series of interactions that begin with the first people we know, our families. With growth, relationships change and evolve. We become acquaintances, friends, coworkers, lovers, and spouses. These and other relationships affect our everyday lives.

The readings in this unit explore relationships on a variety of levels. Family, friends, and lovers form the most basic relationships. Some relationships may be simple, stable, and easy to maintain; others may be complicated, short-lived, or filled with ups and downs. Each of you has, by now, experienced many relationships. As you read, compare your own experiences with those presented in the readings. An author is trying to establish a relationship with you, the reader, in order to share thoughts and experiences. By connecting your experiences with those the author writes about, you will construct meaning and understanding. This relationship forms the basis of the reading process.

■ ■ ■ ■ ■ The Reading Process

What is reading? People often think of it as an important part of life, an enjoyable activity, an essential skill. These points are all true, but there is another valuable way to consider reading—the process by which a reader constructs meaning from text. Constructing meaning is making sense of what you read. Meaning does not come from the author alone. You, the reader, must be an active participant in the process; you bring your language, thoughts, experiences, and knowledge to the text as you build meaning. Because each of us is different, no two readers will ever produce the exact same meaning from a given text. No reader's meaning will ever be exactly the same as the author's meaning.

When does the process of reading begin? Most students think that reading starts as their eyes hit the first word of the first paragraph. In fact, the reading process begins before this point. An effective reader uses strategies before actually reading the body of the text. These strategies help make sense of the text. They include

- previewing the text,
- thinking about what you know about the topic, and
- establishing a purpose for reading.

The process continues while you are reading. As an active, involved reader, you are

- making predictions about the text,
- confirming these predictions,
- visualizing the material, and
- monitoring your comprehension.

After you read the text, the reading process still goes on. You take additional steps to evaluate your understanding of the reading by

- deciding if you have met your purpose for reading,
- questioning your understanding of the text,
- recalling important information, and
- relating information you have read to your own knowledge or experience with the subject.

What you, the reader, do after reading is just as important as what you do before and during reading.

To be an effective reader, you must incorporate *before, during,* and *after* reading strategies into the reading process. Unit I addresses each of these areas.

Unit Objectives

After completing the unit, you will be able to

1. **Understand reading as a process involving both the author and the reader.**

2. **Construct meaning by applying *before*, *during*, and *after* reading strategies.**

1

Before Reading

Theme of Readings: Families

While we try to teach our children all about life, our children teach us what life is all about.
ANGELA SCHWINDT

Families

Father, mother, sister, brother, grandmother, grandfather, uncle, aunt, niece, nephew, cousin are all terms for people who make up our family. Families are groups related by blood, marriage, adoption, or some other long-term relationship or living arrangements. The underlying purpose of a family is often the raising and nurturing of children. Children represent renewal and the cycle of life beginning again. They bring love, laughter, tears, and stress in the best and worst of families. But other factors form strong bonds, too: shared enterprises, stories, histories, the intertwining of relationships, and commitments to common needs and goals.

These days, the traditional structure of a mother, a father, two children, and a dog is no longer the typical American family. Single parent families, same-sex couples, unmarried couples who live together, and blended groups from divorced parents are also families. However "family" is defined, it remains a fundamental element in society, important to each of us individually and as part of the larger, social whole.

Chapter Objectives

After completing this chapter, you will be able to

1. **Preview the reading.**

2. **Connect your knowledge to the author's ideas.**

3. **Establish a purpose for reading.**

Focus on *Before Reading* Strategies

A good athlete knows that before you begin a workout you must warm up. Your muscles need to stretch, and your mind needs to focus on whatever sport you are about to play. These activities will maximize your performance. Before you start to read, you also need to "warm up" your brain. You have to focus your attention on the task at hand and start thinking about what you are going to read. Focus your attention before reading by

- previewing the material,
- thinking about what you know about the topic, and
- establishing a purpose for reading.

These strategies will maximize your reading performance.

Before you read, you need to become familiar with the ideas presented by the author or authors. You can get a sense of what the reading is about by previewing it as follows: First, read the title. Does the title tell you what the topic is? If not, does the title give you any clues or hints? From the clues given, can you make a prediction about the topic? For example, looking at a book by Rudolf Dreikurs, Pearl Cassel, and David Kehoe titled *Discipline without Tears*, you might predict it to be about dealing with children who misbehave. Another person may predict that it is about the personal discipline necessary for success.

After you have thought about the title, scan the chapter titles, and read the information given on the book jacket. For a shorter reading, such as an article, essay, or short story, scan the reading. Are there any headings that can give information about the topic? If there are no headings to preview, look at the first and last paragraphs and glance at the first sentences of the other paragraphs. Was your prediction about the topic correct?

After scanning *Discipline without Tears*, you would find the book to be about strategies for dealing with a wide range of childhood misbehaviors. Think about what you know about the topic. What experiences have you had with this topic in your reading, in the media, or in your life? By starting to think about what you know, you start to connect with the author.

Once you have finished scanning and predicting, establish a purpose for reading. Ask yourself, "Why am I reading this particular chapter, article, or essay?" Are you looking for an understanding of information? For example, you may read the daily newspaper to understand a local community issue better. If you are assigned a reading for a college course, your purpose might be understanding the information taught in that course.

You may read for purposes other than gaining knowledge: you may read for entertainment or to explore an argument and perhaps change your opinion. An article about your favorite hobby would be entertaining but an article discussing two opposing views of gun control might lead you to explore the argument and change or strengthen your opinion. Your purpose depends on what you are reading and why you are reading it.

By previewing, connecting your knowledge, and setting a purpose for reading, you will be a more effective reader. All three *before reading* strategies work together so that you will construct the most understanding of your reading.

■ ■ ■ ■ Short Exercises: *Before Reading* Strategies

Predicting the Topic

Directions: Read the following titles and write your prediction about the topic.

1. *Adoption without Fear* by James L. Gritter

   _____

   _____

   _____

2. *Dr. Tightwad's Money-Smart Kids* by Janet Bodnar

   _____

   _____

   _____

3. "Rethinking the American Family" by Lauren Tarshis

   _____

   _____

   _____

4. *Three Steps to a Strong Family* by Linda Eyre, Richard Eyre, and Stephen Covey

   _____

   _____

   _____

5. "Dining Together Strengthens Ties" *USA Today Magazine*

   _____

   _____

   _____

6. "All In The Family" by John Bingham in *Runner's World*

_____

_____

_____

7. *The Shelter of Each Other: Rebuilding Our Families* by Mary Bray Pipher

_____

_____

_____

8. "Today's Stepmother: Myths and Realities" *Ebony Magazine*

_____

_____

_____

9. *Family Abuse: A National Epidemic* by Marie Hong

_____

_____

_____

10. *The ABC's of Parenting* by Anthony P. Witham, Debbie Hansen, and Jeff Maniglia

_____

_____

_____

Thinking about the Topic

Directions: List what comes to mind when you think about the following topics.

Example: If the topic is *discipline*, the following thoughts may come to mind: My mother sent me to my room when I misbehaved; children need some kind of discipline; spanking is a controversial issue.

1. Curfews

   _____

   _____

2. Sibling rivalry

   _____

   _____

3. Effects of divorce

   _____

   _____

4. Aging parents

   _____

   _____

5. Family vacations

   _____

   _____

6. Adult children returning home

   _____

   _____

7. Changing family structure

   _____

   _____

8. Right to privacy

   _____

   _____

9. Family values

   _____

   _____

10. Managing family money

   _____

   _____

Reading Selections

Selection 1

Brick by Brick

BILL SHORE

Before Reading

Before you read the story, "Brick by Brick," predict what the topic may be. Scan the reading to see if you have correctly predicted the topic. Look at the first and last paragraphs, and glance at the first sentences of the other paragraphs. Think about the topic and relate what you know to "Brick by Brick." Set a purpose for reading this story. Do you expect to be entertained, to gain knowledge, or to explore an argument?

Note: A list of the parts of speech, their definitions, and the abbreviations used for each part of speech listed in the Words to Preview section is found in Appendix A.

Word to Preview   **manifest**   *(v.)* to show or demonstrate plainly

For years I worked in politics, a career choice that required long hours and a lot of traveling. When Senator Bob Kerrey ran for President in 1992, for example, I helped on his campaign and spent a great deal of time away from my wife, Bonnie, and our two young children, Zach and Mollie.

After the campaign, I came home to learn an important lesson about balancing a career and family, about what kids really need from a dad—and about the building and dismantling of walls.

Shortly before Mollie's third birthday, I had just returned from a series of long trips with the Senator, some of which had lasted six or seven days, with only a quick stop at home to change laundry.

Mollie and I were driving through our Silver Spring, Md., neighborhood on the way back from the grocery store when, from her car seat in the back, she said, "Dad, what street is your house on?"

"What?" I thought I hadn't heard correctly.

"What street is your house on?"

It was a telling moment. Although she knew I was her dad and she knew her mom and I were married, she did not know I lived in the same house that she did.

Secret Hide-Out

Though I was able to convince her that we resided at the same address, her uncertainty about my place in her life continued and manifested itself in many ways. A skinned knee sent her toppling toward Mom, not me. A question raised by something overheard at school would be saved for hours until Mom was around to ask.

I realized that not only did I have to spend more time with Mollie, I also had to spend it differently. The more I sensed her distance from me, the more goal-oriented things I tried to do with her—like going to the swimming pool or to the movies.

If Mollie and I didn't have some specifically scheduled activity, I would typically go off and work on chores. For maximizing time and being productive, it made perfect sense.

When it was time to read a bedtime story, Bonnie would call me after the rest of the pre-sleep routine had been completed, and I would walk into Mollie's room like a dentist who waited until the patient was prepped so he wouldn't have to waste a minute's time. It was the way I felt, and I'm sure now it was the way it made Mollie feel too.

A turning point came one summer evening. Mollie was growing increasingly frustrated trying to build a "secret hide-out" in the back yard. The sun was setting, and Mollie should have been winding down for bed, except that the thin slate tiles she tried to prop against one another kept falling over. She'd been at it for days, sometimes with a neighboring friend, sometimes on

Family bonds extend through the generations and help to stregthen family ties. (Jean Claude Lejeune/Stock Boston)

her own. When the walls fell for the last time, cracking as they did, she burst into tears.

"You know what you need to make this work, Molls?" I said.

"What?"

"You need about 60 bricks."

"Yeah, but we don't have 60 bricks."

"But we could get them."

"Where?"

"The hardware store. Get your shoes on and hop in the car."

We drove the three or four miles to the hardware store and found the bricks. I started to load them, a few at a time, onto a big, flat cart. They were rough and heavy, and I realized that I had my work cut out for me. After being loaded onto the cart, they would need to be unloaded into the Jeep, and then unloaded yet again at the house.

"Oh, please, let me do that, Dad. Please!" Mollie begged.

If I let her, we'd be there forever. She would have to use two hands just to pick up one of them. I glanced at my watch and tried to keep my impatience in check.

"But sweetie, they're very heavy."

"Please, Dad, I really want to," she begged again, moving quickly to the pile of bricks and hoisting one with both hands. She lugged it over to the cart and laid it next to the handful I'd placed there.

This was going to take all night.

Mollie walked back to the pile and carefully selected another brick. She took her time making her choice.

Then I realized she wanted it to take all night.

It was rare for the two of us to have time like this alone together. This was the kind of thing her older brother, Zach, would usually get to do: impulsive, past bedtime, just the two of us. Only with Zach, in maybe typically male fashion, I would see this as a task to finish quickly, so that we could go build the wall. Mollie wanted this moment to last.

Mollie's Moment

I leaned back against one of the wood pallets and took a deep breath. Mollie, working steadily at the bricks, relaxed and became chatty, talking to me about what she'd build, and about school and her girlfriends and her upcoming horseback-riding lesson. And it dawned on me: here we were buying bricks to make a wall, but in truth we were actually dismantling a wall, brick by brick—the wall that had threatened to divide me from my daughter.

Since then I've learned what her mother already knew: how to watch a TV show with Mollie even if it isn't a show I wanted to see; how to be with her without also reading a newspaper or magazine, to be fully present. Mollie doesn't want me for what I can give her, for where I can take her, or even for what we can do together. She wants me for me.

Selection 2   **Parents Are Strange Animals . . . Aren't We?**

RAY MORRIS

Before Reading   Before you read the poem, "Parents Are Strange Animals . . . Aren't We?"
predict what the topic may be. Scan the poem to see if you have correctly
predicted the topic. Think about the topic. Relate what you know to "Parents
Are Strange Animals . . . Aren't We?" Set a purpose for reading this poem. Do
you expect to be entertained, to gain knowledge, or to explore an argument?

Parents are strange animals ....aren't we?
    When our kids are just babies it's
      "My aren't we so big!"
      "He's just like a little adult."
      "She's so much a lady."
      "They grow up so fast."
    But when they're teenagers it's
      "When are you going to grow up?"
      "You act like you were just born yesterday."
      "Act your age."   10

Parents are strange animals ....aren't we?
    When our kids are just babies we can
      take anything that comes off, out of, or from
          their little baby bodies.
      Whether it's drool from their mouths,
      vomits from their stomachs,
      wiping 'yuchs' from their noses,
      and, of course, those diapers!
    But when they're teenagers it's
      "You're disgusting!"   20
      "You make me sick."
      "I don't have to take that from you."

Parents are strange animals ....aren't we?
    When our kids are just babies we
      Dress them as little sailors or cowboys,
      or as miniature Barbie Dolls.
      We put on them 'Barney the Dinosaur' shirts,
      'Elmo' sneakers,
      Let them run around in 'Winnie the Pooh' underwear.
    But when they're teenagers it's   30
      "Where did you ever learn how to dress?"
      "You look like a freak!"
      "How can you dare to be seen out in public."

Parents are strange animals ....aren't we?
    When our kids are just babies it's
        "See my baby."
        "He has my eyes."
        "She has my facial expressions!"
    But when they're teenagers it's
        "You look like the devil."   40
        "Your child did this!"
        "I don't know you."

Parents are strange animals ....aren't we?
    When our kids are just babies,
            We'll wind up the toy that plays "Twinkle Twinkle Little Star"
                Hundreds of times,
            We'll teach them "Inky Dinky Spider" day in and day out
                    Till they have all the words and the gestures down pat
        And how can we ever forget . . . "I love you, You love me . . ."
    But when they're teenagers it's   50
        "I can't believe this music you're listening to!"
        "It's sickening"
        "Same thing over and over."

Parents are strange animals ....aren't we?
    It seems many of the things
        That make us so proud of our babies,
        Are the very same things
        We condemn in our teenagers!

Why are parents such strange animals?
    Is it because when our kids were just babies,   60
        We acted more like them, than they did us?
    Is it because when our kids are teenagers,
        We refuse to admit we used to be just like them?
    Is it because we cherish the fond times that our babies offer
        And dread the "uncherishable" times our teenagers offer?
    Is it because when our kids were just babies,
        They copied our personality.
    But when they're teenagers,
        They develop their own personality,
            which now, in turn, makes them "rebellious"?   70

Parents are strange animals ....aren't we?
    We're so quick to remember
        How strange our teenagers are,
    And just as quick to forget that
        They're the product of our genetics!

Parents are strange animals ....aren't we?
　　When our kids are just babies,
　　　　We do all we can to make them know
　　　　　　How much we love them,
　　　　　　How much we cherish them,
　　　　　　How very important they are to us.
　　But when they're teenagers
　　　　. . .Well . . . What can we say? . . .

Parents are strange animals .... aren't we?

80

84

Selection 3

Four Generations

JOYCE MAYNARD

Before Reading

Before you read "Four Generations," predict what the topic may be. Scan the story to see if you have correctly predicted the topic. Think about the topic. Relate what you know to "Four Generations." Set a purpose for reading this story. Do you expect to be entertained, to gain knowledge, or to explore an argument?

Words to Preview

pancreas	*(n.)* gland behind the stomach
jaundice	*(n.)* yellowish discoloration
pogrom	*(n.)* organized massacre of minority group
cossack	*(n.)* a people of southern Soviet Union who were generally organized in a cavalry unit
covet	*(v.)* to wish for excessively
elocution	*(n.)* style of public speaking
knish	*(n.)* a piece of dough stuffed with potato, meat, or cheese and baked or fried

M y mother called last week to tell me that my grandmother is dying. She has refused an operation that would postpone, but not prevent, her death from pancreatic cancer. She can't eat, she has been hemorrhaging, and she has severe jaundice. "I always prided myself on being different," she told my mother. "Now I *am* different. I'm yellow."

My mother, telling me this news, began to cry. So I became the mother for a moment, reminding her, reasonably, that my grandmother is 87, she's had a full life, she has all her faculties, and no one who knows her could wish that she live long enough to lose them. Lately my mother has been finding notes in my grandmother's drawers at the nursing home, reminding her, "Joyce's husband's name is Steve. Their daughter is Audrey." In the last few years she hasn't had the strength to cook or garden, and she's begun to say she's had enough of living.

My grandmother was born in Russia, in 1892—the oldest daughter in a large and prosperous Jewish family. But the prosperity didn't last. She tells stories of the pogroms and the cossacks who raped her when she was 12. Soon after that, her family emigrated to Canada, where she met my grandfather.

Their children were the center of their life. The story I loved best, as a child, was of my grandfather opening every box of Cracker Jack in the general store he ran, in search of the particular tin toy my mother coveted. Though they never had much money, my grandmother saw to it that her daughter had elocution lessons and piano lessons, and assured her that she would go to college.

But while she was at college, my mother met my father, who was blue-eyed and blond-haired and not Jewish. When my father sent love letters to my mother, my grandmother would open and hide them, and when my mother told her parents she was going to marry this man, my grandmother said if that happened, it would kill her.

Not likely, of course. My grandmother is a woman who used to crack Brazil nuts open with her teeth, a woman who once lifted a car off the ground, when there was an accident and it had to be moved. She has been representing her death as imminent ever since I've known her—25 years—and has discussed, at length, the distribution of her possessions and her lamb coat. Every time we said goodbye, after our annual visit to Winnipeg, she'd weep and say she'd never see us again. But in the meantime, while every other relative of her generation, and a good many of the younger ones, has died (nursed usually by her), she has kept making knishes, shopping for bargains, tending the healthiest plants I've ever seen.

After my grandfather died, my grandmother lived, more than ever, through her children. When she came to visit, I would hide my diary. She couldn't understand any desire for privacy. She couldn't bear it if my mother left the house without her.

This possessiveness is what made my mother furious (and then guilt-ridden that she felt that way, when of course she owed so much to her mother). So I harbored the resentment that my mother—the dutiful daughter—would not allow herself. I—who had always performed especially well for my grandmother, danced and sung for her, presented her with kisses and good report cards—stopped writing to her, ceased to visit.

But when I heard that she was dying, I realized I wanted to go to Winnipeg to see her one more time. Mostly to make my mother happy, I told myself (certain patterns being hard to break). But also, I was offering up one more particularly fine accomplishment: my own dark-eyed, dark-skinned, dark-haired daughter, whom my grandmother had never met.

I put on my daughter's best dress for our visit to Winnipeg, the way the best dresses were always put on me, and I filled my pockets with animal crackers, in case Audrey started to cry. I scrubbed her face mercilessly. On the elevator going up to her room, I realized how much I was sweating.

Grandma was lying flat with an IV tube in her arm and her eyes shut, but she opened them when I leaned over to kiss her. "It's Fredelle's daughter, Joyce," I yelled, because she doesn't hear well anymore, but I could see that no explanation was necessary. "You came," she said. "You brought the baby."

Audrey is just 1, but she has seen enough of the world to know that people in beds are not meant to be so still and yellow, and she looked frightened. I had never wanted, more, for her to smile.

Then Grandma waved at her—the same kind of slow, finger-flexing wave a baby makes—and Audrey waved back. I spread her toys out on my grandmother's bed and sat her down. There she stayed, most of the afternoon, playing and humming and sipping on her bottle, taking a nap at one point, leaning against my grandmother's leg. When I cranked her Snoopy guitar, Audrey stood up on the bed and danced. Grandma couldn't talk much anymore, though every once in a while she would say how sorry she was that she wasn't having a better day. "I'm not always like this," she said.

Mostly she just watched Audrey. Sometimes Audrey would get off the bed, inspect the get-well cards, totter down the hall. "Where is she?" Grandma kept asking. "Who's looking after her?" I had the feeling, even then, that if I'd said, "Audrey's lighting matches," Grandma would have shot up to rescue her.

We were flying home that night, and I had dreaded telling her, remembering all those other tearful partings. But in the end, I was the one who cried. She had said she was ready to die. But as I leaned over to stroke her forehead, what she said was, "I wish I had your hair" and "I wish I was well."

On the plane flying home, with Audrey in my arms, I thought about mothers and daughters, and the four generations of the family that I know most intimately. Every one of those mothers loves and needs her daughter more than her daughter will love or need her some day, and we are, each of us, the only person on earth who is quite so consumingly interested in our child.

Sometimes I kiss and hug Audrey so much she starts crying—which is, in effect, what my grandmother was doing to my mother, all her life. And what makes my mother grieve right now, I think, is not simply that her mother will die in a day or two, but that, once her mother dies, there will never again be someone to love her in quite such an unreserved, unquestioning way. No one else who believes that, 50 years ago, she could have put Shirley Temple out of a job, no one else who remembers the moment of her birth. She will only be a mother, then, not a daughter anymore.

Audrey and I have stopped over for a night in Toronto, where my mother lives. Tomorrow she will go to a safe-deposit box in the bank and take out the receipt for my grandmother's burial plot. Then she will fly back to Winnipeg, where, for the first time in anybody's memory, there was waist-high snow on April Fool's Day. But tonight she is feeding me, as she always does when I come, and I am eating more than I do anywhere else. I admire the wedding china (once my grandmother's) that my mother has set on the table. She says (the way Grandma used to say to her, of the lamb coat), "Some day it will be yours."

▪ ▪ ▪ ▪ Portfolio Activities

Integrating Ideas

The three readings reflect various family situations. Think about one of your own family experiences. What were your reactions? How did your parents' or guardians' reactions differ from your own? If and when you are a parent, what would you do differently in these or other situations? Reflect on these ideas in writing or in class discussion.

Extending Concepts

People relate to each member of their family differently. Whom in your family are you particularly close to? What is it about that person that makes you comfortable? In what ways has he or she supported you, and how have you helped that person in return? Write about your relationship.

Collaborative Activity

In groups, first define the concept of family, including the members and their roles. Next choose a television program that portrays a family, and describe the TV family and its members and roles. Then discuss how the groups' definition of family fits the TV family. Report back to the class as a whole on your findings.

Additional Portfolio Suggestion

A literacy autobiography tells the story of your development as a reader and writer. This process began when you were very young and continues throughout your life. Explore your growth as a literate person to better understand your current abilities. A series of questions to guide you are provided in Appendix B of this text.

Chapter Summary Graphic Organizer

Before Reading

Preview
- Read the title
- Predict the topic

Connect
- Scan the story
- Think about what you know

Establish Purpose
- Knowledge
- Entertainment
- Argument

2

During Reading

Theme of Readings: *Friendship*

A real friend is one who walks in when the rest of the world walks out.
    WALTER WINCHELL

■ ■ ■ ■ Friendship

Friendship is a special bond that you have with certain people. It keeps your life from being lonely and makes life more fun and meaningful. You can sit in a room full of people, but without a friend you are still alone. Whom will you talk to? Who knows how you feel? Who will share this time? Friends help make the good times better and the hard times more bearable.

It is the freedom to choose your friends that makes friendship special. Friends share interests, attitudes, problems, and experiences. If you share an interest in music, together you may listen to music, play instruments, or write lyrics to a song. Hours may be spent talking about the perfect sound system for a car. Common computer knowledge may lead to developing a Web site or new software. Friends provide companionship, the sharing of information, and insights. Similar interests enhance a friendship.

Friends also depend on and trust each other. They give advice and emotional support when it is needed most. They listen. Maintaining a friendship is not automatic, however. Ralph Waldo Emerson said, "The only way to have a friend is to be one." You have to work at being a good friend. It takes time, energy, and commitment, but friendship is its own reward.

Chapter Objectives

After completing this chapter, you will be able to

1. **Predict as you read.**
2. **Visualize the reading.**
3. **Monitor your comprehension.**

Focus on *During Reading* Strategies

As a passenger in a car, you don't usually pay attention to the roads and turns the driver takes. You do not take an active part in getting to the destination. When you change from being the passenger to being the driver, you may not remember an exact route to a place you have been driven to many times—sometimes you get lost. Many students read as if they are a passenger in a car; they do not become involved in what they are reading and often find themselves lost.

How many times have you finished reading something and were unable to remember what it was about? It doesn't matter whether you read a newspaper, magazine, novel, or textbook. You went through the "motions" of reading but didn't retain the information because you were not involved with what you were reading.

You begin your involvement using the *before reading* strategies. To continue the process, you need to focus on the reading and work at constructing meaning. To accomplish this, you will predict, visualize, and monitor your comprehension while you read.

Prediction

As you read, words, phrases, and sentences trigger thoughts about what may happen in the reading. Your mind is always ahead of where your eyes are on the page, continuously predicting what the next word or idea will be. As you read, you confirm those predictions that are correct or those that are not. At the same time, you continue to make new predictions.

For example, a student reads the first sentence of a story: "I was sure he was coming to get me." The student makes several predictions about the story: Someone is afraid of an attack, someone is waiting for a ride, or someone is looking forward to an excursion. As the student continues to read, the student begins to confirm his or her predictions. The reader realizes that a little boy was having a nightmare—no one was going to be attacked, and no one was waiting for a ride. The student adjusts the predictions and continues to make new ones as he or she reads the story.

Whether your predictions are correct is not important. It is the process of making those predictions that connects you to the author and actively involves you in the reading.

Visualization

The strategy of taking words and ideas from a reading and forming a mental picture is visualization. Effective readers create images as they read. Readers' images are unique because their visualizations depend on their own experiences. For instance, if a story describes a castle in Germany, a reader who has visited that country will picture one image. Someone who has never traveled to Europe may picture a castle they saw on television or

Cinderella's castle at Disneyworld. Your mental image will depend on your background and experiences. As you read, your mental pictures change or are modified. The process of visualization further strengthens your connection to the author.

Monitoring Comprehension

Every day you drive your car to work, school, or home without ever thinking about what is happening in the car's engine. If you never check the oil of your car, it may run well for a while, but eventually it will break down. In the same way, if you were to withdraw money from your checking account without keeping track of the balance, your checks would eventually bounce. You need to check, or monitor, these and other daily activities to prevent problems.

If you read an entire chapter but remember little or nothing of what you read, you have not checked your understanding while you were reading. Just as you need to monitor activities in your life, you must monitor your comprehension. You must realize that you are in charge of constructing meaning from what you read.

Be actively involved in monitoring your comprehension as you read. Use the following techniques:

- Continually ask yourself, "Does this make sense?"
- Carry on a conversation in your head about the reading.
- Mentally state, in your own words, what the author is saying.

For example, while reading a magazine article about unsafe foods, you may start to think about what the author is saying about beef and deadly bacteria. Could you explain the reading to another person? If the reading does not make sense or if you are unable to explain it, your comprehension has broken down.

Effective readers recognize or monitor these breakdowns in comprehension and take actions to repair them. If you realize you do not understand, stop reading and attempt to figure out where the problem began. Was it with a word, a phrase, or a sentence? Reread the section and look for a clearer understanding. You may have thought that stopping and rereading are actions to be avoided; on the contrary, they are a crucial part of effective reading. Monitoring your comprehension allows you to understand if you are connecting to the author.

■ ■ ■ ■ ■ Short Exercise: *During Reading* Strategies

The following exercise demonstrates *during reading* strategies. After you read the suggested predictions, visualizations, and monitoring statements that are given in italics, try predicting, visualizing, and monitoring on your own. Talk about your responses with your classmates.

"The Dinner Party"

EXCERPTED FROM *AMONG FRIENDS* BY LETTY COTTIN POGREBIN

Five years ago at my house, a well-known actor-screenwriter asked the others gathered around the dinner table to give him some ideas for a script in progress.

I see a fancy table with candles and special dishes and lots of crystal and silver with eight or ten nicely dressed people sitting and chatting. [Visualizing]

The movie is about friendship, he explained.

I wonder what movie this is going to be. I bet it will be like that old movie, The Big Chill. [Predicting]

I need to know what role friendship plays in the average person's life.

By "role," I think the speaker means whatever part friendship does play is very important in a person's life. [Monitoring]

I think the people at this dinner party will say friendship is very important in their lives. [Predicting]

What do you look for in a friend?

I look for someone who will support me and be there when I need a friend. [Monitoring]

How many really good friends do you have and how often do you see them?

What does he mean by "really good friends"? I don't think you have to see someone often to consider that person a really good friend. [Monitoring]

I picture my friend Debbie; she is a really good friend. We do lots of things together. [Visualizing]

What do you do together?

_____

_____

Could you stay friends after a serious fight?

_____

Did you ever lose a meaningful friend?

_____

_____

Do you keep making new ones?

_____

_____

_____

Is there such a thing as having too many friends?

_____

_____

_____

Are you a good friend to the friends in your life?

_____

_____

_____

The minute he stopped to take a sip of wine, the other seven of us started talking at once—unlike nuclear arms and Central America, friendship was a subject on which each of us was an expert.

_____

_____

_____

What's more, how often did we get the opportunity to contribute to an artist's conceptual formulations, especially when our pearls of wisdom might one day be repeated by a star on the silver screen?

_____

_____

_____

An hour later, long after finishing dessert, we were still at the table, mining friendship for all it was worth.

_____

_____

_____

At first, I chalked it up to good conversation.

_____

_____

■ ■ ■ ■   Reading Selections

Selection 1

Real Friends
CATHERINE WEISKOPF

Before Reading   Before you read the story, "Real Friends," predict what the topic may be. Scan the story to see if you have correctly predicted the topic. Think about the topic and relate what you know to "Real Friends." Set your purpose for this story. Do you expect to be entertained, to gain knowledge, or to explore an argument?

Words to Preview

catalyst	*(n.)* substance that increases the rate of chemical reaction
reciprocal	*(adj.)* experienced by both sides
reappraise	*(v.)* to evaluate again
exalt	*(v.)* to glorify; praise

During Reading   As you read "Real Friends," continue to predict what will happen in the article, visualize the story, and monitor your understanding. Use the guide questions that are printed in the margins of the reading to help you with this process.

Can you picture your friends?

What qualities do you look for in a friend?

riends: They can make a boring class bearable; a blustery day warm; a teeth-grinding worry disappear. Friends are an important part of your life. The 1996 Mood of American Youth Survey found friends were the number-one reason why teens liked school, and being with friends was the number-two nonschool activity. You will have many different friends over the course of your life, but what draws you to certain people? What qualities do you look for in friends? For that matter, why do you even need friends?

What Makes You Friends

What's a catalyst?

Do you share the same attitudes as your friends?

I predict people look for _____ and _____ in friends.

Are you and your friend major basketball fans? Do you both have the same strong views about recycling? Maybe you've both survived a common tragedy. At all ages, common interest is the catalyst for friendship. This doesn't mean friends are similar in every way, but you are similar in the ways that are important to you. Adam Bonjour, age 15, says his friendships developed "because we have a lot of things in common. We like to do the same stuff together." Similarities with friends tend to change as you get older, but they are always there. Faye Steuer noted in her book, *The Psychological Development of Children,* that friendships involving younger children have more behavioral similarities while adolescent friendships tend more toward similarities in attitude.

When Helen Swanson is looking for a friend, she looks for someone who is "funny, not too serious, and nice." Adam Bonjour wants friends who are "thoughtful, kind, honest, and fun." Marcus Schneider wants his friends to have "intelligence, kindness, and be nonconforming." Everyone wants friends who are nice, kind, and supportive. Beyond these traits, you want friends who are similar to you. If you are artistic, you want friends who are the same. If you value honesty and thoughtfulness, you look for friends who have the same values. What do the experts say people look for in friends? One recent study found certain aspects of friendship appear to be present at all ages: "similarity, emotional supportiveness, shared activities, confiding, and reciprocal liking, trust, and acceptance."

Was my prediction confirmed?

Friendship—Not All Peaches and Cream

Do you have a mental image of a time when a friend hurt you?

Sometimes people get messed up about what friendship means. You may expect a friend to never be late. You may expect a friend to never disagree. But friends aren't copies of yourself, and friendships aren't perfect. Anytime people are close, they're bound to hurt one another's feelings. But you need to balance what they've done wrong with what they've done right.

It is also important to remember being a real friend isn't always easy. Sometimes, to be a real friend, you have to be brutally honest and tough. Real friends may take keys away from a drunk friend even if it might mean the loss of his or her friendship. Real friendship isn't all peaches and cream.

Making and Keeping Friends

Every friendship starts with a smile, a hello, and a simple icebreaker, writes psychologist Dr. Lillian Glass in an article about attracting terrific people. The icebreaker can be homework or the news or the weather.

How do you develop friendships?

When you're interested in becoming friends with an acquaintance, first think about what you look for in a friend. There's an old saying, "To have a friend is to be a friend." It's true. Are you a good friend? Lesson one on developing friendship is to show interest in the other person. Be a good listener, show your interest, and treat the person as if he or she is special.

Once you've spent time and energy developing friends, you need to put that same energy into keeping them. So how do you keep friends? "I keep friends by staying loyal. I always keep appointments, and I'm always honest," says Marcus Schneider. It all boils down to showing your friends the respect and appreciation that you want from them.

Better Than an Apple a Day?

Do you share respect and appreciation with your friends?

You know friends make your life better, but did you know studies show they also improve both your psychological and physical health? A study done by D. Buhrmester in 1990 found, "Those who had closer friendships saw themselves as more competent and sociable and having higher self-esteem than youngsters without close friends." Friendships may be beneficial in part because they allow you to talk about your problems. According to Brant R. Burleson, professor of communications at Purdue University, talking about your troubles helps you clarify them. "Discussing a traumatic event helps the distressed person get some distance on it—reappraise it— and integrate new perspectives on it within a broader view of life."

How do friends make your life better?

Good friends are also good for your physical health. In a study done at the University of Texas, researchers found, "Social support boosts the immune system, improves the quality—and possibly the length—of life, and helps reduce heart disease." In other words, a good friendship can be just as good as an apple a day at keeping the doctor away.

Friends—they increase your health and your happiness and possibly even lengthen your life. The glories of friendship have been exalted in poetry and vocalized in songs. Perhaps one of the best songs about the nature of friendship is "Lean on Me," written by Bill Withers. "Lean on me when you're not strong and I'll be your friend—I'll help you carry on. For I know that it won't be long 'til I'm gonna need somebody to lean on."

Selection 2

Facing the Limitations of Long-Distance Friendships Can Be Downright Traumatic

CATHERINE WALSH

Before Reading

Before you read "Facing the Limitations of Long-Distance Friendships Can Be Downright Traumatic," predict what the topic may be. Scan the entire story to see if you have correctly predicted the topic. Think about the topic, and relate what you know to the reading selection. Set your purpose for reading. Do you expect to be entertained, to gain knowledge, or to explore an argument?

Words to Preview

empathy   *(n.)* understanding of another's situation or feelings
balk   *(v.)* to refuse abruptly
proverbial *(adj.)* expressed in a short saying; commonly spoken of

During Reading

As you read "Facing the Limitations of Long-Distance Friendships Can Be Downright Traumatic," continue to predict where the author is headed, visualize the story, and monitor your understanding. Use the limited guide questions in the margin to help you with this process; add your own comments, questions, or descriptions as you read.

Are you familiar with the movie, *It's A Wonderful Life*?

Georgi Bailey of Bedford Falls was lucky. "The richest man in town" didn't have to worry about keeping in touch with friends around the planet. If cyberspace competing long-distance phone companies and frequent-flier programs had been around when the film *It's a Wonderful Life* was made, ol' George might have been both poor and perplexed.

How would he have kept his priorities straight? Whom would he have built houses for first—folks in Barcelona, Bedford Falls, or Bangladesh? "No man is a failure who has friends," said Harry Bailey in a toast to his brother at the movie's end. But the folks who emptied their wallets, purses, and piggy banks for George Bailey after his building-and-loan lost $8,000 were as familiar, as unchosen, as family. Fifty-plus years after the film's debut, friendship (like family life) has become a lot more complicated.

Can you picture the scene?

"It's a pain in the neck to have too many friends," a journalist I know said recently. "You can't keep up with them." This acquaintance made his observations at a farewell party for another journalist, a man I considered a friend but hadn't seen in nearly a year. I'd sat beside "Rick" during nine months of employment at a small daily newspaper in the Boston area. During long days in the newsroom we shared stories we were writing on deadline and stories of lives we had lived and hoped to lead. I provided an empathetic ear while Rick reflected on girlfriend troubles; he gave me romantic advice in return. We goofed around at parties.

Why is friendship complicated today?

Driving the hour's distance to the farewell gala, I found myself flooded with memories—the notes Rick taped to my computer praising my writing, the hug he gave me when I burst into tears one day at work, the support he provided as I wrestled to the ground a difficult decision to leave day journalism for a freelance career.

Over the din of a crowded bar, I congratulated Rick on his new job and promised to call him soon. But I haven't—so far. I'd planned to send Rick a Valentine's Day card, but I haven't done that either—yet.

Celebrating friendships past and present, near and far that have blessed my life: this was my goal for Valentine's Day. I wanted to paste a humorous photo of myself on folded construction paper and send these homemade cards to 40 friends around the country and abroad. I relished the idea of going beyond the holiday's sticky romantic sentiment; besides, I needed to make up for the fact that I'd been too busy in December to write my annual Christmas letter. But alas, alas. Valentine's Day has come and gone; I've managed to mail only three cards. Maybe I'll get the rest out in time for St. Patrick's Day.

Do you ever procrastinate?

Now mind you, a few days prior to Valentine's Day my sister ribbed me about procrastinating on my cards. "Just sit down and write them, for goodness' sake," she exclaimed. But my sister hadn't lived for significant stretches of time in England, the American Southwest, and the Midwest. I wanted to follow her advice, truly. I opened my address file on the computer one night, thinking that I would do the cards in alphabetical order. But I didn't get past B. I discovered I lacked the new address of an Ohio friend, a woman whose values I cherished and whom I'd scarcely been in touch with since her wedding a year ago. I called her with every intention of talking just for two minutes.

For an hour and a half, this friend and I probed the directions our lives had taken. We discussed her mixed feelings about moving far from her family while her husband pursued the next stage in his medical career. In between tackling my career dilemmas and romantic hopes, we laughed again at jokes we'd shared ages ago. Buoyed by my friend's humor and insight her faith and wisdom, I got off the phone feeling as though I'd just eaten a half-dozen warm chocolate chip cookies and drunk the most cold, delicious water imaginable. More than full, I found that my energy to turn out cards efficiently had dissipated.

How do you keep in touch with friends who have moved away?

Maintaining friendships in a mobile age requires efficiency, alas. But human nature balks at such demands; given their druthers most folks still prefer the proverbial chat over the back fence to e-mail. Coming together for personal encounters, however, requires planning, prioritizing, and sometimes making painful choices. Do I go to Pam and Joe's wedding in Boise or visit Joyce, Pete, and their new baby in Cedar Rapids? Facing the limitations of long distance friendships can be downright traumatic. Yet the joys of friendship nourished over time and distance more than make up for the trauma.

A few hours after I turn this essay over to my editors, I'll go to the airport to pick up a friend I haven't seen for six years.

My visit with Nuala during a stopover in England in 1991—I was on my way to India—lasted less than 24 hours. Our previous visit, in Boston in 1984, lasted a few days. On a whim, I called Nuala last fall and informed her that that day was the 15th anniversary of my arrival in England for my junior year abroad. Deciding we wanted to keep in closer touch, we began sending e-mail often to each other. Turned out that Nuala had a frequent-flier ticket that had to be used by spring. We'll head to New Hampshire for an extended weekend of skiing and conversation. I can't wait to see her.

Selection 3

Can Men and Women Just Be Friends?

Jet Magazine

Before Reading

Before you read "Can Men and Women Just Be Friends?" predict what the topic may be. Scan the entire story to see if you have correctly predicted the topic. Think about the topic; relate what you know to "Can Men and Women Be Friends?" Set your purpose for reading. Do you expect to be entertained, to gain knowledge, or to explore an argument?

Word to Preview   **platonic**   *(adj.)* a spiritual relationship that rises above physical desire

During Reading

As you read "Can Men and Women Just Be Friends?" continue to predict where the author is headed, visualize the story, and monitor your understanding. There are no guide questions given. As you read, write your own comments, questions, or descriptions in the margins.

Opposites seem to attract. And men and women are as opposite as it gets. So can the two genders merge as just friends, putting aside their natural attractions and sexual desires?

Everyone *JET* polled agrees that men and women can have truly platonic relationships. In fact, the experts and those who've experienced such relationships all think platonic relationships are healthy and enriching. However, some conditions have to be present for healthy, enriching platonic relationships to begin and develop.

Self-control is a key element needed to make platonic relationships work, according to Dr. Sheron C. Patterson, senior pastor at Jubilee United Methodist Church in Duncanville, TX.

"We need self-control," she explains. "It stems from knowing yourself. Once you know what you can take and what you can handle, you can more comfortably interact with someone else."

She also said both parties need to be "certain and secure that they want to be platonic." And a platonic relationship should be conducted in "well-lit public places."

"You can not meet a man in a dark corner at midnight and expect the relationship to remain platonic."

Patterson, who conducts relationship seminars for singles and married couples, emphasizes the importance of the places people in platonic relationships hang out. She says they should not hang out in the same places where there are several romantic couples who are being affectionate. "You can have the best intentions in the world, but I do believe Satan will slip in," she contends.

Dr. Allen Carter, a psychologist in Atlanta, points out that platonic relationships should have a defined purpose.

"What's the purpose of this relationship?" he says, is a key question. 'To make any relationship, from marriage to someone who shares an office with you, powerful, you have to get clear on what's the purpose of this relationship."

Carter explains that this means being honest and open. If one party begins to feel something for another, "put it on the table," he advises. "Say 'Yes, I'm feeling something for you . . . should we let this pass by?'"

Honesty is one reason Valda Williams, 31, of Washington, D.C., says she is able to have three males as close, platonic friends. She says she "lets them know up front" if she's not interested or if she's just looking for friendship.

Williams' relationship with James Hill, 30, of St. Louis, began when they were students at St. Louis University.

"I'm like a little brother to her, and she's a big sister to me," Hill says about their relationship. And he says while he was attracted to Williams, her honesty in the beginning let him know nothing would happen.

And even now, after 12 years of friendship, the two don't see their relationship going past the platonic state.

"I know I can never date my sister," Hill points out.

"That would be incest," Williams quips.

But despite the success of some, other people don't think platonic relationships can work. One reason, according to Dr. Tracy Shaw of UCLA, is that "people confuse intimacy and sexuality."

Intimacy is "where you can develop a close, supportive relationship with someone," she suggests. "If that in fact happens with an individual of the opposite sex, there may be a tendency to believe that the next step is for some sort of romantic component to take place."

But that does not have to be the case. A male and female can be intimate without being sexual, Shaw says. "Friendships between men and women don't have to end in romance."

She points to several of her "healthy, satisfying, supporting relationships" with platonic friends. She says most of them developed out of work relationships with colleagues or individuals she's known over the years. Some even resulted from old romantic relationships.

"As time has passed and feelings have healed," she says of the once-romantic relationships, "they've developed into platonic relationships."

Turning once-romantic relationships into platonic ones isn't always easy, says Dr. Ronn Elmore, whose books *How to Love a Black Woman* and *How to Love a Black Man* look at the differences between men and women.

Often people are "too tired, too hurt, or too angry to even figure out" what it means to have a friendship with each other.

He also says a person should be leery of platonic relationships when he or she doesn't let anyone know about it. "If it's (relationship) a secret, there's something going on that probably is unhealthy."

But those instances aside, Elmore says platonic relationships can be vital.

Platonic relationships can be "truly beneficial because men and women are so different and we speak such different languages. It helps us become bilingual. It expands our own ability to speak both languages."

Portfolio Activities

Integrating Ideas

Now that you have read three selections about friendship, define and describe your concept of friendship. Think about the friends that you have or had. What was it about these relationships that made them good or bad friendships? Reflect on these ideas in writing or in class discussion.

Extending Concepts

Opinions vary on whether men and women can be just friends. Have you had a friend who was of the opposite sex? Was that friendship different from a friendship with someone of the same sex? Write your opinion about men and women having friendships. Support your view by describing your experiences or those of others.

Collaborative Activity

In a group, compose a list of questions to use for an interview about friendship. Then, using these questions, interview someone in the class to learn about his or her concept of friendship. After the interview, share your findings with the group.

Additional Portfolio Suggestion

Look back at the model of *during reading* activities on page 21. Using a reading of your choice, create a similar model with your comments, questions, and descriptions. Use at least ten consecutive sentences from the story.

Chapter Summary Graphic Organizer

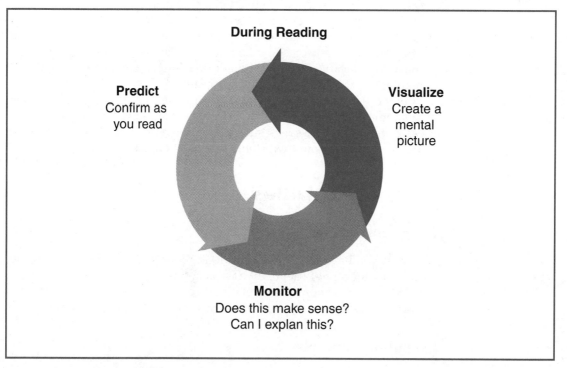

During Reading

Predict
Confirm as
you read

Visualize
Create a
mental
picture

Monitor
Does this make sense?
Can I explain this?

3

After Reading

Theme of Readings: Love

A heart that loves is always young.

<small>GREEK PROVERB</small>

Love

Pick up a magazine. Listen to the radio. Watch a television show. View a movie. Read a novel. Share a conversation. One theme is easy to find in all of these activities—love. Since ancient times, love has been an enduring and inspiring topic in literature and the arts. To love and be loved is a life-long goal, sought after by young and old. You can find recipes for love; descriptions of lost love; and poems, cartoons, and greeting cards about love. Some cultures even dedicate a day to love—St. Valentine's Day.

Preoccupation with love begins when you are very young. Small children pretend to be married and play house. Ten-year-olds claim boyfriends and girlfriends, even though they barely speak to each other. Teenagers struggle with the insecurity of dating as they approach adulthood. All have one goal in mind—receiving and giving love.

As preoccupied as each of us may be with the pursuit of love, love is not always easy to find or to keep. Maintaining a long term love relationship in today's society, may be one of the most difficult things you do. Like friendship, it takes time, energy, and commitment; it also takes communication skills, the ability to compromise, and a touch of luck. Whether it lasts a month or a lifetime, a loving relationship is one of life's great experiences.

Chapter Objectives

After completing this chapter, you will be able to

1. **Evaluate your understanding of the reading.**
2. **Review and recall the ideas presented in the selection.**

Focus on *After Reading* Strategies

An article in your favorite magazine catches your eye. You scan it, find it interesting, and read the entire article. When finished, you toss the magazine aside without a second thought. Even though you became actively involved in reading by using *before reading* and *during reading* strategies, your reading remains unfinished. If you neglect to do anything after you read, the reading process is incomplete. Effective readers evaluate their understanding of the reading to complete the process.

To evaluate your understanding, you must review the reading and recall information. Ask yourself, "Did I meet my purpose for reading?" "Did I understand what I just read?" "Were there any confusing parts that I need to reread?" "What is important to remember?" "Can I relate the information to my knowledge or experience?" These questions will guide you in evaluating your understanding. You increase your memory of what you read by reviewing and recalling the information.

To understand *after reading* strategies, read the following excerpt from Leo Buscaglia's *Living, Loving & Learning* and the model questions and responses that follow.

> Don't miss love. It's an incredible gift. I love to think that the day you are born, you're given the world as your birthday present. It frightens me that so few people even bother to open up the ribbon! *Rip it open! Tear off the top!* It's just *full* of love and magic and life and joy and wonder and pain and tears. All of the things that are your gifts for being human. Not only the really happy things—"I want to be happy all the time"—no, there's a lot of pain in there, a lot of tears. A lot of magic, a lot of wonder, a lot of confusion. But that's what it means. That's what life *is*. And all *so exciting*. Get into that box and you'll never be bored.
>
> I see people who are always saying, "I'm a lover, I'm a lover, I'm a lover. I really believe in love. I act the part." And then they shout at the waitress, *"Where's the water?!"* I will believe your love when you show it to me in action. When you can understand that everybody is teaching everybody to love at every moment. And when you ask yourself, "Am I the best teacher?" and if your answer is "Yes"—great. Go around—listen to how many times a day you say, "I love," instead of, "I hate." Isn't it interesting that children, as they learn the process of language, always learn the word "no" years before they learn the word "yes"? Ask linguists where they hear it. Maybe if they heard more of "I love, I love, I love," they'd say it sooner and more often.

Review the excerpt. What is important to remember?

The author feels love and life are gifts for being human. Life is exciting, and if you see it that way, you'll never be bored. The author feels that we are teaching each other about love. We need to hear the word love more often.

What is the author's definition of love?

Love is a gift to be opened and experienced.

How do people's actions differ from their beliefs about love?

People say one thing but do another. For example, they will say they believe in love but yell at the waitress over getting a glass of water.

■ ■ ■ ■ Short Exercises: *After Reading* Strategies

The following selections are excerpts from *Don't Sweat the Small Stuff . . . and It's All Small Stuff* by Richard Carlson. After you read, use the questions to help you evaluate your understanding and review and recall the selection.

Tell Three People (Today) How Much You Love Them

RICHARD CARLSON

Author Stephen Levine asks the question, "If you had an hour to live and could make only one phone call—who would you call, what would you say, and why are you waiting?" What a powerful message!

Who knows what we are waiting for? Perhaps we want to believe we will live forever, or that "someday" we will get around to telling the people we love how much we love them. Whatever the reasons, most of us simply wait too long.

As fate would have it, I'm writing this strategy on my grandmother's birthday. Later today, my father and I are driving out to visit her grave site. She died about two years ago. Before she passed away, it became obvious how important it was to her to let her family know how much she loved us all. It was a good reminder that there is no good reason to wait. Now is the time to let people know how much you care.

Ideally, you can tell someone in person or over the phone. I wonder how many people have been on the receiving end of a phone call where the caller says, "I just called to tell you how much I love you!" You may be surprised that almost nothing in the world means so much to a person. How would you like to receive the same message?

If you're too shy to make such a phone call, write a heartfelt letter instead. Either way, you may find that as you get used to it, letting people know how much you love them will become a regular part of your life. It probably won't shock you to know that, if it does, you'll probably begin receiving more love as a result.

1. Review "Tell Three People (Today) How Much You Love Them." What is important to remember?

   _____

   _____

   _____

   _____

2. Why is it important to tell people that you love them?

   _____

   _____

Spend a Moment, Every Day, Thinking of Someone to Love

Earlier in this book I introduced the idea of spending a moment, each day, thinking of someone to thank. Another excellent source of gratitude and inner peace is to spend a moment, every day, thinking of someone to love. Remember the old saying, "An apple a day keeps the doctor away"? The love equivalent might read, "Thinking of someone to love each day keeps your resentment away!"

I started consciously choosing to think of people to love when I realized how often I could get caught up in thinking about the opposite—people who irritate me. My mind would focus on negative or strange behavior, and within seconds I was filled with negativity. Once I made the conscious decision, however, to spend a moment each morning thinking of someone to love, my attention was redirected toward the positive, not only toward that one person, but in general throughout the day. I don't mean to suggest that I never get irritated anymore, but without question it happens much less frequently than it used to. I credit this exercise with much of my improvement.

Every morning when I wake up, I close my eyes and take a few deep breaths. Then I ask myself the question, "Who shall I send love to today?" Instantly, a picture of someone will pop into my mind—a family member, a friend, someone I work with, a neighbor, someone from my past, even a stranger I may have seen on the street. To me, it doesn't really matter who it is because the idea is to gear my mind toward love. Once the person to whom I'm directing the love is clear, I simply wish them a day filled with love. I might say to myself something like, "I hope you have a wonderful day filled with loving kindness." When I'm finished, which is within seconds, I usually feel that my heart is ready to begin my day. In some mystical way that I can't explain, those few seconds stick with me for many hours. If you give this little exercise a try, I think you'll find that your day is a little more peaceful.

3. Review "Spend a Moment, Every Day, Thinking of Someone to Love." What is important to remember?

_____

_____

_____

4. How does the author start each day?

_____

_____

Fill Your Life with Love

I don't know anyone who doesn't want a life filled with love. In order for this to happen, the effort must start within us. Rather than waiting for other people to provide the love we desire, *we* must be a vision and a source of love. We must tap into our own loving-kindness in order to set an example for others to follow suit.

It has been said that "the shortest distance between two points is an intention." This is certainly true with regard to a life filled with love. The starting point or foundation of a life filled with love is the desire and commitment to be a source of love. Our attitude, choices, acts of kindness, and willingness to be the first to reach out will take us toward this goal.

The next time you find yourself frustrated at the lack of love in your own life or at the lack of love in the world, try an experiment. Forget about the world and other people for a few minutes. Instead, look into your own heart. Can you become a source of greater love? Can you think loving thoughts for yourself and others? Can you extend these loving thoughts outward toward the rest of the world—even to people who you feel don't deserve it?

By opening your heart to the possibility of greater love, and by making yourself a source of love (rather than getting love) as a top priority, you will be taking an important step in getting the love you desire. You'll also discover something truly remarkable. The more love you give, the more you will receive. As you put more emphasis on being a loving person, which is something you can control—and less emphasis on receiving love, which is something you can't control—you'll find that you have plenty of love in your life. Soon you'll discover one of the greatest secrets in the world: Love is its own reward.

5. Review "Fill Your Life With Love." What is important to remember?

_____

_____

_____

6. How can you be a source of greater love?

_____

_____

_____

Practice Random Acts of Kindness

There is a bumper sticker that has been out for some time now. You see it on cars all across the nation (in fact, I have one on my own car). It says, "Practice Random Acts of Kindness and Senseless Acts of Beauty." I have no idea who thought of this idea, but I've never seen a more important message on a car in front of me. Practicing random kindness is an effective way to get in touch with the joy of giving without expecting anything in return. It's best practiced without letting anyone know what you are doing.

There are five toll bridges in the San Francisco Bay Area. A while back, some people began paying the tolls of the cars immediately behind them. The drivers would drive to the toll window, and pull out their dollar bill, only to be informed, "Your toll has been paid by the car ahead of you." This is an example of a spontaneous, random gift, something given without expectation of or demand for anything in return. You can imagine the impact that tiny gift had on the driver of the car! Perhaps it encouraged him to be a nicer person that day. Often a single act of kindness sets a series of kind acts in motion.

There is no prescription for how to practice random kindness. It comes from the heart. Your gift might be to pick up litter in your neighborhood, make an anonymous contribution to a charity, send some cash in an unmarked envelope to make someone experiencing financial stress breathe a little easier, save an animal by bringing it to an animal rescue agency, or get a volunteer position feeding hungry people at a church or shelter. You may want to do all these things, and more. The point is, giving is fun, and it doesn't have to be expensive.

Perhaps the greatest reason to practice random kindness is that it brings great contentment into your life. Each act of kindness rewards you with positive feelings and reminds you of the important aspects of life—service, kindness, and love. If we all do our own part, pretty soon we will live in a nicer world.

7. Review "Practice Random Acts of Kindness." What is important to remember?

_____

_____

_____

_____

8. What is the greatest reason to practice random acts of kindness?

_____

_____

_____

■ ■ ■ ■ Reading Selections

| Selection 1 | **Fear of Failure** |
| | DAVE BARRY |

Before Reading	Before you read "Fear of Failure," predict what the topic may be. Scan the reading to see if you have correctly predicted the topic. Think about the topic. Relate what you know to "Fear of Failure." Set your purpose for reading. Do you expect to be entertained, to gain knowledge, or to explore an argument?
Words to Preview	**viable** (adj.) practical; capable of existence as an independent unit
	ambience (n.) special atmosphere or surrounding
During Reading	As you read "Fear of Failure," continue to predict where the author is headed, visualize the story, and monitor your understanding. Write your comments, questions, or descriptions in the margin as you read.

As a mature adult, I feel an obligation to help the younger generation, just as the mother fish guards her unhatched eggs, keeping her lonely vigil day after day, never leaving her post, not even to go to the bathroom, until her tiny babies emerge and she is able, at last, to eat them.

But today I want to talk about dating. This subject was raised in a letter to me from a young person named Eric Knott, who writes:

"I have got a big problem. There's this girl in my English class who is really good looking. However, I don't think she knows I exist. I want to ask her out, but I'm afraid she will say no, and I will be the freak of the week. What should I do?"

Eric, you have sent your question to the right mature adult, because as a young person I spent a lot of time thinking about this very problem. Starting in about eighth grade, my time was divided as follows:

Academic pursuits: 2 percent

Zits: 16 percent

Trying to figure out how to ask girls out: 82 percent

The most sensible way to ask a girl out is to walk directly up to her on foot and say, "So, you want to go out? Or what?" I never did this. I knew, as Eric Knott knows, that there was always the possibility that the girl would say no, thereby leaving me with no viable option but to leave Harold C. Crittenden Junior High School forever and go into the woods and become a bark-eating hermit whose only companions would be the gentle and understanding woodland creatures.

"Hey, ZITFACE!" the woodland creatures would shriek in cute little Chip 'n' Dale voices while raining acorns down upon my head. "You wanna DATE? HAHAHAHAHAHA."

So the first rule of dating is: Never risk direct contact with the girl in question. Your role model should be the nuclear submarine, gliding silently beneath the ocean surface, tracking an enemy target that does not even begin to suspect that the submarine would like to date it. I spent the vast majority of 1960 keeping a girl named Judy under surveillance, maintaining a minimum distance of 50 lockers to avoid the danger that I might somehow get into a conversation with her, which could have led to disaster:

Judy: Hi

Me: Hi

Judy: Just in case you have ever thought about having a date with me, the answer is no

Woodland creatures: HAHAHAHAHAHA

The only problem with the nuclear-submarine technique is that it's difficult to get a date with a girl who has never, technically, been asked. This is why you need Phil Grant. Phil was a friend of mine who had the ability to talk to girls. It was a mysterious superhuman power he had, comparable to X-ray vision. So, after several thousand hours of intense discussion and planning with me, Phil approached a girl he knew named Nancy, who approached a girl named Sandy, who was a direct personal friend of Judy's and who passed the word back to Phil via Nancy that Judy would be willing to go on a date with me.

Thus it was, that, finally, Judy and I went on an actual date, to see a movie in White Plains, N.Y. If I were to sum up the romantic ambience of this date in four words, those four words would be: "My mother was driving."

After what seemed like several years we got to the movie theater, where my mother went off to sit in the Parents and Lepers Section The movie was called, *North to Alaska,* but I can tell you nothing else about it because I spent the whole time wondering whether it would be necessary to amputate my right arm, which was not getting any blood flow as a result of being perched for two hours like a petrified snake on the back of Judy's seat exactly one molecule away from physical contact.

So it was definitely a fun first date, featuring all the relaxed spontaneity of a real-estate closing, and in later years I did regain some feeling in my arm. My point, Eric Knott, is that the key to successful dating is self-confidence. I bet that good-looking girl in your English class would LOVE to go out with you. But YOU have to make the first move. So just do it! Pick up that phone! Call Phil Grant.

After Reading

Connecting Meaning

1. How does the title, "Fear of Failure," reflect the author's view of dating?

_____

_____

_____

2. Who is Phil Grant, and why would Eric call him?

_____

_____

_____

_____

3. Recall the details of the author's date with Judy.

_____

_____

_____

_____

Selection 2   ## Y Not Love?

HELENE STAPINSKI

Before Reading   Before you read "Y Not Love?" predict what the topic may be. Scan the story to see if you have correctly predicted the topic. Think about the topic. Relate what you know to "Y Not Love?" and set your purpose for reading. Do you expect to be entertained, to gain knowledge, or to explore an argument?

Words to Preview

cohorts	(n.) group of people, associates
macro-trend	(n.) large trend
neotraditionalism	(n.) a return to belief in traditional values
pundit	(n.) a learned person
jaded	(adj.) emotionally hardened
endocrine	(adj.) dealing with glands that secrete hormones

During Reading   As you read "Y Not Love?" continue to predict where the author is headed, visualize the story, and monitor your understanding. Write your comments, questions, or descriptions in the margin as you read.

Ryan K. has searched all his life for his soul mate, and when he finally finds her, he will romantically propose marriage, rather than living together. He will have sex with his bride for the first time on their wedding night. He has no respect for women who sleep around. But that doesn't stop him from wearing Between the Sheets cologne.

On a recent date with a potential mate, Ryan (cologne liberally applied) wore a suit and took Bachelorette No. 1 on a traditional night-out-dinner and a play. He almost bought her flowers, but then thought twice about it, figuring it would be awkward for her to lug a bouquet around all night. When he's feeling a bit more adventurous, he might take a date to play miniature golf or even go bowling.

Though he fits the profile of the classic male of the 1950s, Ryan is not from the Ozzie-and-Harriet generation.

He is a 19-year-old snowboarder from Vail, Colorado, a college freshman majoring in business at Georgetown University who is looking for love in all the right places. And in many ways, he's more idealistic than his baby boomer parents ever were, at least when it comes to matters of the heart—and more conservative, too. Picture Eisenhower, but with a pierced eyebrow.

"The soul mate thing is so huge," Ryan says. "I still believe there's one person out there that you're meant for. It sounds naive. But this generation kind of has a trust in fate. When I talked to my mom about it, she told me she could have married seven or eight different people, that my father was the best choice at the time. Not 'He was my true love.' I was like, 'Oh, thanks.'"

With Ryan and his cohorts in mind, market analysts are predicting a values shift for Gen Y lovers—whose dating, mating, and child-rearing habits may be more like those of their grandparents than like the cast of Melrose Place.

"One of the macro-trends we're seeing is neotraditionalism," says Kirsty Doig, vice president of Youth Intelligence, a market research and trend forecasting group based in New York City. "These kids are fed up with the superficialities of life. They have not had a lot of stability in their lives. It's a backlash, a return to tradition and ritual. And that includes marriage. It's all about finding 'the right one'—as opposed to sleeping around."

Though census data has yet to reflect the trend—marriage and child-bearing have continued to occur at later ages, and living together is still on the rise—the pundits all agree: We're headed for a second coming of family values. And with it, boosted sales of white wedding gowns, subscriptions to bridal magazines, and perhaps a future surge in sales of Pampers.

"This generation is very much into the spirituality of love," says Doig. "They're much more optimistic than Generation X . . . They know they'll find their soul mate."

Last year, when asked if they would get married if they found the right person, 80.5 percent of 18-to-24-year-olds answered a resounding "Yes!" Only 69 percent of Gen X—the 25-to-34-year-olds—held the same romantic view, according to the General Social Survey of the University of Chicago.

Rather than base their lives on people like Sylvester Stallone—whose daughter was nine months old when he and mom, Jennifer Flavin, wed in 1997—Generation Ys are more likely to follow the example set by young Macaulay Culkin, the *Home Alone* star raised in a turbulent, common-law marriage, who tied the knot with his 17-year-old girlfriend last year.

People like Culkin—and even snowboarding business majors like Ryan—are what marketing consultant Liz Nickles of Chicago-based Nickles & Ashcraft calls the early adopters: opinion and style leaders who set the trends. "They don't show up on the government charts," she admits, "but the rest of the population follows them."

Nickles, who's been conducting surveys with partner Laurie Ashcraft for the past 18 years, predicts a surge in teen marriage and a trend toward bigger families, whether because of the threat of AIDS or simply as a rebellion against what their free-lovin', baby boomer parents did in the '60s. Or perhaps more importantly, what Mom and Dad did in the '80s.

"[Gen Y's] role models were mothers focused on their careers," says Nickles. "But today you can have a career, and your first priority can still be your home. For these young women, their heart is in the home."

In their latest survey, "The New Millennium Woman," Nickles and Ashcraft found that 82 percent of 20-to-24-year-olds thought motherhood was the most important job in the world, compared to 72 percent in the more jaded 25-to-34-year-old Gen X category.

Sociologist Linda Waite, codirector of the Alfred P. Sloan Center on Parents, Children and Work at the University of Chicago, says that because children usually rebel against their parents, it makes sense that Generation Y may get hitched earlier. "Part of the women's movement," she explains, "was involved in trying to make sure women weren't trapped in bad marriages. Certainly some marriages are bad, but marriage has its advantages, too."

Perhaps the younger set knows instinctually what Waite has spent years researching—that married people are much more healthy psychologically and physically than those who are just living together. For women, according to Waite's forthcoming book, *The Case for Marriage* (Harvard University Press), the state of matrimony improves their access to health insurance, provides safer places to live, and even boosts their endocrine and immune systems. Men reap the benefits as well, with improved careers and extended life spans.

After Reading

Connecting Meaning

1. Did you meet your purpose for reading? Explain.

_____

2. How would you explain Ryan's concept of "a soul mate"?

_____

_____

3. Review the author's examples of a return to more traditional values.

_____

_____

_____

_____

_____

Selection 3

True Love

PATRICIA JENSEN

Before Reading

Before you read "True Love," predict what the topic may be. Scan the story to see if you have correctly predicted the topic. Think about the topic. Relate what you know to "True Love." Set your purpose for reading: to be entertained, to gain knowledge, or to explore an argument.

Words to Preview

schottische (n.) a round dance in two-quarter time
proficient (adj.) performing with expert correctness

During Reading   As you read "True Love," continue to predict where the author is headed, visualize the story, and monitor your understanding. Write your comments, questions, or descriptions in the margin as you read.

The big band era was an exciting time in America. Live music and dancing was the fashion. As a young woman, I loved to dance. Along with my three sisters and my neighborhood girlfriends, we could be found at the Trianon Ball Room on Saturday nights.

I could waltz, two-step, jitterbug, polka, and schottische. During the summer, we would go to the lakes to dance, for they would always have live music.

One particular evening, a man asked me to dance. He was pleasant but not an extraordinary dancer, and he talked all the time. Little did I know then, what an impact he would have on my life.

We danced the fox-trot and then came a jitterbug rhythm, and he still would use the same old steps. This annoyed me. As the dance ended, he deposited me next to my sister and asked us if we would like a soft drink. "Sure," she said. As we finished our drink, he reached over and took my hand and led me out onto the dance floor, same old two-step again.

When we had completed our dance, I excused myself and headed for the ladies' lounge. I wasted time there. By now he would surely have another partner. I strolled out and there he was! . . . HORRORS . . . I thought he is like glue to wallpaper and couldn't seem to get rid of him.

We danced the last dance and he asked to take me home. "No!" I said. "My father's rules are my sister and I go together, my sister and I come home together." "May I have your phone number?" he asked. "All right." At least over the phone I could say no.

He never called me.

The following Sunday, I took the bus to see a girlfriend who lived on Alki Avenue, and I had to transfer to another bus. While I waited at the bus stop, he drove up in a new car and opened the passenger door and said, "Hi!, get in."

"No, I am waiting for my bus."

The bus approached and stopped behind him while he just sat. The bus driver honked and he still just sat. It didn't appear that he would ever move so I jumped into the car.

We drove off around Alki beach and talked and then I said, "That green house is where my friend lives and I get off." He drove past the house and kept on going. I yelled "Let me out!!" Panic stricken, I fumbled to find the door handle.

"All right! Did I miss your stop?" he calmly replied. He made a u-turn and stopped at her door.

"How did you find me?" I asked him. "I went to your house and visited with your father, he told me where you would be."

Often he would phone and say, "Pat, I want to go to the movies." I would yell, "NO!" and a half hour later he would be at my door.

Sometimes there were long hesitations over the phone before he announced his message. What an unusual person I thought, but my family adored him, especially my father and brother.

When my brother bought his first car and took him for a ride, the faulty wiring burned up. He was there to help him repair it and teach him mechanics.

Two months had gone by before he told me he was stone deaf and had been educated at the Iowa State School for the Deaf. He relied on lip reading and was very proficient at it. He could talk and also used sign language to communicate.

After I realized the problem, I learned to cope. We never talked to each other over the phone, or in the dark, and I learned to face him when speaking. He was always such a happy person and very good for my personality.

We often went dancing and I even taught him a few new steps. What I didn't realize was that I was falling in love with that big Dane from Iowa.

Six months later, he asked me to marry him and gave me a beautiful diamond ring.

We were married in Seattle and had a happy marriage for forty-three years.

After Reading

Connecting Meaning

1. What is the time period of the story? What clues helped you to figure out the answer?

   _____

   _____

   _____

2. Pat thought the young man she met at the dance was very unusual. What was the reason for the young man's unusual behavior?

   _____

3. Review and recall the events of the story.

   _____

   _____

   _____

Portfolio Activities

Integrating Ideas

The three selections you have read deal with the idea of love on different levels. Relate each of the readings to different people in your life who exemplify the level of love shown in the story. Reflect on these ideas in writing or in class discussion.

Extending Concepts

"Fear of Failure" describes the author's extensive efforts to ask someone out on a date and the date itself. Write a description of your own experiences on these topics.

Collaborative Activity

Local newspapers contain advice columns, like "Dear Abby" or "Ann Landers." Each group will choose several letters dealing with love and its problems. Discuss the problem without reading the columnist's reply. The group will draft its own reply in letter form. Compare the group's response to the columnist's response.

Additional Portfolio Suggestion

The more you read, the more comfortable you will be with the reading process. There are many books dealing with the topic of love. Choose one that interests you, read it, and write a book review. A book review should include a brief summary of the book, your opinion of the book, and why you hold this opinion. Would you recommend the book to others?

▪ ▪ ▪ ▪ Chapter Summary Graphic Organizer

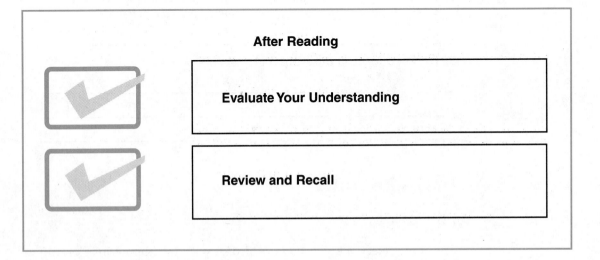

After Reading

Evaluate Your Understanding

Review and Recall

Review

Unit 1

The Reading Process

In this unit, you examined reading as a three step process. By using *before*, *during*, and *after reading* strategies, you are better able to construct meaning from what you read. Your active involvement in this process includes the following strategies:

Before Reading

Preview the reading.
- Read the title.
- Make a prediction about the topic.
- Scan the story.

Connect your knowledge to the author's ideas.
- Think about what you know about the topic.

Establish a purpose for reading.
- Do you expect to be entertained, to gain knowledge, or to explore an argument?

During Reading

Predict as you read.
- Confirm predictions.

Visualize the story.
- Create mental pictures.

Monitor your comprehension.
- Carry on a mental conversation with the author.
- Does the reading make sense?
- Converse mentally about the reading.
- Has comprehension broken down?
- If so, stop and reread.

After Reading

Evaluate your understanding.
- Review the story.

- Did I meet my purpose for reading?
- Did I understand what I just read?
- Were there any confusing parts?
- Can I relate the information to my knowledge or experience?
- Recall.
  - What is important to remember?

■ ■ ■ ■ Unit Review: Graphic Organizer

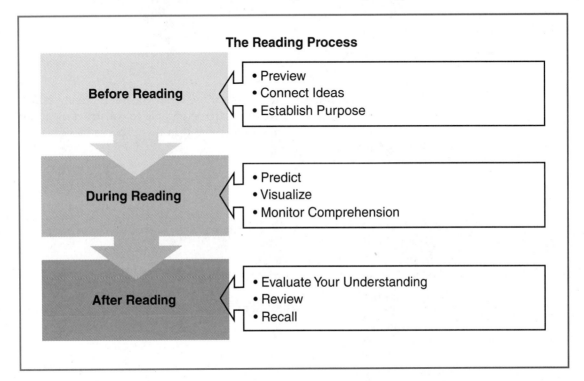

The Reading Process

Before Reading
- Preview
- Connect Ideas
- Establish Purpose

During Reading
- Predict
- Visualize
- Monitor Comprehension

After Reading
- Evaluate Your Understanding
- Review
- Recall

Portfolio Suggestion

Responding to reading in a variety of ways helps you to think critically about what you are reading. A reader response journal is an important way of evaluating your understanding and connecting reading and writing. In a reader response journal, you go beyond writing a simple summary of what you are reading:

- What did you find to be interesting or thought provoking?
- What experiences have you had that you can relate to what you are reading?
- What is your opinion of the reading or the author?
- Can you make a prediction about the story?

You may include any other thoughts about your reading. Other possibilities for reader responses are found in Appendix C.

Vocabulary Strategies

Theme of Readings: Heroism

A hero is no braver than an ordinary man, but he is braver five minutes longer.

RALPH WALDO EMERSON

■ ■ ■ ■ ■ Heroism

For centuries, the concept of heroism applied only to figures of mythology and legend. In Greek and Roman mythology, for example, Hercules was a man of divine ancestry who showed courage, strength, and boldness. Other cultures have similar, "larger than life" figures whose stories were often told to teach values, create a group identity, and entertain listeners.

As time passed, the need for these stories was still important, but the concept of heroism was extended to real people. George Washington fought for his country, shared the hardships of Valley Forge with his men, and chose to become president instead of king. He was admired for honesty, courage, leadership, and compassion and came to be viewed as an American hero. Similarly, Charles Lindbergh was called a hero for being the first person to fly across the Atlantic Ocean by himself, and Rosa Parks was hailed for standing her ground against segregation on buses. In all of these cases heroes had courage, goals, beliefs, and a willingness to make personal sacrifices for what is important.

Heroes are found among family, friends, teachers, and neighbors. A passing motorist pulls an accident victim from a burning car. A twelve-year-old girl saves her little brother from drowning in the local lake. An ordinary person put to a test may accomplish an extraordinary feat. Whoever they may be, heroes will continue to inspire us.

▪ ▪ ▪ ▪ Vocabulary Strategies

The ordinary feat of reading may at times seem extraordinarily difficult if you are not familiar with the words used by an author. You may ignore a word rather than dust off the dictionary. Sometimes you feel you know the word but can not clearly express its meaning. Without a clear understanding of the words, you are unable to grasp an author's concepts. Increasing your vocabulary will expand your knowledge and improve your reading.

To improve your vocabulary, you can use a variety of strategies. Through context clues, some sentences will provide enough information for you to determine a word's meaning. The general sense of the reading may also help you to predict the definition of a word. Your knowledge of word parts, roots, prefixes, and suffixes can be applied to unknown words. No one method will help you learn the meaning of every word, but together these strategies will help you increase your vocabulary.

To help you remember new words, you will want to try recording their meanings in several ways. Graphic organizers (diagrams of words) show definitions, related terms, examples, and concepts. They create a picture of a particular term that will help you visualize the meaning. Word cards may also be used if they include more than a definition.

These vocabulary strategies reflect the activities that make you an effective reader. You will predict, visualize, and monitor your understanding of words as you apply these strategies to construct meaning for the entire selection.

Unit Objective

After completing this unit, you will be able to understand multiple strategies to increase vocabulary knowledge.

4

Vocabulary Strategies

Theme of Readings: Contemporary Heroes

There lives in each of us a hero awaiting the call to action.

H. JACKSON BROWN, JR.

Contemporary Heroes

Contemporary heroes come from all walks of life. They are men and women who have answered their own personal call to action. The stories in this chapter are about two heroes widely proclaimed by the media. The third person is less well known and may not be familiar to you.

As part of the Mercury 7 Program, John Glenn was among the first group of American astronauts to enter outer space; in 1962, he became the first American to orbit the earth. He later went on to a successful career in government and politics. In 1998, at the age of 77, he braved the dangers of space again and became America's oldest astronaut.

Well known for her work in the entertainment industry, Oprah Winfrey turned her fame into an instrument for good. After learning of the molestation and death of a four-year-old child, Oprah Winfrey set into motion legislation to protect children. Her commitment to social change provides a contemporary role model.

Joe Foss is known for his work as the first commissioner of the American Football League and for his television show, "The American Sportsman." In 1943, he was awarded the Congressional Medal of Honor for his bravery and service as a pilot during World War II.

Under different circumstances, each of these people answered a "call to action." They represent only a few of the contemporary heroes who may inspire you to do the same.

Chapter Objectives

After completing this chapter, you will be able to

1. **Use context clues to define a word.**
2. **Use word parts to construct word meaning.**
3. **Create graphic organizers to improve vocabulary knowledge.**

Focus on Vocabulary Strategies

Vocabulary in Context

When you open a jigsaw puzzle box, a thousand individual pieces wait to be assembled into one scene. Hold up a piece of the puzzle, and you can not recognize the finished picture. To help you to figure out where the piece fits, you use clues such as the shape and color of the piece, the picture on the box, and your own sense of how to put the puzzle together. As you find surrounding pieces, the picture begins to emerge.

When you open a book, you see a thousand different words. It is only when you put these words together while reading that they make sense. Sometimes a word is unfamiliar to you, but you can use clues found in the context—the surrounding words, ideas, and punctuation—to understand the meaning of the word.

Using the context clues of definition, explanation, example or illustration, logic, and contrast will help you give meaning to unfamiliar words. Following are examples of these clues:

Definition/Synonym   Sometimes a sentence provides a direct definition or a synonym of the unknown word.

> *Example:* Molly Brown became better known as "Unsinkable Molly Brown" for her <u>prowess</u>, or superior courage, during the *Titanic* disaster.

Explanation   An explanation of the unknown word may be found in other words in the sentence or paragraph.

> *Example:* Charles Lindbergh gained fame as the first aviator to complete a solo <u>transoceanic</u> flight. His nonstop flight across the Atlantic Ocean began May 20 on Long Island, New York, and ended May 21, 1927, in Paris, France.

Example/Illustration   An unfamiliar word may be followed by an example or illustration that leads you to its meaning.

> *Example:* Jackie Robinson, the first player to break the color barrier in major league baseball, endured <u>discriminatory</u> acts against him as he grew up. For example, the local swimming pool was "for whites only."

Logic   Sometimes a word's meaning may come indirectly from the ideas presented in the sentence or paragraph. Use your own thoughts and experiences as a basis to predict the meaning of the word.

Example: <u>Pandemonium</u> broke loose at the Olympic games when Florence Griffith Joyner (Flo Jo) set a world record for the women's 100-meter dash in 1988.

Contrast   A word's meaning may be found in a sentence or paragraph that states the opposite meaning.

Example: Joe Foss is a relatively unknown World War II hero when compared to <u>prominent</u> heroes such as George Patton and Dwight D. Eisenhower.

Short Exercises: Context Clues

Rosa Parks is a hero of the Civil Rights Movement in America, and Mahatma Gandhi led the people of India in their successful struggle for independence from Britain.

Directions: Read the following sentences about Rosa Parks and Mahatma Gandhi. Define each of the underlined words using context clues.

1. In the 1930s, the education that most black children like Rosa Parks received was minimal, leaving many of them qualified only for <u>menial</u> or domestic jobs.

   _____

2. In the South, the treatment of blacks on the public bus system was one of the most frustrating of everyday <u>indignities</u>. Black passengers were required to give up their seats for any whites who wanted to sit. Blacks could not sit forward of any white passenger and were always told to "move to the back of the bus."

   _____

3. In 1955, Rosa Parks was arrested for refusing to give up her seat on the bus to a white person. This action was <u>momentous</u>, touching off a thirteen-month bus boycott in Montgomery, Alabama, and giving civil rights activists national attention. Eventually the events in Montgomery led to the Supreme Court decision outlawing segregation on buses.

   _____

4. Rosa Parks did not <u>succumb</u> to the hardships put upon her by society. She rose above them and went on with her life.

   _____

5. In 1999, President Clinton <u>bestowed</u> the nation's highest civilian honor upon Parks, giving her the Congressional Gold Medal.

_____

6. The British passed many <u>exorbitant</u> laws against the people of India to keep strict control over the country. Gandhi felt these laws were unfair.

_____

7. Many of the protests led by Gandhi were <u>illicit</u>, and he had often been jailed.

_____

8. Gandhi was a <u>revered</u> leader with hundreds of followers. He reminded the people of their duty to love one another and to resist the British through nonviolent means.

_____

9. Achieving independence from Britain was not a <u>facile</u> accomplishment. It was seventeen years from Gandhi's first march until the British granted India self-government.

_____

10. Mahatma Gandhi's <u>doctrines</u> or teachings were a great influence on another heroic figure of our time, Martin Luther King.

_____

Word Parts

The use of context clues is one strategy for finding the meaning of unknown words. If the sentence does not contain these clues, you may use your knowledge of word parts to help you to figure out the meaning. Word parts are segments of words that have consistent meanings that can be used to define the whole word. These segments are prefixes, suffixes, and roots.

Prefix

A **prefix** is a word part added to the beginning of a word that changes the meaning of a word. For example, the meanings of *unicycle, bicycle,* and *tricycle* differ because of the prefixes *uni, bi,* and *tri,* indicating one, two, or three wheels.

Suffix

A **suffix** is a word part added to the end of a word that often changes a word from one part of speech to another. Adding the suffix "*-ment*" to the verb *encourage* changes it to the noun *encouragement.*

Root

A **root** is a word part or word to which prefixes and suffixes can be added. For example, *graph* is a root that can stand alone as a word. Its meaning can be expanded by adding a prefix, a suffix, a prefix and a suffix, or another root—for example, *autograph, graphing, biography, telegraph.*

It is important to note that a certain combination of letters can be a word part in some instances but not in others. For example, the prefix *"pre-"* means "before" as in *preview* or *precaution.* In words such as *precious* and *preach,* "pre" is not a prefix.

Short Exercises: Word Parts

Dr. Jonas Salk is recognized as a hero for his development of the first polio vaccine. Dr. Shirley Jackson was appointed head of the U.S. Nuclear Regulatory Commission in 1995, making her the first woman and the first African-American to lead the agency.

Directions: Read the following sentences about Jonas Salk and Shirley Jackson. Define the underlined words using your knowledge of word parts. You may refer to the list of common word parts in Appendix E.

1. Jonas Salk is an American <u>epidemiologist</u> and medical researcher who was born in New York City in 1914.

   _____

   _____

2. While still a student, Salk became interested in bacterial vaccines. These vaccines could be made from a preparation of dead bacteria, which would immunize without <u>inducing</u> the infection.

   _____

3. Salk is noted for developing the vaccine that causes the building of <u>antibodies</u> against several types of polio, a crippling disease of the 1950s.

   _____

4. Salk became an <u>international</u> hero as millions of parents were relieved of the anxiety that their child might die or be crippled for life.

   _____

5. Jonas Salk is one of the founders of the field of <u>psychoneuroimmunology.</u>

   _____

   _____

6. Dr. Jackson <u>superceded</u> many obstacles in her academic and professional career. She was ostracized by many in her freshman class in 1965 for being one of two black women at the Massachusetts Institute of Technology.

_____

7. Four years into her post at the Nuclear Regulatory Commission, Jackson had won considerable praise for restoring <u>credibility</u> to a troubled agency.

_____

8. Rensselear <u>Polytechnic</u> Institute asked Dr. Jackson to become the head of their institution. This would make her the first African-American woman to head a major research institution.

_____

9. and 10. Dr. George Campbell, Jr., president of the National Action Council for Minorities in Engineering stated, "Jackson's <u>visibility</u> and <u>extensive</u> network of scientists will draw more people of color to Rensselear and to the fields of mathematics and science."

_____

_____

Graphic Organizers

Using context clues and word parts, you are able to figure out some unknown words as you read. To continue to expand your vocabulary knowledge, you may want to use other effective strategies to learn and remember new words. Graphic organizers are visual representations of the words, their meanings, and related terms.

Concept of Definition Map

One easy and effective organizer is a **concept of definition map** (Figure 4-1) originally developed by Schwartz and Raphael (1985). It helps you understand a vocabulary word by answering three key questions: What is it? What is it like? What or who are some examples?

Word Maps

A **word map** (Figure 4-2) based on common word parts can also help you expand your vocabulary. A word map is a chart on which your knowledge of one word part is expanded to a group of other words that use that word

Figure 4-1
**Concept of
Definition Map**

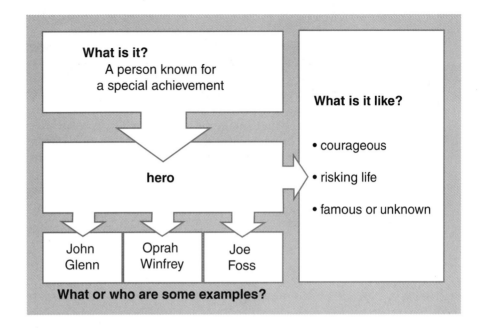

Figure 4-2
Word Map

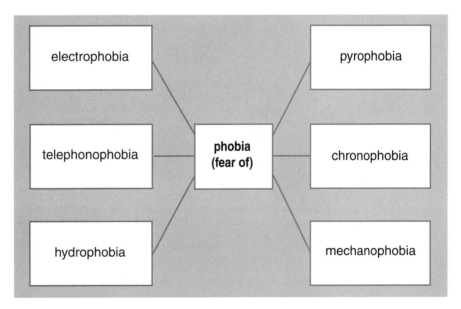

part. For example, if you know the word *phobia* means "fear of," you can use that knowledge to figure out the meaning of the word *cardiophobia*, the fear of heart disease, or *technophobia*, the fear of technology. Use an organizer to help learn and remember related words. You may wish to add the definition under each word.

Word Cards

Graphic organizers represent one way of increasing your vocabulary knowledge. Another method to learn and remember new vocabulary is the use of word cards. On your card, write a troublesome word, its definition, and its pronunciation. To make sure that your word card will be meaningful to you, include one or more of the following: a sentence that uses the word, a visual image or picture that you associate with the word, or a graphic organizer for the word. Constructing one card for each difficult word will provide study cards that can be reviewed to increase your vocabulary knowledge.

No one strategy can be used for all words. As you apply them to various readings, you will learn to choose the most appropriate strategy for the words you need to learn and remember.

■ ■ ■ ■ Short Exercises: Concept of Definition Maps

Directions: A model of a concept of definition map was provided previously. Complete the concept of definition maps by filling in the blanks. The first one has been started for you.

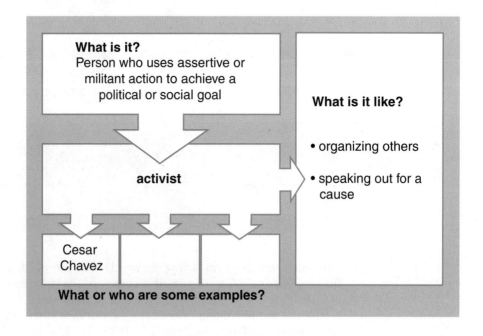

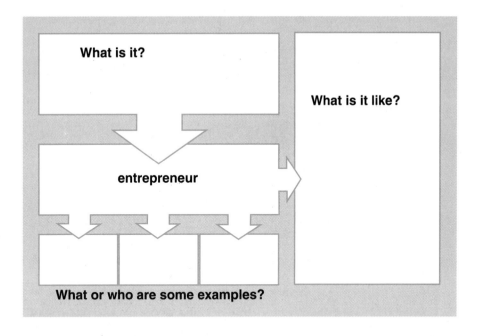

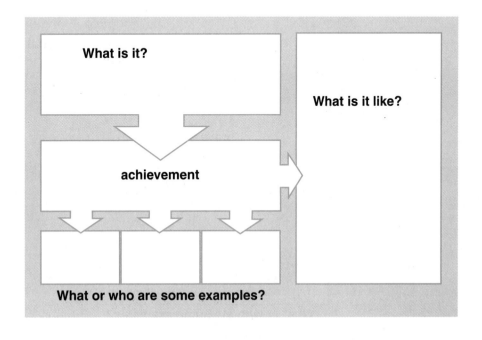

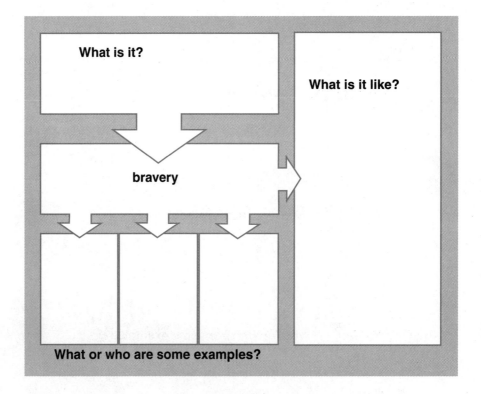

What is it?

What is it like?

infamous

What or who are some examples?

What is it?

What is it like?

bravery

What or who are some examples?

Short Exercises: Word Maps

Fill in the following word maps with other vocabulary words that use the common word part at the center. You may wish to add the definition of the word beneath it. You can check your answers using a dictionary. Add more lines as necessary to expand.

1.

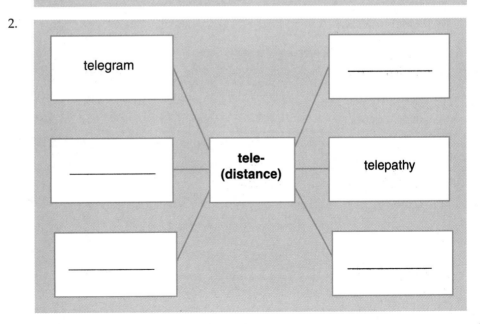

2.

3. Create a word map for the root *port*.

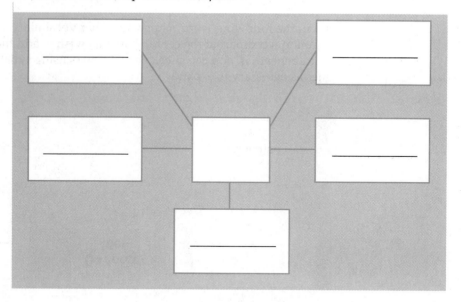

4. Create a word map for the root *graph*.

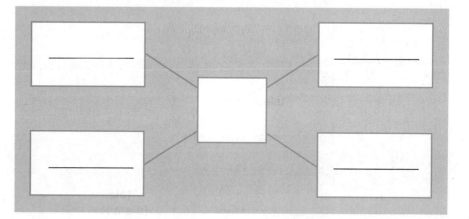

5. Create a word map for the root *duct*.

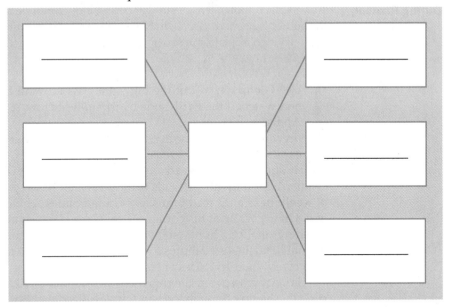

■ ■ ■ ■ Reading Selections

Selection 1

John Glenn: Man with a Mission

WILLIAM R. NEWCOTT

Before Reading   Before you read "John Glenn: Man with a Mission," predict what the topic may be. Scan the article to see if you have correctly predicted the topic. Think about the topic. Is outer space a frontier to explore for people of all ages? Have you ever thought of being a space pioneer? Relate what you already know about space exploration and the astronaut, John Glenn, to this topic. Set your purpose for reading. Do you expect to be entertained, to gain knowledge, or to explore an argument?

Words to Preview

triumphant	*(adj.)* celebrating in success	
emblazon	*(v.)* to adorn	
insignia	*(n.)* a badge or emblem	
scrub	*(n.)* a scraggly tree or shrub	
gantry	*(n.)* a massive vertical frame used in assembling a rocket	
speculate	*(v.)* to guess	
adrift	*(adv.)* without direction or purpose	
advocate	*(n.)* a supporter or defender	
trepidation	*(n.)* a state of alarm or dread	
fester	*(v.)* to become an increasing source of irritation	

During Reading As you read "John Glenn: Man with a Mission," continue to predict where the author is headed, visualize the story, and monitor your comprehension. Write your comments, questions, or descriptions in the margin as you read.

John Glenn gazed out the big square window in the orbiter *Discovery* and watched the Earth slide by 345 miles below. A tear came to his eye. And stayed there.

"In zero gravity a tear doesn't roll down your cheek," he later recalled. "It just sits there on your eyeball until it evaporates."

He smiled, embarrassed a little. But he was clear-eyed on this day in December 1998, a month after his triumphant return to space and just a couple of weeks before his four terms as a United States senator would come to an end. On the walls of his corner office in the Hart Senate Office Building in Washington, D.C., hung mementos of legislative victories, photos of presidential handshakes, tributes to him as America's first man in orbit, in 1962. And everywhere, pictures of his beloved wife, Annie.

Sitting across from Glenn, who was illuminated like a museum piece by sunlight slanting through the window, I realized that this was the first time I'd encountered the senator in a suit and tie. For months I'd followed his training at the Johnson Space Center in Houston and at the Kennedy Space Center in Florida, and virtually all he'd worn were blue zippered flight outfits, bulky orange pressure suits, polo shirts emblazoned with the mission insignia.

Even at age 77, John Glenn seemed to be made for an astronaut's gear, and vice versa. Back in the beginning it was that way too.

Early on the morning of Glenn's space shuttle flight, I drove through the Florida scrub to the Kennedy Space Center by way of the Cape Canaveral Air Station, where the original Mercury rockets were launched. It was still long before dawn as I approached the abandoned site of launch complex 14. The Mercury gantry is gone. The blockhouse is a conference center. The ghosts of a space program in its infancy whisper through the sea grapes.

Thirty-six years earlier, at this spot on a morning much like this, a man in a silver space suit trudged from a trailer carrying his briefcase-size life-support system, an alien headed for the office. Above him a nine-story-tall rocket groaned under the pressure of refined kerosene fuel and hissed billowing clouds of vented liquid oxygen.

A countdown, a roar, a pencil-shaped craft rose into the Florida sky. Five hours later it was all over: John Glenn, the first American to see three sunrises in a single day, sat bobbing in the Atlantic, awaiting pickup by the destroyer U.S.S. *Noa.*

He was a national hero. Although two other U.S. astronauts, Alan Shepard and Gus Grissom, had pierced the boundary of space before him in short suborbital flights, Glenn cast a spell on the American people that never quite wore off. There were parades, speeches, honorary degrees, and a medal

On October 27, 1998, John Glenn gives thumbs up upon his arrival at Cape Canaveral for his historic flight. (SYGMA)

from the President. But what John Glenn really wanted, and what he genuinely expected, was his next shot. America was going to the moon, and John Glenn planned to be there.

"I wasn't concerned when I wasn't put back in the astronaut rotation right away," he says. "They gave me some administrative work to do, and I kept asking about being sent up again, and they kept telling me, 'Headquarters says not yet. Not yet.'"

Some speculate that President John F. Kennedy didn't want to risk losing the space program's greatest hero in an accident.

"Unfortunately I never got to ask him," said Glenn. "And I got tired of waiting around. So I left the space program."

A year later, adrift from the Marines for the first time in his adult life, Glenn went into business. He became president of Royal Crown International and eventually achieved political legend status: Four times Ohioans sent him to the Senate.

"I figured my time in space had come and gone," he said. "I'd given the space program a good run, I thought, and that was it."

He has always remained an advocate of NASA and the space program though. Within hours of the space shuttle *Challenger* accident in 1986, Glenn was in Florida with the crew's families to offer sympathy and to lend his support to the space program. His influence has been key in keeping the International Space Station program alive.

It was while doing research in support of the space station that Glenn stumbled upon what ultimately became his ticket back.

"Over the years," Glenn said, "NASA has observed more than 50 changes that occur in the human body in space. And nine or ten of these are very similar to things that happen in the process of aging. Things like loss of muscle strength. Bone density loss. Cardiovascular changes. Changes in balance and coordination.

"My idea was to send an older person up and study the body's reaction to space flight—see if there were differences between younger and older people. For example, how long was the recovery period after returning to Earth? Shorter or longer for an older astronaut?

"I went over to NASA to talk to Dan Goldin, the administrator. I made no bones about it—I wanted to be the person to do it."

As dusk fell over Florida, I wandered to the top of the Kennedy Space Center press mound, a small hill where the NASA public information office and network broadcast booths perch. "Not since the shuttle's return to flight in 1988 have so many members of the press converged upon this place . . . ."

The routine on October 29 bore more than a passing resemblance to that Mercury morning in 1962. The drive to the pad, the ride in the gantry elevator, the walk across a metal bridge to the waiting spacecraft. The strap-in, the closing of the hatch, the long wait.

A few minutes of trepidation—five private planes buzzing into, and finally out of, restricted airspace—and then *Discovery* rose into the afternoon sky on a tongue of fire. As an estimated quarter million observers crawled back home fighting ten-mile-an-hour traffic jams, the shuttle crew orbited the globe at five miles a second.

Space travel used to be a young man's game, but when John Glenn went into orbit aboard *Discovery*, four generations of men and women could gaze into the sky and think, That could be me someday. At the same time Glenn was looking down and doing some thinking of his own.

"It's quite something," he said, "to look down on this blue planet, seeing that little film of air that surrounds it. You fly over the Mediterranean, over the Middle East—and it's so beautiful. You wonder why in the world humans can't solve all the problems they've created and left to fester over the centuries.

"I was at the Houston airport on my way back to Washington recently when this older guy walked up to me, all excited. He shook my hand and said, 'Boy, you're changing my life!' I said how's that? He said, 'I'm 74, and ever since I was a kid I've wanted to climb Mount Kilimanjaro. I haven't done it, and I kept putting it off. And now I'm gonna do it!' And all the time his wife is standing behind him, just shaking her head.

"So I may have killed a man on Kilimanjaro, for all I know. But I've noticed something. I've noticed that maybe because of all this, people are seeing themselves in a way they haven't before. They're realizing that older people have the same ambitions, hopes, and dreams as anybody else. I say you should live life based on how you feel and not by the calendar."

The measure of John Glenn's achievements may someday be the familiar sight of grandparents waving good-bye to grandchildren at Gate 36 of the Los Angeles Space Port. And don't be surprised by the gentleman with the sky blue eyes you see in line there.

"Annie says no more space travel," Glenn grins. "Well, I've never fully committed to that."

After Reading

Word Connections

1. Glenn was "illuminated like a museum piece by sunlight slanting through the window." Which words in this sentence help you to define *illuminated?*

   _____

   _____

   _____

2. Alan Shepard and Gus Grissom completed short suborbital flights even before John Glenn. Define the prefix *sub-*. Create a word map for this word part.

3. Use your knowledge of word parts to help you to define *cardiovascular.*

   _____

   _____

   _____

Connecting Meaning

1. What careers other than astronaut did John Glenn pursue?

   _____

   _____

   _____

   _____

2. What research questions ultimately supported Glenn's ticket back to space?

_____

_____

_____

_____

_____

3. John Glenn's initial space venture was followed by a return to space in 1998 at the age of 77. Why do you think Glenn chose to take this risk again?

_____

_____

_____

_____

Selection 2

Oprah Winfrey

FROM *AMERICAN HEROES: THEIR LIVES, THEIR VALUES, THEIR BELIEFS*
ROBERT B. PAMPLIN, JR. AND GARY K. EISLER

Before Reading

Before you read "Oprah Winfrey," predict what the topic of this article may be. Scan the story to see if you have correctly predicted the topic. Think about the topic. Oprah Winfrey is famous for her national television talk show. Do you know anything about other parts of her life? Should famous people use their fame to help others? Think about what you already know about Oprah Winfrey. Set your purpose for reading. Do you expect to be entertained, to gain knowledge, or to explore an argument?

Words to Preview

abduct	*(v.)* to kidnap	
compensate	*(v.)* to counterbalance; to make a payment to	
advocacy	*(n.)* active support	
prestigious	*(adj.)* having the high regard of others	
pedophile	*(n.)* adult who has a sexual attraction toward a child	
irrevocably	*(adj.)* impossible to retract or take back	

During Reading   As you read this selection about Oprah Winfrey, continue to predict what may happen next in the article, visualize the story, and monitor your comprehension. Write your comments, questions, or descriptions in the margin as you read.

T he death of Angelica Mena, a four-year-old Chicago girl who had been molested, strangled, and thrown into Lake Michigan by Michael Howarth, who had been convicted twice before of abducting and raping children, set Oprah Winfrey in motion. After she saw the reports on the evening news in mid-February 1991, something snapped. "I didn't know the child, never heard her laughter," Winfrey said. "But I vowed that night to do something, to take a stand for the children of this country."

Winfrey had long been concerned about child victimization. She had learned that experts maintain that abuse victims seek control in their adult lives to compensate for the helplessness they experienced as abused children, tending to abuse children themselves. That she was abused as a child herself, according to that explanation, could account for Winfrey's personal motivation. She'd talked about the issue on her show and sent checks to child advocacy groups.

This time, however, she went to see former Illinois Governor James Thompson, a partner in the prestigious Chicago law firm of Winston & Strawn. Thompson helped her draft child protection legislation for the entire country. "When millions of people look to you to both set an example and add your voice to theirs, it empowers you to do more than you ordinarily might," the former governor said of Winfrey's fight. "This is a woman with extraordinary commitment."

Winfrey was only thirty-seven in 1991 when she went to Washington, D.C., with her own idea of the law in her hands: The National Child Protection Act, which became known as "the Oprah Bill." The bill required states to register the names and social security numbers of and other information about anyone convicted of child molestation and report it to the U.S. Justice Department. That information becomes available through the FBI to employers screening job applicants for positions in which the applicant would have access to children. (At the time, only California, Iowa, Florida, Minnesota, Texas, and Washington had such reporting systems; in one year, these states had discovered sixty-two hundred individuals, convicted of serious crimes, who sought jobs as child-care providers.)

In Washington, although it is unusual for citizens to prepare legislation themselves, Winfrey won the support of Senator Joseph Biden, chairman of the Senate Judiciary Committee on Child Abuse, who agreed to sponsor the bill, as did Representative Patricia Schroeder. "[Biden] asked for some changes, which we agreed to, and he said 'We'll have hearings in two weeks.' I was stunned," Winfrey reported.

"This is the best proposal that's come before us," Biden told his committee. "The idea is simple: that you must do everything you can to detect the convicted criminal before . . . another tragedy takes place."

At a hearing, Winfrey told the committee, "Everybody deals with their pain differently. Some become overachievers like me, and others become mothers who kill. Pedophiles seek employment where they will be in contact with children," she testified. "There are millions upon millions of silent victims in this country that have been and will continue to be irrevocably harmed unless we do something to stem this horrible tide.

"I wept for Angelica, and I wept for us, a society that apparently cares so little about its children that we would allow a man with two previous convictions for kidnapping and rape of children to go free after serving only seven years of a fifteen-year sentence."

Following the hearing, Winfrey recounted her own experience with child abuse at a press conference. "You lose your childhood when you've been abused. My heart goes out to those children who are abused at home and have no one to turn to."

Her arguments were convincing. Oprah Winfrey enjoyed the satisfaction of personally witnessing President Bill Clinton sign the bill into national law. Clinton said, "Not unlike the Brady Bill, this law creates a national database network. This one can be used by any child-care provider in America to conduct a background check to determine if a job applicant can be trusted with our children."

With the bill safely on the books, Winfrey now plans to lobby for mandatory sentencing of child abusers. "We have to demonstrate that we value our children enough to say that when you hurt a child, this is what happens to you," Winfrey said. "It is not negotiable."

She and the women of her staff have also formed a "Big Sister" group with two dozen teenage girls from a Chicago housing project in which drugs and crime are prevalent. Winfrey invites the teens to her place for pajama parties and takes them to plays and social gatherings. But she also gives them dictionaries with orders to learn five new words a day.

After Reading

Word Connections

1. Abuse victims seek to control their adult lives to compensate for childhood abuse. In what other situations do people feel the need for *compensation*?

   _____

   _____

2. Oprah Winfrey was a children's rights advocate. Create a concept of definition map for the term *advocate*.

Diagram:

Connecting Meaning

1. Oprah Winfrey vowed "to take a stand for the children of this country." In what ways did she take action?

   _____

   _____

   _____

   _____

2. In your own words, describe the requirements of The National Child Protection Act.

   _____

   _____

   _____

   _____

   _____

3. How is The National Child Protection Act like the Brady Bill?

_____

_____

4. Do Oprah Winfrey's actions against child abuse fit your definition of heroic? Why or why not?

_____

_____

_____

Selection 3

Joe Foss

FROM *THE GREATEST GENERATION*
TOM BROKAW

Before Reading

Before you read "Joe Foss," predict what the topic of the article may be. Scan the story to see if you have correctly predicted the topic. Think about this topic. Does a hero have to be famous or rich? Do you know any heroic people from World War II or other times? Relate what you already know about heroes to Joe Foss. Set your purpose for reading. Do you expect to be entertained, to gain knowledge, or to explore an argument?

Words to Preview

quintessential	*(adj.)* purest or most typical instance or example
barnstorm	*(v.)* to appear, as at fairs, in exhibitions of stunt flying
arouse	*(v.)* to awaken from sleep
careen	*(v.)* to swerve while in motion
exploit	*(n.)* an act or deed, especially a heroic one
accolade	*(n.)* expression of approval, praise
swagger	*(n.)* a walk with a boastful manner

During Reading

As you read this selection about Joe Foss, continue to predict what is ahead in the article, visualize the story, and monitor your understanding. Write your comments, questions, or descriptions in the margin as you read.

Those of us who lived have to represent those who didn't make it.

N o one would ever accuse Joe Foss of slowing down. Even now, at the age of eighty-two, he inhales life in big, energetic drafts. He is in many ways the quintessential World War II hero. He grew up poor on a farm in South Dakota at the height of the Depression. He lost his father when he was a teenager. He was inspired to fly when he saw another midwesterner, Charles Lindbergh, on a barnstorming tour. He worked at a gasoline station after high school to earn money for college and flying lessons. After playing football and graduating from the University of South Dakota, he enlisted in the Marine Corps in 1940. He quickly became one of the Marines' most gifted pilots, and when war broke out, he spent a year working at Pensacola as an instructor.

In the fall of 1942, Foss shipped out to Guadalcanal as the executive officer of a squadron of Marine F-4 Wildcat fighter planes. Foss remembers they were at sea, with their planes on a carrier, "wondering what it would really be like to finally be in the war." They found out quickly enough when they were aroused from their berths in the middle of the night with the news that Japanese submarines were in the area and the pilots would have to launch their planes early.

Foss, who now lives in Scottsdale, Arizona, remembers that once the squadron was off the carrier and headed for Guadalcanal, "I knew what war was going to be like. As we came in low to Henderson Field on Guadalcanal, we could see bomb craters all around, and the antiaircraft guns were firing at Jap planes overhead. When we landed, the Marines on the ground gave us a big reception, cheering and everything." Those Marines were happy to have the help. They had been fighting steadily since August just to gain control of the field and hang on to it.

Foss said to one of the Marine fliers who had been there awhile, "Well, I guess you veterans will show us around." Foss says the Marine answered. "Oh, you'll be veterans, too, by tomorrow." Actually, it took a week. On October 16, 1942, Foss shot down his first Japanese Zero. By November 19 he had shot down twenty-three, an extraordinary number, but the skies over the Pacific were filled with fighter planes and bombers as the United States and the Japanese battled for control of the air and the sea lanes leading to the mainland of Japan.

In fact, on the day he shot down his first Zero, Foss was nearly shot down himself. In those days, aerial combat was practically face to face. Foss and the other pilots didn't have laser-guided weapons and sophisticated computer systems telling them when to shoot. Those aerial battles were accurately called "dogfights," two snarling high-powered fighter planes twisting and turning, each trying to get the advantage, the pilots hitting the buttons to fire the machine guns, while they continued to fly at speeds of up to 300 miles an hour at altitudes ranging from just a few feet off the ocean surface to high in the clouds.

The F-4 Wildcat was not as quick or as responsive as the Japanese Zero, so when Foss's plane was hit, he knew he was in trouble. He had three Zeros on his tail as he went into a steep dive and then a big, wide turn, trying to get back to Henderson Field with a dead engine and his propeller freewheeling. "The Zeros stayed right behind me," he says, "and as I cleared the hill to land at Henderson they unloaded all their lead at me." Foss landed the plane at full speed, with no flaps and little control in what is called a "dead stick" landing. The F-4 careened across the runway and skidded to a stop just short of some palm trees. Later his ground crew counted more than two hundred bullet holes in the plane. Foss, then twenty-seven years old, sat in his cockpit, badly shaken, thinking, Why did I ever leave the farm? Suddenly he heard the cheers of the ground crew, "kids eighteen and nineteen years old who had watched it all," he recalls, "and I said to myself, Well, you're a leader, Joe. You're in it all the way now, and from that point on I was just a full blower."

By January 1943, Foss had shot down twenty-six enemy planes, equaling Eddie Rickenbacker's record from World War I. He had been shot down and forced to ditch at sea, swimming through the Pacific waters for twelve hours until he was rescued by island natives in a dugout canoe. Two days later he was back in the air.

His exploits included a breathtaking maneuver in which he dove directly toward a Japanese battleship to deliberately draw fire and make it easier for other American planes to torpedo the vessel. As he started his dive he radioed to the rest of the squadron, "Keep it steep, girls, keep it steep." He figured a plane coming straight down would be a difficult target for the battleship guns. He was right, but it was an extremely risky maneuver. When Foss pulled out at the last moment, he was so close to the ship he could see the Japanese officers on the bridge.

He was indestructible. Though he was knocked off the flight line for six weeks by a bout of malaria, he came back to fly again. Foss, who had learned to shoot pheasants and ducks on the wing as a boy on the South Dakota prairie, was a warrior of the old school, mourning the losses of friends from his squadron but never crying. He carried a Bible and a pair of dice in his flight-suit pockets, wore a leather helmet, and chewed on a cigar when he was on the ground. He had a Marine's vocabulary and a bellowing voice. One of his squadron members would say of him, "All the balls of any man who ever walked the earth."

In the spring of 1943, the Marines decided Captain Foss had done his share and brought him home to a hero's welcome, less than a year after he had shipped out. He was awarded the Congressional Medal of Honor and was put on the cover of *Life* magazine, the ultimate press accolade during the war. He had a hero's swagger but a winning smile to go with his plain talk and movie-star looks. Joe Foss was larger than life, and his heroics in the skies over the Pacific were just the beginning of a journey that would take him to places far from that farm with no electricity and not much hope north of Sioux Falls.

After Reading   **Word Connections**

1. During World War II, Joe Foss engaged in dogfights. Define the term *dogfight* as given in the story.

_____

_____

2. "He had been shot down and forced to ditch at sea, swimming through the Pacific waters for twelve hours until he was rescued by island natives in a dugout canoe." What does *ditch* mean in this sentence? What are other meanings of the word?

_____

_____

_____

3. Joe Foss was the quintessential World War II hero. In your own words, define *quintessential*.

_____

_____

Connecting Meaning

1. Joe Foss received awards for his World War II heroism. Describe his heroic exploits.

_____

_____

_____

_____

2. Compare World War II aerial combat to present-day aerial combat.

_____

_____

_____

_____

_____

Portfolio Activities

Integrating Ideas

The selections you have read describe the actions of three heroes. Although each of their situations was unique, as heroes they share common characteristics. What heroic qualities do they embody? What other traits do you see as heroic? Reflect on these ideas in writing or in class discussion.

Extending Concepts

America's first spacemen and World War II heroes represented America's hopes and dreams. Think about the changes in America since the early 1960s. What are the hopes and dreams of today? Write about a contemporary hero who represents these hopes and dreams.

Collaborative Activity

Who are the heroes of today? Create groups of four students. Each student will survey twenty-five students with the following questions: Do you have a hero? Who is it? After bringing the results back to the group, the findings will be compiled and presented to the class.

Additional Portfolio Suggestion

To show your understanding of the vocabulary strategies presented, create several concept of definition maps and word maps with words of your choice.

▪ ▪ ▪ ▪ Chapter Summary Graphic Organizers

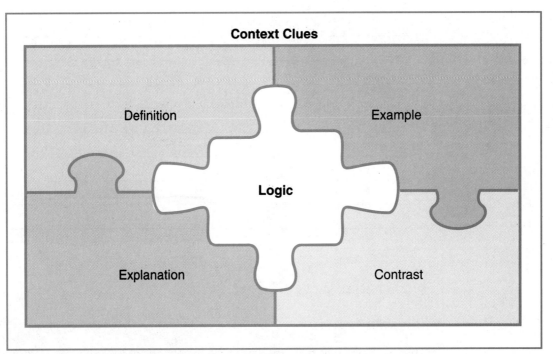

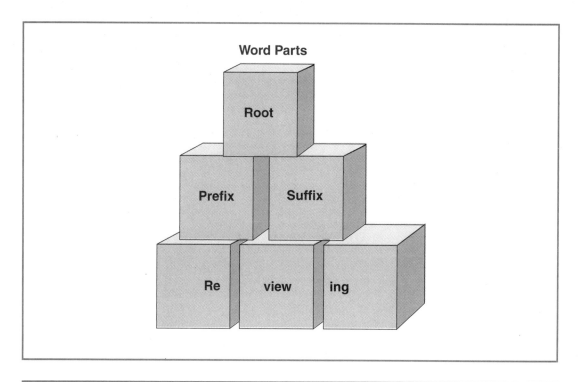

Word Parts

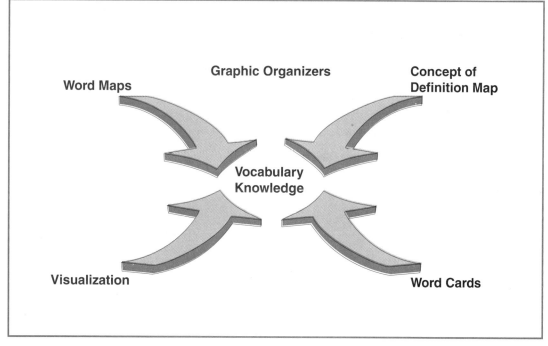

Graphic Organizers

Review

Unit 2

Vocabulary Strategies

In this unit, several strategies were presented to help you figure out, learn, and remember unfamiliar vocabulary. Expanding your vocabulary will increase your understanding while reading.

Context clues allow you to predict a word's meaning by using the surrounding words or the sense of the sentence. Five types of context clues were identified: definition, explanation, example, logic, and contrast.

Word parts also provide information that can be applied to unknown words. Prefixes, suffixes, and roots give you a base of knowledge for use with new words.

To help you to remember, you may record the meanings in several ways. A word map expands the word parts by providing other words that use that part. A concept of definition map helps you to understand vocabulary by answering three questions: What is it? What is it like? What or who are some examples? These are only two of many graphic organizers that you may use.

As you construct meaning for a reading selection, you will predict, visualize, and monitor your understanding of words as you apply these vocabulary strategies.

■ ■ ■ ■ Unit Review: Graphic Organizer

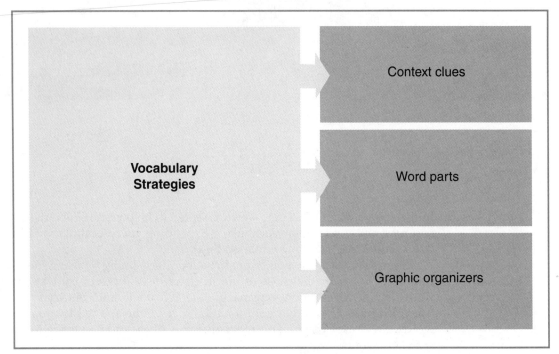

Portfolio Suggestion

Choose a comic book hero such as Batman, Spiderman, or Wonder Woman. Write an essay identifying their heroic qualities. Compare these heroes to real-life heroes.

3

Main Ideas

Theme of Readings: *Fear*

You can measure people . . . by the way they respond to challenge.

DWIGHT D. EISENHOWER

Fear

Fears . . . we all have them. When we are young, we lie in bed frozen with fear of the dark or an open closet door, sure an unseen monster is coming to get us. We may be afraid of a neighbor's dog, a crash of thunder, a bad dream, or an unfamiliar place. As we grow, our fears change. With or without good reason, some of us are afraid of spiders, flying, public speaking, new technology, illness, or death. Others fear crowds, confined spaces, high places, or guns. It is human nature to have some fears, even in adulthood.

For most people, fears are simply part of life. Some of them are justified; they come and go as life changes. There are true dangers in the world which one needs to be on guard against. Sometimes, however, fears become so overwhelming that they are paralyzing; they cross the line and become phobias. Phobias are such intense fears that they are no longer manageable. A phobia keeps a person from going on with everyday life. For example, people commonly fear dentists but will go regularly anyway to keep their teeth healthy. A dentalphobic experiences extreme, paralyzing fear at the thought of a visit to the dentist's office and will avoid this situation at all costs. Likewise, someone may be nervous about flying but will nonetheless get on the plane headed for an exotic dream vacation. A person with a phobia of flying is limited to trips by land, rail, or water: phobias restrict life experiences.

While some people's lives are made narrow by fears, others relish the excitement and challenge of coming face-to-face with danger in their work or leisure time. Policemen, firemen, astronauts, and military personnel, for example, often get great satisfaction from their difficult jobs. They still feel fear on occasion, but ideally they have the bravery, experience, training, equipment, and teamwork to bring threatening situations to a good conclusion.

Other people enjoy pursuing death-defying sports or hobbies, such as sky diving, mountain climbing, or tornado chasing. A great number of us like the excitement that comes from watching others face fearful situations or from experiencing as spectators "safe" danger, such as high-wire circus acts or air shows. We as a nation spend many entertainment dollars to see action/adventure and horror movies, attend car races, watch "X-Game" extreme sports events, and go on ever-more-frightening roller coaster rides.

People with common fears, those with phobias, and those who challenge themselves to confront fear, all handle fear differently. How you deal with your fears depends on your experiences and your personality. If you are like most people, your fears and your attitude toward your fears will have had a significant impact, either positive or negative, on your life.

Main Ideas

As a student, you may hesitate to participate in a class discussion about a reading. You may not be clear on its main points. By using the *before, during,* and *after reading* strategies, your understanding will improve.

1. Before you read, predict the topic of the reading. Ask yourself, "Who or what is this paragraph or selection about?"

2. While you read, establish a mental conversation to keep yourself focused on the reading and connected to the topic. Ask yourself, "What does the author want me, the reader, to understand or remember about this topic? What is the author's main idea?" Whether directly stated or not, the main idea is supported by details that allow you to understand or visualize the reading better. Identify the examples, explanations, or facts that support the author's main point. Major supporting details establish the main idea, while minor details simply add interest.

3. After you read, the topic, the main idea, and the supporting details will come together as you evaluate your understanding. Ask yourself, "Were there any confusing parts? What is important to remember?" Having the ability to identify the topic, the main idea, and the supporting details will enhance your comprehension and make you a more effective reader.

Unit Objectives

After completing this unit, you will be able to

1. **Identify the topic of a selection.**
2. **Determine the stated or unstated main idea of a paragraph or longer selection.**
3. **Recognize the major and minor supporting details of a paragraph or longer selection.**

Topics and Main Ideas

Theme of Readings: *Phobias*

The oldest and strongest emotion of mankind is fear.

H. P. LOVECRAFT

Phobias

We all have fears, but at what point do they interfere with our lives? Many of us jump at the sight of a spider crawling on our leg. A bumpy plane ride may make us nervous. But what if a fear becomes so intense that it makes normal life impossible? Then that fear would become a phobia.

A phobia is an intense and persistent fear of a specific object, situation, or activity. The anxiety is usually out of proportion to the real situation, and the victim is fully aware that the fear is irrational. Because of this fear, the phobic person leads a restricted life. A salesperson who is terrified to fly has to limit business to areas that can be visited by land, rail, or water. A person with an extreme fear of elevators must use the stairs to get to a friend's tenth-floor apartment.

Phobic anxiety is different from other forms of anxiety because it is focused on a particular object or event. When confronted with the object of their phobia, people often experience physical symptoms. A rapid, pounding heartbeat, stomach disorders, nausea, diarrhea, frequent urination, a choking feeling, flushing of the face, sweating, trembling, and faintness are some common symptoms.

Through various types of therapy, some phobic people are able to confront their fears. More commonly, however, they avoid the situation or object that causes the fear—an avoidance that limits the phobic's life experiences.

Chapter Objectives

After completing this chapter, you will be able to

1. **Identify the topic of a paragraph or longer selection.**
2. **Determine the stated main idea of a paragraph.**
3. **Determine the stated main idea of a longer selection.**

Focus on Topics and Main Ideas

When you were little, did you ever wonder how something worked? For example, the telephone was a fascinating item. It rang, you could talk into it, and you could hear someone else talk to you. You may have taken the telephone receiver and pulled out the parts to figure out how it worked. To understand how something works, you sometimes have to examine the parts. The topic and the main idea are the parts you need to identify to get a better understanding of what you are reading.

Topic

The topic is the general subject of a paragraph or longer selection. You can usually express the topic in one or two words. Using *before reading* strategies, you can identify the topic of what you are reading by previewing the title, scanning the reading, and asking yourself, "Who or what is this paragraph or selection about?"

Stated Main Idea

After confirming the topic, read the selection. While reading, ask yourself, "What does the author want me, the reader, to understand or remember about this topic?" The answer is the main idea of the paragraph or selection.

Authors will often state their main idea in one or two sentences toward the beginning of the selection. This statement is referred to as the main idea statement or the topic sentence. While the main idea statement is frequently found early in the reading, there is no rule as to where it will be located. The author may place it in the beginning, middle, or end of a paragraph or selection. As you read, look for a stated main idea.

To sum up, find the topic of the selection by asking yourself, "Who or what is this paragraph or selection about?" To find the main idea, ask yourself, "What does the author want me, the reader, to understand or remember about this topic?"

To understand the difference between topic and the stated main idea, read the following paragraph:

Phobias are very treatable. In *Prevention* magazine (July 1992), a psychologist reports as many as 90 percent of people with phobias recover or show significant progress after treatment. Effective therapies include relaxation techniques, thinking about the reality of the situation, and gradual exposure to the source of fear. People with mild phobias often treat themselves using self-help groups and books. With more intense phobias, a few sessions with a good therapist will often relieve the problem. Severe phobias may require more intensive therapy.

What is the topic *of this paragraph?*

The topic is phobias, a brief answer to the question, "Who or what is this paragraph about?" Notice that the term "phobias" was mentioned five times by the writer.

What is the stated main idea *of the paragraph?*

The main idea statement, "Phobias are very treatable," answers the question, "What does the author want the reader to understand or remember about the topic of phobias?" The main idea statement tells us that phobias can be treated.

Short Exercises: Topics and Stated Main Ideas

Following are ten paragraphs dealing with the concept of phobias. The first five paragraphs come from *Fears and Phobias* by Margaret Hyde. The remaining paragraphs were taken from a 1994 *Cosmopolitan* article, "Who's Afraid of the Big, Bad Phobia?" written by Stephen Rae.

Read each paragraph and complete these activities:

1. State the topic of each paragraph in one or two words.
2. Underline the sentence that contains the main idea.

1. A phobia is a real fear, but it is a reaction that is out of proportion to a specific situation or thing. Phobias cannot be voluntarily controlled, and they lead to total avoidance of the feared situation. One classic case of phobia concerns Professor William Ellery Leonard, who was terrified by a locomotive when he was a child. This had such far-reaching effects that his phobia virtually kept him a prisoner in the university town where he taught. Professor Leonard described seizures that terrified him. When his anxiety attacks occurred, he had to retreat to what he felt was a safe place.

   Topic: _____

2. Someone shouts "Fire!" in a theater, and fear spreads through the auditorium. People rush toward the exits, and the crush of the crowd is so great that no one can get through a doorway. Bodies are jammed together in a panic that need not have been. Intelligent leadership could have kept the crowd's fear under control and prevented many deaths.

    Topic: _____

3. Almost everyone knows the look and sound of fear. Suppose a cry pierces the distant air. You can tell from the sound that someone is frightened, even though you have no idea what is causing the fear. You can picture the distorted face of the person. The eyes are open, and the muscles of the lower eyelids are tense. The upper eyelids are raised, and so are the eyebrows. Eyebrows appear to be straightened, and there are horizontal wrinkles across the forehead. This is the physical face of fear.

    Topic: _____

4. You are probably not the only one to experience fear in the meadow. Other animals respond to the environment with different senses and may experience varying amounts of fear because of your presence. The ant that crawls nearby lives in a very limited world and does not see you as it follows the track from its anthill to a source of food. The ant puts its nose to the ground, smelling its way with no fear that you might step on it and extinguish its existence. But if you crush some other ants, it will exhibit some apparent signs of fear. No one really knows if the ant you have been watching is frightened by the crushed members of its own species, but it will appear to be frantic. This reaction may be due to the odor of the damaged ants. You, of course, will have no fear of the harmless, little ant crawling through the grass beside you.

    Topic: _____

5. Sometimes a phobia can be extinguished by having another person demonstrate that the feared situation or object is not harmful. Take the strange case of a nineteen-year-old woman. The object of her phobia was earthworms. Although this did not restrict her life in any great way, she avoided picnics in the grass or other areas where earthworms might be found. Watching another person handling earthworms to bait a fishhook, mixing them in the soil of a flowerpot, and coming to no apparent harm might have lessened her fear.

    Topic: _____

6. Irrational, involuntary terrors are this country's most prevalent mental-health problem, afflicting more than twenty-three million Americans.

Clinicians group phobias into three categories: specific, like fear of heights or driving; social, revolving around the fear of committing in public some act the sufferer perceives will lead to embarrassment or ridicule (speaking, eating, signing one's name); and agoraphobia, a complex set of fears and avoidance behaviors that can result in a person's becoming completely housebound. Phobias, in turn, are part of a larger group of anxiety disorders—including panic disorder, obsessive-compulsive behavior, post-traumatic stress syndrome—that the National Institute of Mental Health estimates afflicts 12.6 percent of the population.

Topic: _____

7. Antianxiety and depression drugs such as Xanex and Prozac can prove useful in treating phobias, but many therapists say their use should be limited and not form the basis for treatment. "We don't want to cover over people's fears with drugs," says Dr. Natalie Schor. "Our goal is to allow phobics to experience some anxiety so they can learn to be less afraid." Conventional psychoanalysis, she and other phobia experts note, is useless in treating these problems. What seems to work best—and treatment for phobias yields the highest rate of success of any type of psychotherapy, with more than 90 percent of patients finding some relief—is a combination of cognitive and behavioral approaches, with supporting medication if necessary.

Topic: _____

8. What other phobias are common? Fear of dentists is a big one. "Here in Seattle we did an epidemiological study of one thousand people and found that about seven percent described themselves as either terrified or very afraid of dentists, and another thirteen percent as somewhat afraid," said Tracy Gertz, a psychologist with the Dental Fears Research Clinic at the University of Washington. "I see men and women who haven't been to a dentist in thirty years. They are either self-referred because they have a toothache or have been sent to us by a dentist who throws his hands up and says, 'You clearly need dental work, but I can't treat you.'"

Topic: _____

9. Technophobia—fear of technology—is another common problem, and one that's growing. "People aren't just afraid of computers," says Larry Rosen, a psychology professor at California State University in Dominguez Hills. "These days, almost everything in your house has technology: computers embedded in the VCR, microwave, coffeepot. We're finding that people are uncomfortable with all of them." Up to 25 percent of the population "are true technophobes." Rosen adds, "They avoid technology at all costs.

If you force them to use something that involves it, they'll have all the symptoms of a true anxiety reaction: sweaty palms, nervousness, quickened heartbeat. Maybe their mind goes blank."

Topic: _____

10. Even Thanksgiving, that most American of holidays, strikes terror in the hearts of many—and not just those with Aunt Mary phobia. Turkey phobia, says Donald Dossey (founder of Phobia Institute of Asheville, North Carolina), is a serious condition based on excessive worry over being able to cook the bird correctly. Each year, he notes, the Butterball® Turkey Hotline fields thousands of frantic phone calls on the days before the event; last year the Federal Government set up a toll-free 800 number to help alleviate national turkey anxiety. Being a turkey failure is not an easy thing to live down, Dossey points out, "We're afraid that if we don't do it exactly right, the ghost of Norman Rockwell will come after us."

Topic: _____

■ ■ ■ ■ Reading Selections

Selection 1

Virtual Therapy

FROM *PSYCHOLOGY TODAY*

Before Reading

Before you read "Virtual Therapy," predict what the topic may be. After scanning the story to see if your prediction was correct, think about what you already know about virtual activities. Have you ever heard of virtual reality or played a virtual reality game? How did it feel? Did you like the experience? Think about ways virtual reality may be used. Relate what you know about virtual reality to its use in psychology. Set your purpose for reading.

Words to Preview

brink	*(n.)*	edge of a steep slope
consolation	*(n.)*	comfort
virtual	*(adj.)*	not existing in actual fact
truncated	*(adj.)*	appearing to end abruptly
don	*(v.)*	to put on
perceive	*(v.)*	to become aware of through any sense
peer	*(v.)*	to look intently
endure	*(v.)*	to carry on through hardships

During Reading

As you read "Virtual Therapy," continue to predict events, visualize the story, and monitor your comprehension. What is the author telling you about virtual therapy and its use in medicine?

The bridge suddenly ends at midspan, and you're standing on the brink, staring down at the icy waters below. Your heart is racing, your palms are sweating. The sole consolation: the bridge exists only on a computer chip.

Welcome to virtual reality, until now, a technology in search of a purpose. Psychologist Ralph Lamson, Ph.D., of the Kaiser Permanente Medical Group, says it's just the thing to help acrophobes overcome their fear of heights.

Don the special helmet and the real world is replaced by a computer-generated universe. As you turn your head, the headgear senses the movement and alters the image accordingly. Turn the handgrip and you seem to move forward or backward, allowing you to tour this cyberworld at your own pace.

More than 60 patients (average age, 54) have explored the bridge in 40-minute sessions. They begin their travels in a cafe and gradually make their way to a raised wooden plank outside. To cross the plank, they must confront their phobia. Patients perceive the plank's height differently—some see it as 10 feet, some as 10 stories—but the experience can be dizzying, even if it isn't real.

"When people look down, their heart rate and blood pressure go up," Lamson says. "They get a little shaky. They say, 'Oh my God, I can't do this.'" Lamson encourages patients to stay where they are until they feel comfortable.

The plank leads to the bridge, where the truly daring can peer over the edge of the truncated span. By the time the patients return to the plank, they are somewhat desensitized, and their vital signs are closer to normal. High technology, indeed!

After treatment, more than 90 percent of the participants successfully endured a 15-story ride in a glass elevator and completed self-assigned tasks ranging from cleaning out their roof gutters to driving across the Golden Gate Bridge. Benefits were still apparent after three months.

One woman who wouldn't climb above the second step on a ladder now mountain climbs. Her next destination: Lassen Peak, 10,453 feet.

After Reading

Word Connections

1. What do *acrophobes* fear?

_____

2. In "Virtual Therapy," the only *consolation* to standing on the brink on the bridge was that the bridge existed only on a computer chip. People often *console* each other after a sorrowful event. How are these words related?

_____

3. In this reading, patients perceived heights very differently. Create a concept of definition map for *perception*.

Diagram:

4. After treatment, phobics endured a fifteen-story ride in a glass elevator. What kinds of situations have you *endured*?

_____

_____

_____

_____

_____

Connecting Meaning

1. Virtual reality has gone beyond entertainment. What is the stated main idea of "Virtual Therapy"?

_____

_____

_____

2. Describe the desensitization process patients go through to reduce their fear of heights.

_____

_____

_____

_____

3. After treatment, what are some activities that demonstrate a reduced fear of heights?

_____

_____

_____

Selection 2

Red Flag

FROM *FIVE WHO CONQUERED FEAR*
CATHY PERLMUTTER

Before Reading

Before you read "Red Flag," predict what the topic may be. After scanning the story to confirm your prediction, think about the topic. How do you react to injections, violent movies, and the sight of blood? Do you avoid them? Does your heart race uncontrollably? Do you get nauseous or faint? Relate what you know or have experienced to this selection that describes how a teenager's phobia affected her life. Set your purpose for reading.

Words to Preview

queasy	(adj.) nauseous, uneasy, troubled
onset	(n.) beginning
fiasco	(n.) complete failure
neurologist	(n.) doctor who deals with nervous system disorders
hierarchy	(n.) ranking from highest to lowest or lowest to highest
provoking	(adj.) troubling the nerves or peace of mind
squeamish	(adj.) easily nauseated or sickened

During Reading

As you read "Red Flag," continue to predict events, visualize the story, and monitor your comprehension. What is the author telling you about blood and injury phobia?

Injections, violent movies, and the sight of blood make many people queasy. But for some, the problem gets out of hand. It's called a "blood and injury phobia." Blood and injury phobia is a little different, though. Like other phobic reactions, it starts with a rapid rise in heart rate. But then, blood pressure and heart rate drop dramatically, and the person usually faints.

Sarah McKinley, 17, a high school senior, faced down a severe phobia of this kind with the help of the staff of the Center for Stress and Anxiety Disorders at the State University of New York at Albany. (We've changed Sarah's name.)

Although Sarah was young, the sudden onset of her phobia is exactly like that of many older adults, notes the Center's Dr. Albano. "It even happens in physicians, who after years of treating injuries suddenly start fainting at the sight of them."

In grammar school, if we had to watch a gory film, I closed my eyes during the bloody parts. That wasn't unusual; everyone else did the same thing as I did.

But then, one day about a year ago, I was sitting in homeroom, reading a newspaper, when I saw a photograph of bloody palm prints on a wall. I looked at it and passed out. That was the first time.

The school sent me home. I knew that looking at the photograph had completely grossed me out, but I didn't worry about it too much.

Then came a sort of turning point. In a social studies class, they showed us an incredibly bloody movie about the Civil War. A soldier was blown up, and I fainted right there.

After that I started fainting about once a week. Then twice a week, then every day, then four or five times a day. The Gulf War was going on at that time, so magazines and newspapers were full of bloody images and ideas. In English class, we'd read stories in which people were injured, and those scared me. In biology class, talking about body parts made me faint. I think my imagination was too vivid. My mom and I drove by an auto accident once, and even though I couldn't see the injuries, I imagined them, and fainted. I couldn't look at any kind of raw meat.

It got so bad that when a teacher handed me back a math test with corrections written in red ink, I thought of blood. The next thing I knew, I was lying on the ground.

No one was really sure what was going on. Early on, I was brought to an emergency room. What a fiasco. The guy kept asking me if I was pregnant! Then he decided there was nothing wrong with me. Another doctor told my parents I'd have to be on medications for the rest of my life.

We went to a neurologist, and he said my brain was fine. He said I needed to see a psychologist, that what I actually had was a phobia. My parents found the Center for Stress and Anxiety Disorders.

They asked me to write out a hierarchy, starting with the situation I found least anxiety provoking, and working all the way up to the scariest. At the bottom of my list I wrote down things like, looking at a Band-Aid and seeing something red. At the top, the scariest things I listed were seeing someone bleeding and watching a gory movie.

The psychologists told me that most people with phobias must be taught to relax in scary situations. But people who faint need to learn the opposite response—how to tense up our bodies and keep them tense, so our blood pressure doesn't drop and we don't pass out.

First I practiced tensing and holding with separate muscle groups, like the hands, the arms, and the legs. Then I learned to tense and hold all the muscles at the same time. I learned to do it sitting, standing up, in a variety of positions.

Then the therapists asked me to choose music that made me feel cheerful. I picked Billy Joel music and brought in my favorite tape. That's when we were ready to start working on the hierarchy list.

At first I had to write the word blood over and over again. I'd tense all my muscles, and sometimes they'd play the Billy Joel music that I liked. We'd do that until I was completely comfortable writing "blood" and then move up to the next level. They'd bring in pieces of raw meat, scary pictures, gory movies. I'd tense and listen to the music.

By the end of about three months, I wasn't fainting anymore and could do all the things on my hierarchy without feeling nervous.

My final tasks were to have my blood drawn and to watch a hip operation. When I went to get my blood drawn, the doctor couldn't find my vein, so he let me draw his blood! I was fine, even though I probably hurt him! And I actually found the hip operation interesting. I think the therapist who came along with me was more upset than I was. He'd never seen an operation, and I noticed he kept his arms folded, which is one way of doing the tension exercise without anyone knowing.

I'll probably always be a little bit squeamish about blood and injuries. But nowadays, it's no big deal.

After Reading   **Word Connections**

1. "In grammar school, if we had to watch a gory film, I closed my eyes during the bloody parts." What synonym for *gory* is given in this sentence?

   _____

2. Develop a concept of definition map for *anxiety*.

   Diagram:

3. Sarah wrote out her hierarchy of anxiety provoking situations. Write your own *hierarchy* of situations that frighten you from the least frightening to the most frightening.

_____

_____

_____

Connecting Meaning

1. What is the stated main idea of "Red Flag"?

_____

_____

_____

_____

2. How does the main idea relate to the title?

_____

_____

_____

3. Name three items that caused an extreme reaction in Sarah, items which most people handle without unusual upset.

_____

_____

_____

_____

_____

4. Most people with phobias must learn to relax. What was different about Sarah's treatment?

_____

_____

_____

_____

_____

Selection 3	# Help! I Think I'm Dying! DR. ABBOT GRANOFF

Before Reading   Before you read "Help! I Think I'm Dying!" predict the topic. After scanning the story to see if your prediction is correct, think about the feeling of panic. Have you ever experienced panic? Relate what you know to the author's experiences with panic attacks; set your purpose for reading.

Words to Preview

reassure	*(v.)*	to restore confidence to
entangle	*(v.)*	to twist together in a confusing mass
tar baby	*(n.)*	a situation or problem from which it is virtually impossible to disentangle oneself
EKG	*(n.)*	electrocardiograph; instrument used to diagnose heart problems
pervasive	*(adj.)*	present throughout
linger	*(v.)*	to be slow in parting or quitting
bout	*(n.)*	a period of time spent in a particular way
onset	*(n.)*	a beginning or start
mimic	*(v.)*	to copy or imitate
vague	*(adj.)*	not clearly expressed

During Reading   As you read "Help! I Think I'm Dying!" continue to predict events, visualize the story, and monitor your comprehension. What does the author want you to know or remember about panic attacks?

My eyes popped open. It was dark. The clock said 3:24 A.M. I knew I was dying. I had severe crushing pain in the middle of my chest. I was having a heart attack even though I was only thirty-six years old. I had just started my psychiatric practice four years ago. It was a struggle driving sixty miles a day to three hospitals, my office, and endless meetings. My wife and I had just purchased a lot and started our dream house. It took me every weekend for two years to clear it with a pick, shovel, chain saw, and ax. We interviewed eleven architects, worked with three and had to sue one for taking us on a royal ride. We finally found an architect that designed the house we wanted and had broken ground one month ago.

All the sacrifices of time and energy put into studying in college to get the grades to get into medical school. All the sacrifices of time and energy studying in medical school to learn the art and science of medicine. All the sacrifices of time and energy taking call every fourth night in internship and residency with the sixty, seventy, eighty hours per week to refine the knowledge. Two years of sacrifice serving my country in the army. Not now, after all the long, hard work and sacrifice of becoming a psychiatrist. I couldn't die now.

I checked my pulse. It was 90 beats per minute. My heart felt like it was going to jump out of my chest. I felt hot. I was sweating, and my fingers felt numb. My hands were shaking. I was so scared that I felt nauseous and thought I would vomit. My breathing was shallow and rapid. I had to get to the emergency room. I felt so dizzy. Time seemed to stand still. Everything was in slow motion.

I was sitting up in bed. My wife rolled over and asked me what was wrong. I didn't want to scare her, so I told her I didn't feel well and was going out for a drive. I'd never done this before and she was both surprised and concerned, but I reassured her and told her to go back to sleep. I didn't want to die in front of her. I felt like a fool, and I didn't want her to see me like this. I quickly got dressed and drove to the hospital five minutes from my house. I left the car outside the emergency room door and ran in. I grabbed the first doctor I saw who happened to be a friend and told him to hook me up to an EKG. I was having a heart attack and was sure I was dying. We didn't even bother checking me in through admissions. He grabbed a nurse and had her help him set up the EKG. I felt a little relief that I had made it this far. At least if my heart stopped, there was a chance I could be revived.

My friend looked at the EKG. I was waiting to hear the bad news. He said it looked fine! What? There must be some mistake! The chest pain was now gone, and my heart rate was down to the low 80s, but I was still frightened out of my wits, and I knew I was dying. I asked him to recheck the EKG, and I asked to look at it. Again he said it was fine, and I could find no abnormality either.

What was going on? How could I be having a heart attack, know I was going to die, and yet have a normal EKG? He suggested that I just lie back and relax, and he would continue to monitor me.

I began to feel embarrassed and foolish. I still felt frightened, but the fear was beginning to subside. The numbness, dizziness, nausea had gone away. The only thing left was fear and that continued to subside.

My friend continued to check on me. He asked if I had been under any stress lately. Of course I had and explained the tar baby I was entangled in. He said that what I was experiencing was stress. There was nothing physically wrong with me. I argued how could that be. I was a psychiatrist and understood stress and its symptoms. Besides I had experienced lots of stresses in my life, and nothing ever felt like this did. The shame and embarrassment continued to grow until that made me feel uncomfortable enough to want to get out of there. It was 1½ hours later. The symptoms were gone, and I was no longer fearful that I was dying.

I went home. My wife was worried sick. She asked me what happened. I told her. She was bewildered that I would drive myself to the ER rather than letting her take me. What if I lost consciousness while driving?

I didn't want to listen to her logic and told her I was feeling okay now. Whatever it was, it was all over or so I thought.

I cut back on the four-to-five cups of coffee I was drinking each day, figuring that I had to reduce my stress levels. I tried to spend a little less time at the new house, but there were always decisions to be made and problems to be solved. Fortunately, my practice slowed down a little, but that added a different kind of stress. How could I afford the house if I wasn't working full time? Well, I just wouldn't think about it. I would do my best and let the chips fall where they may.

I found it difficult to get to sleep. Somehow I became fearful that I would again awake in the middle of the night panicky. That never happened again.

Six week later, I was driving from my house to my first hospital to make rounds. It began to start all over again. The tightness in my chest. The severe chest pain, rapid heart beat, hot and sweaty, rapid and shallow breathing, numbness in my fingers, nausea. I knew I was going to die this time. I was fifteen minutes away from the hospital in the middle of an expressway. I'd never make it. Slow motion returned.

I hoped I wouldn't accidentally run my car into anyone else and hurt or kill them if I blacked out. I began to cry for fear of my wife and children having to get along without me. I knew I was going to die. But this is what had happened before, and there was nothing wrong with my heart. It was just stress.

I took my pulse, and although it was about ninety beats per minute, it was regular and strong. I had no pain in my left shoulder, neck, jaw, or arm. The kind of pain that a heart attack generally causes. Could this be stress again? I sure didn't want to embarrass myself in front of my colleagues again.

By the time I got to the hospital, the overwhelming fear was gone. What remained was a less pervasive lingering fear. I put on the best mask I could and walked into the ER and asked one of the nurses to hook me up to an EKG. I told her I had a small bout of chest pain, and although I didn't think it was anything, I just wanted to make sure it wasn't. She looked concerned and hooked me up. After running the full EKG, she unhooked me and I read it. It looked okay to me. One of the ER doctors had come over to check me out. He reassured me the EKG was normal. I thanked them both and slowly walked to the doctors' lounge to think.

This was getting weird. I thought I must be going crazy. I couldn't live like this, but what could I do?

I decided to call a psychiatrist friend in Chicago. Maybe he could help explain what was happening to me. I called him that night and described the symptoms. He said, "You had two panic attacks." I had known them as anxiety attacks or hyperventilation syndrome. But the only symptoms were anxiety, a rapidly beating heart and hyperventilation. These were just beginning to be defined in the early 1980s with the new "DSM-III," *Diagnostic and Statistical Manual of Mental Disorders*. This text was a major breakthrough in diagnosis because it clearly listed all the possible symptoms of each disorder. It described the usual age of onset of each illness and listed other illnesses which could mimic it. It made diagnosis more of a science than a guess, and it standardized the diagnosis of mental disorders.

Stress was too vague a term to grasp. So I got all the material I could relating to panic disorder and began to learn in depth what I had experienced.

I began diagnosing, treating, and understanding panic attacks, panic disorder, and phobias. Although I have since had several minor bouts of anxiety, fortunately I have never experienced another panic attack again.

After Reading

Word Connections

1. Find two synonyms for *panic attacks* given in the story.

   _____

   _____

2. Describe the situation the author was referring to as "the tar baby I was entangled in."

   _____

   _____

   _____

   _____

   _____

3. According to the author, panic attacks are often misdiagnosed and inadequately treated. Create a word map for the prefix *mis-*, which means badly or wrongly.

   Diagram:

Connecting Meaning

1. What is the main idea of "Help! I Think I'm Dying!"?

   _____

   _____

2. Describe the physical symptoms that Dr. Granoff experienced when he thought he was dying.

   _____

   _____

   _____

   _____

3. What was the true cause of Dr. Granoff's symptoms?

   _____

   _____

   _____

4. What is DSM-III? Why is it so important in the diagnosis of mental disorders?

   _____

   _____

   _____

   _____

■ ■ ■ ■ **Portfolio Activities**

Integrating Ideas

Using virtual reality and psychological therapy, patients in these readings were desensitized of their fears. Do you think anyone is really cured of a phobia? Reflect on the causes of phobias. Are they genetically or environmentally caused? Support your answers with examples in writing or in class discussion.

Extending Concepts

In "Red Flag," Sarah used music to help relieve her anxiety. In writing, describe the kinds of music you use to relieve anxiety. What other reasons do you have for listening to music? Describe your favorite music and how it affects your state of mind.

Collaborative Activity

In groups, discuss and record reactions and feelings toward fearful and gory situations. View a movie that reflects the theme of this chapter, for example, *Arachnophobia, Vertigo,* or one of the films in the *Friday the Thirteenth* series. Discuss the main idea of the movie and your reactions to the fearful and gory situations within the film.

Additional Portfolio Suggestion

Using Internet access, search the Web for information about phobias. Compile a list of phobias and their descriptions.

▪ ▪ ▪ ▪ Chapter Summary Graphic Organizer

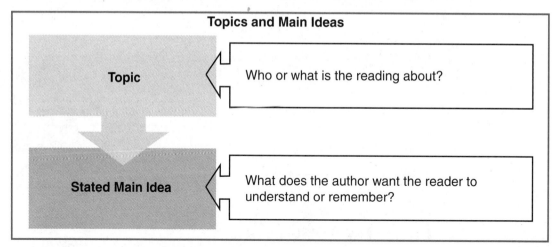

Topics and Main Ideas

Topic

Who or what is the reading about?

Stated Main Idea

What does the author want the reader to understand or remember?

CHAPTER

6

Unstated Main Ideas

Theme of Readings: Taking Risks

A good scare is worth more to a man than good advice.

EDGAR WATSON HOWE

Taking Risks

How many risks have you taken in your life? Many would say that everything is a risk. Getting up in the morning, driving in traffic, living in urban areas, playing the lotto, falling in love are all risks. You can lose money, time, or life itself by taking risks. But is there anything to gain? Take all risks away and life is no longer an adventure. You cannot grow or experience what life has to offer without risks. Because of this fact, people commonly accept a number of risks as part of life.

The majority of people feel that acceptable risks are those that do not risk bodily harm. Some people, however, thrive on taking chances. Street luge competitors combine traditional luge and skateboarding as they race down a street, flat on their back at sixty mph. Although they wear protective helmets, street lugers lack brakes, seatbelts, and seats. Bungee jumpers secure elastic cords to their ankles, leap, and drop hundreds of feet before enjoying the sudden recoil. To provide the ultimate skiing experience, heliskiers are lifted by helicopter to mountain tops that cannot be reached by any other means. For casual observers, these thrill seekers seem to have no fear. In reality, risk takers don't feel an absence of fear but rather a fear overcome or enjoyed. The challenge satisfies their quest for the exciting adrenaline rush.

Some people choose professions that place them at extraordinary risk. Police officers and firefighters place their life at risk as part of their job. Bomb squads handle bomb threats and possible explosive devices. Medical specialists working with deadly viruses run the risk of contracting fatal diseases. Likewise, scientists who chase tornadoes to record information for study place themselves in incredible danger.

The risks you have taken in life may not be this extreme. The level of acceptable risk differs for everyone. Fearsome or fearless, we choose a variety of experiences to make our life a unique adventure.

Chapter Objective

After completing this chapter, you will be able to determine the unstated main idea of a paragraph or selection.

■ ■ ■ ■ Focus on Unstated Main Ideas

Are you able to figure out what is being implied but not directly expressed in each of the following situations?

- It's the week before Valentine's Day, and a woman stops to gaze at every diamond ring she sees in jewelry store windows at the local mall.
- A father places a "Warning—Health Hazard" sign on his teenager's bedroom door.
- A dog sits by the door with a leash in his mouth.

In life we often have to figure out what is being implied but not stated. In reading a paragraph or selection, the same is sometimes true. Often an author will not state the main idea in one or more sentences but will expect you to figure it out from the information given. In these cases, you must draw a conclusion that is implied but not directly stated.

Whether the main idea is stated or unstated, identify the topic of the paragraph by asking yourself, "Who or what is this paragraph or selection about?" As you read, ask yourself, "What does the author want me to understand or remember about the topic?" If there is not a single sentence that answers this question, look at all of the important information in the reading and draw your own conclusion about the main idea. Your conclusion is the unstated main idea, which you will then express in one or two sentences.

As you read the following paragraph, draw your own conclusion about the main idea. Compare your answer with the one given.

> Years ago, planning a vacation meant deciding whether to go to the beach, visit out-of-state relatives, or tour historical landmarks. If adventurous, a person might have chosen to go camping or fishing. Today people plan vacations around activities such as rock climbing, bungee jumping, or white-water rafting. An adventurous vacationer may go ice climbing or shark diving or even attend an outdoor survival school.

Who or what is this paragraph about?

The topic of this paragraph is vacations. All four sentences relate to this topic.

What does the author want me to remember about this topic?

The types of vacations have changed over the years. The words *years ago* and *today* establish a comparison with types of vacations given for each time frame.

■ ■ ■ ■ **Short Exercises: Unstated Main Ideas**

Read each paragraph. Identify the topic and express the author's unstated main idea in a complete sentence.

1. Expert parachutists on graphite boards twist and turn while free falling 13,000 feet. Skysurfing did not exist in 1990. Today it attracts thousands of devotees. BASE jumping (**B**uildings, **A**ntennas, **S**pans, **E**arth) involves parachuting off fixed objects such as radio towers or bridges. It was officially established in 1980 and now lures hundreds of people. Ten years ago rock climbers numbered in the tens of thousands; currently, an estimated half-million Americans enjoy clinging to cliffs.

   Topic: _____

   Main Idea: _____

   _____

2. Tie a secure, super strong, elastic cord around your ankles, close your eyes, and jump down hundreds of feet into the air. Suddenly the elastic snaps back, and you enjoy the weightless recoil of a bungee jump. For many, this amusement park activity leads to a trip to the doctor or chiropractor to help relieve neck or back pain. Others are not so lucky. In 1997, trapeze artist Laura Patterson died when a bungee cord broke during rehearsals for a Super Bowl halftime show. Yet the sport of bungee jumping is still pursued.

   Topic: _____

   Main Idea: _____

   _____

3. A person who wouldn't even think about taking a physical risk may stand in front of a large audience to sing. Another may never skateboard but will invest thousands of dollars on a stock tip. A third person is frightened by the thought of parachuting out of a plane but will change careers without a moment's hesitation. Which kind of risk would you take?

   Topic: _____

   Main Idea: _____

   _____

4. With winds approaching 300 miles per hour, a storm bears down on Wichita Falls, Texas. The awesome power of a Texas tornado draws a photographer from Australia to witness its fury. Multiple Texas tornadoes attract a team of meteorologists from Japan to collect data. An Oklahoma scientist establishes a base in Lubbock, Texas, to study the legendary storms of the state. Even filmmakers focus on Texas to illustrate the power of deadly and destructive tornadoes.

   Topic: _____

   Main Idea: _____

   _____

   _____

5. Early explorers took extreme risks to discover new lands. Ancient Hawaiian kings surfed in the treacherous waters off the island shores. In the early 1900s, people went over Niagara Falls in a barrel or stood on the wing of a flying biplane in search of new thrills. The French used the word "extreme" in the 1970s to describe a type of backcountry skiing so dangerous that if you fell you died. In the 1990s, those who sought excitement practiced skateboarding, BMX bike riding, street luging, and wakeboarding.

   Topic: _____

   Main Idea: _____

   _____

6. Roger Stoneburger started bungee jumping in 1980, before it was regulated. He loves skiing off cliffs, riding his mountain bike from great heights into airbags, and jumping off bridges. Lately he gained a foothold in his dream job—the stunt industry—with an offer to double for John Malkovich and do stunt work on Don Johnson's CBS show, "Nash Bridges." (Adapted from *You Can Buy A Thrill: Chasing the Ultimate Rush* by Rebba Piirto Heath)

   Topic: _____

   Main Idea: _____

   _____

7. ESPN's "Extreme Games" series and recent movies like *Point Break* and *Drop Zone* glorify extreme sports. Interest in mountaineering seems to pick up after articles and films like *Cliffhanger*. National advertising spots have sold everything from salsa chips to carrier services using the visual impact of extreme sports. "You can't watch a day of TV without seeing someone jumping out of an airplane," says Chris Needels, executive director of the U.S. Parachute Association. Stoneburger worked as a

consultant on a recent Frito-Lay spot that showed Chris Elliot jumping from a blimp to dip a Tostito chip into a jar of salsa on the middle of the football field. (Adapted from "You Can Buy A Thrill: Chasing the Ultimate Rush" by Rebecca Piirto Heath)

Topic: _____

Main Idea: _____

_____

8. "Five . . . four . . . three . . . two . . . one . . . see ya!" and Chance McGuire, 25, is airborne off a 650-foot concrete dam in northern California. In one second he falls 16 feet, in two seconds 63 feet, and after three seconds and 137 feet he is flying at 65 MPH. He prays that his parachute will open facing away from the dam, that his canopy won't collapse, that his toggles will be handy, and that no ill wind will slam him back into the cold concrete. The chute snaps open, the sound ricocheting through the gorge like a gunshot, and McGuire is soaring, carving S-turns into the air, swooping over a winding creek. He lands, packs his chute, and lets out a war whoop. It is a cry of defiance, thanks, and victory. (Adapted from "Life on the Edge" *Time Magazine*)

Topic: _____

Main Idea: _____

_____

9. America was founded by risk takers fed up with the English Crown. It was expanded by pioneers who risked life and limb to settle in new areas. Lewis and Clark, Thomas Edison, Frederick Douglas, Teddy Roosevelt, Henry Ford, and Amelia Earhart bucked the odds and took perilous chances. (Adapted from "Life on the Edge" *Time Magazine*)

Topic: _____

Main Idea: _____

_____

10. At 47, Vicki Hendricks has laughed in the face of death more than once. Her idea of a good time is running with the bulls in Spain or white-water rafting in Mexico. She wanted to go to a great white shark dive next month but that conflicted with the national free-fall convention, a gathering of skydiving enthusiasts, which she plans to attend. (Adapted from *The Type T Personality* by Debbie Geiger)

Topic: _____

Main Idea: _____

_____

■ ■ ■ ■ Reading Selections

Selection 1

Mud and Guts

ROBERT LAFRANCO

Before Reading

Before you read "Mud and Guts," predict what the topic may be. After scanning the story, think about your last vacation. What did you do for fun? Did it involve any risk? If you could design your dream vacation, what would it be like? Relate your ideas about vacations to people who plan risky vacations. Set your purpose for reading.

Words to Preview

garish	*(adj.)* loud and flashy
ravine	*(n.)* a deep narrow passage with steep, rocky sides
mettle	*(n.)* courage
fraught	*(adj.)* filled with the specified element
camaraderie	*(n.)* goodwill among friends

During Reading

As you read "Mud and Guts," continue to predict where the author is headed, visualize the story, and monitor your comprehension. What does the author want you to know about risky vacations?

Slouched in a tattered leather chair in the dingy lounge of Mike's Sky Rancho in Baja California, Mexico, 39-year-old Michael Ellis peels off the garish superhero gear he's worn all day. It has carried him through 150 miles of dust, rocks, and cactus. In the dim light behind him, you can make out a travel poster on the wall of the terrain he's just passed through. The poster shows a tangled heap of four jeeps piled up in a desert ravine.

This is fun? The all-day trip from Ensenada to Mike's by dirt bike was a bruising journey that ended with an hour-long, high-speed race up an un-paved pretzel of a trail. With a swarm of Kawasaki dirt bikes shrouded by dust clouds and headed directly into a blinding late-day sun, the trail's every turn—with threatening drops and no guardrails alongside—was a po-tential catastrophe.

Twelve riders started out, but only ten were sitting with Ellis in the lounge. Sam Woo, the 43-year-old president of his own graphic design firm, smacked into a horse and broke his collarbone and five ribs. It took 11 hours to get him to the care of a San Diego hospital. Keith Galanti, a 35-year-old stockbroker, was missing but was found after dark frantically trying to find the group—with no gas, no money, and no Spanish.

"When you do this kind of sport, you don't worry about the little in-juries—they always heal," mused a stitched-up C.J. Ramstad, as he limped toward his macho medicine: a sizzling steak and a cold beer. "It's the big one—the spinal injury—that's the one that scares you."

But not enough to spoil the fun. Mission Viejo, California-based Baja OffRoad Tours, run by 47-year-old Baja 1000 champion Christopher Haines, is booked [solid]. This year Haines expects to top last year's full slate of 300 riders; some of them are first-time dirt bikers, and some have never straddled a motorcycle before. Haines's past tours have included a management group from Oppenheimer Capital and several Young President Organization chapters.

"In my business I gamble huge every day," says Ellis, the owner of Matrix Communications, a Minneapolis-based telecommunications company. "This is just gambling in a different way."

Maybe it's the absence of war in this generation, but there is something that drives deskbound people to spend their free time taking unnecessary chances with life and limb. The Englewood, Colorado-based Adventure Travel Business Trade Association says there are about 8,000 United States companies packaging tours for adventurers, generating some $7 billion last year—double the figure of a decade ago. Outward Bound's Wilderness School—a hardy test of physical and emotional mettle—reports a 66 percent increase in executive participation between 1992 and 1996, from 3,000 to about 5,000 people. White-water rafting, shark diving, ballooning, heliskiing, rock and mountain climbing, plant gathering among 35-foot anacondas in the Amazon—if you want to gamble (with your limbs as the chips), someone has packaged a tour for you.

"Risk-taking is the keystone American quality," says Frank Farley, a psychologist at Temple University. "Capitalism is fraught with risk."

Baja is a good place for taking these risks. The barren 1,200-plus-mile peninsula is so harsh that in three centuries of effort the Spanish couldn't successfully colonize it. The Americans passed on it altogether after winning it in the Mexican-American War. Today it is a largely undeveloped theme park for thrill seekers who, unlike Haines's more pampered crowd, travel for weeks along its back trails carrying only gas containers, food, camping gear, and global positioning devices.

"On those trails there is no time to think about work, your office, your life—it's the perfect release," says Robert Horowitz, a vice president at International Management Group who rode with a Baja pack. "Every turn is a complete unknown. The terrain is so threatening you have to focus, or you're skidding straight down a mountainside into a cactus."

There are rewards—camaraderie, challenge, and bragging rights, to name a few.

"When you get in that group your competitive spirit just starts flying," says 38-year-old Lee Whaley, a Minute Maid executive who rode with Ellis last October. "So you twist it a little harder and start stretchin' that envelope a little bit. There were times when I had to pull back and just say, 'Whoa, I'm not a young man anymore. I've got to be at work Tuesday morning.'"

Lately the more extreme consequences have been much in the news. Michael Kennedy's death on the slopes of Aspen on New Year's Eve [1998] stemmed directly from the daredevil notion of playing football on skis. John Denver died in a kit plane accident [several years ago].

Remember, though: Thousands of people do get injured playing golf. What kind of risk is that?

After Reading

Word Connections

1. When experiencing risky activities such as biking in the Baja desert, participants *start stretchin' that envelope*. What does the phrase mean in this context?

   _____

   _____

2. Create a concept of definition map for the word *camaraderie*.

   Diagram:

3. The dirt bikes were shrouded by dust clouds. Give the definition of *shrouded*.

   _____

Connecting Meaning

1. Express the main idea of "Mud and Guts"" in one or more sentences.

   _____

   _____

   _____

2. What two kinds of risks or gambles does Michael Ellis describe?

_____

_____

_____

3. Several reasons for taking vacations that involve a certain amount of risk are mentioned in "Mud and Guts." What are they?

_____

_____

_____

Selection 2

On Her Own Terms

NANCY PRICHARD

Before Reading

Before reading "On Her Own Terms," predict what the topic may be. After scanning the story, think about choices you have made in your life. Have you ever struggled against the odds? Were you comfortable with the outcome? Alison Hargreaves followed her dreams with disastrous results. Think about whether the risk is worth the outcome. Set your purpose for reading.

Words to Preview

diminish	*(v.)* to make smaller
insurmountable	*(adj.)* impossible to overcome
supplementary	*(adj.)* something added to make up for a deficiency
plummet	*(v.)* to fall straight down
anorak	*(n.)* a heavy jacket with a hood
surmise	*(v.)* to make a guess
profoundly	*(adv.)* deeply
mar	*(v.)* inflict damage, spoil
inequity	*(n.)* injustice; unfairness
reticent	*(adj.)* inclined to keep one's thoughts and feelings to oneself
hypocrisy	*(n.)* the practice of stating beliefs or feelings that one does not possess; falseness
K2	*(n.)* the world's second-highest and most deadly mountain

During Reading

As you read "On Her Own Terms," continue to predict where the author is headed, visualize the story, and monitor your comprehension. What does the author want you to know about Alison Hargreaves and her accomplishments?

H er critics felt that she took unacceptable risks, but Alison Hargreaves stayed true to her dreams. In the end, she lost her life—but not the respect she'd earned as one of the world's most accomplished mountaineers.

Alison Hargreaves was a true hero, a fact that her tragic death on K2, the world's second-highest and most deadly mountain, does not diminish. Struggling against seemingly insurmountable odds, the 33-year-old Scot, a mother of two, firmly established herself as an elite mountain climber. She became the first person ever to solo the six classic north faces of the Alps in one season, and the second to climb Mount Everest unassisted by supplementary oxygen or partners. By following the call of her lofty ambitions, she became not just a first-rate female alpinist, but one of the top mountain climbers in the world.

The events surrounding her death are sketchy—but ultimately not surprising. K2, a mountain in Pakistan's Karakoram Range, has earned its deadly reputation by killing one in three climbers who attempt its desolate peak (Everest, by contrast, is fatal to about one out of 10 climbers, and McKinley to one out of 250).

Hargreaves had beaten the odds for nearly two months, battling K2's infamous weather in numerous unsuccessful bids for the summit. She was ready to give up and return home to Scotland. But at the last minute, as the Pakistani porters were packing up the base camp, she and her climbing partner, Rob Slater, decided to stay and launch one final attempt. On August 13, Hargreaves, Slater, and four other climbers reached the top of K2. They radioed base camp to announce their success. Then things went horribly wrong. In less than an hour the wind increased to hurricane force and the already-bitter temperature plummeted. The summit team was not heard from again.

Details of the accident remain a mystery, but two Spanish climbers who had stayed in camp 4 (the last camp before the final push to the summit) confirmed Hargreaves's death. After losing their tents to the wind, the Spaniards bowed to life-threatening cold and exhaustion and began a grim retreat down the mountain. On the descent, they discovered one of Hargreaves's boots, her anorak, and her harness. Farther down they saw signs that at least three climbers had fallen from the summit ridge, a distance of nearly 4,000 feet. They surmised that the climbers had been blown off the top shortly after they relayed news of their success to base camp. As the Spaniards descended to camp 3, they discovered Hargreaves's body, but they were forced to leave it unburied and abandon a further search for bodies in order to save their own lives.

In all, K2 claimed seven of the world's top climbers that night: Hargreaves, three Spaniards, a New Zealander, an American, and a Canadian who turned back earlier than the others but died later at camp 2. They climbed for a variety of shared reasons: a love of the mountains, a passion for adventure, the camaraderie and teamwork, and perhaps the opportunity to gain recognition in the sport they had chosen. Hargreaves's motivation was an echo of her summit partners'; the mountains sent out an irresistible call that she gladly answered.

But in a very real way, Hargreaves's experience differed profoundly from that of her companions. No matter how great her passion and expertise, she was viewed—and judged—first as a woman and a mother. "It's strange," says Karen Dickinson of Mountain Madness, the Seattle guide service that was instrumental in relaying news from the K2 base camp to friends, family, and the public. "Many male climbers have families, but that never seems to be an issue when they're taking huge risks in the mountains. When the seven on K2 were killed, no one asked if the others were fathers; discussion centered on the fact that Alison was a mother."

It wasn't the first time. When Hargreaves ascended the north side of the Eiger in 1988, her success was marred by controversy over the fact that she was more than five months pregnant at the time. "I was pregnant, not sick!" she countered. "In fact, I'd never felt healthier or more energetic in my life." But her reasons had less to do with pregnancy than with a far-reaching personal philosophy. "What kind of mother would I be if I sacrificed climbing for my children? It's what makes me me, and what makes me the good mother that I am."

Whether one agrees with Hargreaves's point of view may be less relevant than the issue of why male climbers—and other risk takers—aren't held to the same standard. Even those who question the choices made by Hargreaves see inequities in the criticism launched at her. John Harlin, editor of *Summit Magazine,* was ten years old when his father died during an attempt on the Eiger. He knows both the sorrow of losing a parent and the joy of ascending a mountain. "Being a parent is an enormous responsibility," he says. "When I heard of Alison's leaving her kids at camp when she went up to solo, I didn't like the sound of it, but I would hesitate to condemn her more than I would a male climber."

Others have been less reticent in their criticism, and Hargreaves's role as a parent continued to overshadow her successes as a climber. Few critics, too, felt it important to note that the children were hardly abandoned but left in the care of their father, Jim Ballard. This was not lost on Hargreaves. "My husband is wonderful with the children," she said flatly. "It's lousy that people don't credit him with his role in parenting. For now, we've chosen our responsibilities, and it works."

In spite of her numerous achievements, it wasn't until May of '95, with her oxygenless solo ascent of Mount Everest, that Hargreaves finally gained broad acceptance from the climbing community. For once, the news reports preceded her name not with "Mother of two . . ." but with "Mountain climber Alison Hargreaves . . . ." It was a hardwon victory for a woman whose accomplishments had been so monumental.

"At times I feel victim to the sexual politics inherent in the sport," Hargreaves said not long before her death. "Men don't like seeing women bettering them at high-altitude climbing. That's not what drives me to climb, but it does provide fuel, if just to set the record straight about what people are capable of."

Hargreaves's capabilities were not in question, and in the final analysis she should be credited with being a fine mountaineer—one who lost in a high-stakes match but who played the game as well as anyone. Perhaps more important though, she brought to light a glaring hypocrisy. "I'm doing something that I'm good at and can hopefully make a living at someday," she said. "It shouldn't matter if I'm female or male, or a mother or not. What should matter is that I do my best with what I have, with what I am."

She wasn't alone in that belief. "Alison made great strides in alpinism, breaking barriers, and setting new standards for women as well as men," says Lydia Brady, the only other woman to have reached the summit of Everest without oxygen. "Not only did she establish herself as a barometer for female alpinists, but she proved herself equal to, or better than, contemporary male alpinists—and on her own terms." In the end, that may be Alison Hargreaves's greatest legacy.

After Reading

Word Connections

1. "By following the call of her lofty ambitions, she became not just a first-rate female alpinist, but one of the top mountain climbers in the world." What is the definition of *alpinist*?

   _____

2. Using context clues found in paragraph five, determine the meaning of *surmised*.

   _____

3. Create a concept of definition map for *ascend*.

   Diagram:

4. Several different prefixes that mean *not* are used in "On Her Own Terms." Identify at least five words that use these prefixes.

_____

_____

Connecting Meaning

1. What does the author want you to understand about Hargreaves's mountaineering accomplishments?

_____

_____

_____

_____

2. What overshadowed Hargreaves's successes as a climber?

_____

_____

3. What does the author identify as Hargreaves's greatest legacy?

_____

_____

_____

4. How do you judge the risks Hargreaves took? Support your opinion.

_____

_____

Selection 3

Riders on the Storm: Tornado Chasers Seek the Birthplace of an Elusive Monster

HOWARD B. BLUESTEIN

Before Reading

Before reading "Riders on the Storm: Tornado Chasers Seek the Birthplace of an Elusive Monster," predict what the topic may be. After scanning the story, think about violent storms. Have you ever experienced a violent thunderstorm, hurricane, or tornado? Have you experienced or seen photos of the damage done by tornadoes? Relate what you know about tornadoes to this selection about scientists who chase tornadoes to increase their knowledge. Set your purpose for reading.

Words to Preview	**troposphere**	*(n.)* the lowest region of the atmosphere
	stratify	*(v.)* to form in layers
	array	*(n.)* impressively large number
	dissipate	*(v.)* to vanish
	spawn	*(v.)* to produce
	barrage	*(n.)* a rapid discharge
	verify	*(v.)* to determine the truth or accuracy of

During Reading   As you read "Riders on the Storm: Tornado Chasers Seek the Birthplace of an Elusive Monster," continue to predict what may happen next in the article, visualize the story, and monitor your comprehension. What information does the author want you to remember about tornado chasers?

It was April 26, 1991, and high over central Oklahoma an intriguing kind of hell was about to break loose. The early-morning transmissions from the National Weather Service weather balloons had been encouraging. As the balloons climbed through the troposphere, their instrument packages recorded sharply dropping temperatures, increasing wind speeds, and rapid shifts in wind direction. Meanwhile, somewhere between three and eight miles up, an intense disturbance in the wind field was approaching from the southwest on a collision course with warm, moist air flowing northward across the Great Plains from the Gulf of Mexico. The collision would ignite thunderstorms. With luck, the thunderstorms would tap the potential energy of the stratified air to trigger more powerful storms known as supercells: vast rotating mazes of updrafts and downdrafts that stretch 50,000 or 60,000 feet upward into the atmosphere, produce magnificent hailstones, and give rise to many of the most powerful tornadoes on earth.

As my team members and I pulled out of the parking lot of the University of Oklahoma at Norman, we thought about those tornadoes. At this time of year the five of us—the driver, Herb Stein; three of my graduate students from the School of Meteorology; and I—thought about little else. Inside the twelve-passenger van our broadband radios, miniature television, and cellular telephone kept up a steady two-way buzz of weather-related chatter. Stored in the rear, where there had been a row of seats, were coils of electrical cables, two tripods, a video camera, data-logging equipment, and a low-power Doppler radar capable of measuring wind speed in rain, hail, and airborne debris at a range of up to three or four miles.

Riding along, we kept up running commentaries into small cassette recorders on our laps. Starting at departure time, just after noon, the tapes would later enable us to reconstruct the trip: hours and minutes elapsed, mileage readings, road signs, changes of direction, cloud sightings, and, incidentally, mood swings. For example: The National Severe Storms Forecast

Storm chasers who risk their lives as they record data about an active tornado were portrayed in the movie "Twister." (The Everett Collection)

Center in Kansas City issues a tornado watch for parts of Kansas and Oklahoma. Inside the van, spirits rise. Along the Kansas-Oklahoma border we spot a promising array of towering cumulus clouds. Spirits soar. The clouds bubble upward but fail to turn into thunderstorms. Spirits sag. And so on throughout the afternoon.

4:15 P.M.: Good news comes in over the National Oceanic and Atmospheric Administration weather band. Back in Norman, the National Weather Service's Doppler radar has detected severe thunderstorms brewing back in northern Oklahoma. Herb Stein makes a U-turn and heads us toward the closest storm. 4:53 P.M.: We catch the storm. Beneath its base, southwest of the precipitation core, a small funnel cloud is forming. The funnel quickly dissipates—no tornado this time—and we follow the storm eastward. To the south a new storm has developed, and we spot two more short-lived funnel clouds. 5:47 P.M.: Yet another funnel appears, this time off to the east. We head toward it but change our minds when another severe-thunderstorm warning suggests even better hunting to the south.

(Later we would learn that the storm we had abandoned continued into southern Kansas, where it gave rise to a large tornado just south of the small town of Winfield. Meanwhile, not far from where we turned back from Kansas, an even worse storm sprang up. It spawned a tornado that cut across Wichita and nearby Andover, killing seventeen people and wreaking more than $150 million worth of damage.)

Approaching our new target storm from the north, we enter Billings, Oklahoma. We pass through town amid the eerie blast of tornado sirens. A barrage of wind-driven hailstones, some as big as baseballs, slams into the van. With such a thick curtain of precipitation blocking the view, we could drive right into a tornado without seeing it. We retreat eastward and get ahead of the advancing precipitation core of the storm. Then we see it: the outline of a funnel, possibly a large tornado, off to the southwest. As we head south to investigate, doubt disappears. The tornado—a huge black cylinder jutting upward into the sky—crosses Interstate 35, the north-south highway to Kansas, toppling everything in its path.

Near Red Rock, Oklahoma, Stein stops the van, but before we can unload the radar and the video camera, he orders us back inside. The tornado is heading straight for us. Now it is our turn to be chased! We speed south, out of the path of the tornado, set the radar up on its tripod and watch in awe as the funnel crosses the road to our north, strewing debris over a damage path half a mile wide. The wind is so fierce that two people have to lean on the radar to keep it from blowing over; the camera cannot be set up at all and must be held by hand. Just a mile north of us, a house is blown off its foundation; half a mile from us, snapped utility poles tumble onto the road. As the tornado moves away from us, its damage path widens to a mile. Later analysis of the data will show that the Doppler radar detected wind speeds of between 270 and 280 miles an hour, the fastest tornado winds ever measured by an instrument.

Even for an experienced storm chaser, the Red Rock tornado was an extraordinary event. People who drive thousands of miles in pursuit of tornadoes might see at most a few a year; people who do not chase them probably will never see any at all. That is why we tornado scientists sometimes envy our colleagues who concern themselves with fixed objects of study such as rocks, microscope slides, or the moon.

Our subjects are more like living creatures—enormous shy animals that appear, fleetingly and unpredictably, at places they choose. Because tornadoes are so elusive and so dangerous, much of the progress in tornado studies has taken place far from the tornadoes themselves, either at the end of a radar beam or over highly simplified models run on computers or in the laboratory. But radars must be cross-checked against reality; models and laboratory experiments must be verified. Ultimately, there is no substitute for ground truth; someone must go to the storm.

After Reading

Word Connections

1. Using context clues, define *supercell*.

_____

_____

_____

2. Define *running commentaries* by using the context of paragraph three.

_____

_____

_____

_____

3. Create a concept of definition map for *dissipate*.

Diagram:

Connecting Meaning

1. With today's advanced technology, why is it necessary to risk lives chasing tornadoes?

_____

_____

_____

_____

2. Why are running commentaries recorded by the scientists?

_____

_____

_____

3. Describe the Red Rock tornado.

_____

_____

_____

_____

Portfolio Activities

Integrating Ideas

In the three readings, the risk takers made individual choices that endangered their lives. If their choice resulted in injury or death, it would have a lasting effect on spouses, family, or friends. What would you consider acceptable risks for your spouse? What would you consider acceptable risks for parents of young children? Reflect on these ideas in writing or in class discussion.

Extending Concepts

How does risky behavior differ in men and women? Are men or women more likely to take physical risks? Emotional risks? Financial risks? Career risks? In writing, state and support your opinion on gender differences in risk taking.

Collaborative Activities

Given an unlimited budget, plan the riskiest vacation that you would venture. Investigate activities, locale, equipment, and costs.

Additional Portfolio Suggestion

"Remember that great love and great achievements involve great risk."

H. Jackson Brown, Jr.

Think about this quotation. Reflect on what it means to you. You may record your thoughts through an essay, poem, music, or art.

Chapter Summary Graphic Organizer

Unstated Main Ideas

Topic

Unstated Main Idea

Look at all important information.

What does the author want the reader to understand or remember?

7

Supporting Details

Theme of Readings: *The Value of Fear*

The only thing we have to fear is fear itself . . .

FRANKLIN DELANO ROOSEVELT

Value of Fear

Given that fear is an unpleasant and undesirable sensation, does it have any value, or is it only the remnant of our caveman days? Twenty-five thousand years ago, humans survived because of fear. Fear activated a physical response that aided survival. Imagine yourself as a caveman, picking berries, when suddenly you come nose-to-nose with a ferocious wolf. At the sight of the wolf, your fear triggers the fight or flight response. Your hypothalmus sends a message to your adrenal glands, and within seconds your body becomes supercharged. Extra energy, sharpened senses, and faster responses result from adrenaline produced by your adrenal glands. You narrowly escape death by running faster than you have ever run before.

In the present day, you have the same internal body parts, and you still have the fight or flight response. Threatening situations cause the same physical responses, but today's wolves are more often internal than external. You react to the threat of layoff from your job, the threat of your spouse leaving you, or the threat of an angry confrontation. Not truly life threatening, these situations cause your fight or flight energy to turn inward and cause stress. If you can overcome your fears of non-life-threatening situations, you will gain the courage to enrich your life.

Sometimes, however, fear signals should not be ignored. Life-threatening situations still exist in today's society. By learning to trust your instincts and intuition, by recognizing those situations that are dangerous, and by learning to distinguish between true fear and baseless worry, you can embrace fear as a gift.

Chapter Objectives

After completing this chapter, you will be able to

1. **Recognize the supporting details.**
2. **Identify supporting details as major or minor.**

Focus on Supporting Details

You and your best friend are invited to a party on Friday night, but you can't go because you have to work. You see your friend the next day and ask, "How was the party?" Your friend replies, "It was great!" and turns to walk away. You get the point—it was a good party—but you need more information. What made it a good party? Your friend tells you there were a lot of people, the food and music were terrific, and some funny things happened. You now understand why the party was great, but you want to know more of the details. Who was there? What kind of food was served? Was the music a deejay or a band? What were some of the funny things that happened?

Major Details

The topic of this conversation is the party; the main idea is that the party was great. The major supporting details are the sentences that explain, clarify, and/or prove the main idea. Major supporting details are essential for understanding the main idea. When your friend explained there were a lot of people, the food and music were terrific, and some funny things happened, you are being presented with the major details. To help identify the major details, ask yourself, "How does the author support the main idea?"

Minor Details

Even though major details explain the main idea, you need more than an outline of main images to create a mental picture. You need minor details as well: examples, definitions, or statistics that illustrate the major details and add more interest and variety to the material. Minor supporting details clarify and explain the major supporting details. They are answers to questions like "Who was at the party?" "What did you eat?" "What kind of music was there?" To help identify the minor details, ask yourself, "How does the author illustrate the major details?"

Read the following paragraph. Then use the following guide questions to help you identify the topic, the main idea, and the supporting details.

> Fear is a great motivator. It motivates children to follow their parents' rules. The threat of being grounded for a week will often ensure that curfew is kept. Schools also use fear as a motivator. The threat of failure or detention is the reason why some students complete their homework and behave in the classroom.

Who or what is this paragraph about?

The topic is fear.

What does the author want the reader to remember or understand about the topic?

Fear is a great motivator.

How does the author support the main idea?

The author states that both parents and schools use fear as a motivator.

How does the author illustrate the major details?

The threat of being grounded and the threat of failure or detention illustrate how parents and schools use fear.

You may find it helpful to create a map (see Figure 7-1) when determining the main idea and supporting details.

Figure 7-1

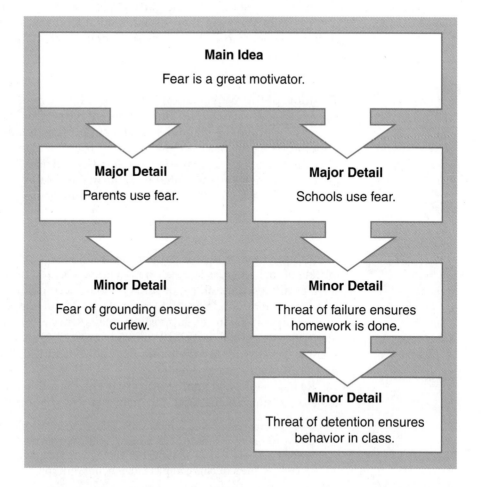

■ ■ ■ ■ Short Exercises: Supporting Details

Read each of the following paragraphs. Identify the topic, the main idea, and the major and minor supporting details by using the guide questions given earlier. Then complete the map or outline provided with your answers.

1. In early man, fear was a tool for human survival through the fight or flight response. The sight of a threatening situation, like a man-eating tiger, caused the hypothalmus gland to release a rush of adrenaline. Adrenaline caused a person to run faster, jump higher, see better, and think faster than he or she did only seconds earlier. In addition, to help humans survive life-threatening circumstances, the fight or flight response caused all unnecessary body functions to stop. Digestion stopped, and the immune system was temporarily shut down.

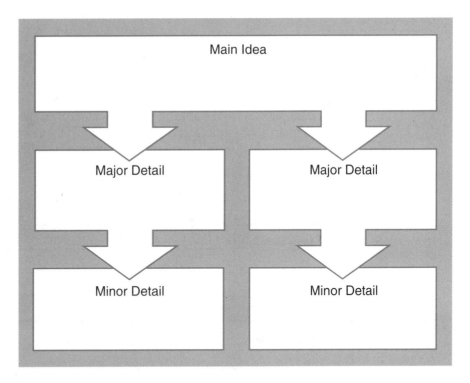

2. In today's world, humans still have the fight or flight response. In response to a threatening situation, such as your boss calling you into the main office when layoffs are expected, your body activates its

fight or flight response. Since you cannot fight or flee, the energy produced by this response is pent up in your body, causing a physical reaction: your heart races, your blood pressure rises, and your palms sweat.

Topic: _____

Main Idea: _____

_____

Major detail: _____

_____

Major detail: _____

_____

Minor detail: _____

_____

3. Fear in the workplace can be used to a manager's advantage. To make fear work, a manager must set up clear expectations and definite consequences for the employees. For instance, an employee must maintain a sales quota. If the sales quota is not met, the employee will face the reduction of sales territory as a consequence.

Topic: _____

Main Idea: _____

_____

Major detail: _____

_____

Minor detail: _____

_____

Minor detail: _____

_____

4. Novels and films capitalize on fear as entertainment. Stephen King has enjoyed phenomenal success as a writer of horror fiction. Books like *The Shining, Cujo,* and *Firestarter* are among his best-selling novels. Horror films have also been a successful means of entertainment. Thousands have flocked to scream in fear at movies like *The Haunting* or *Friday, the Thirteenth.*

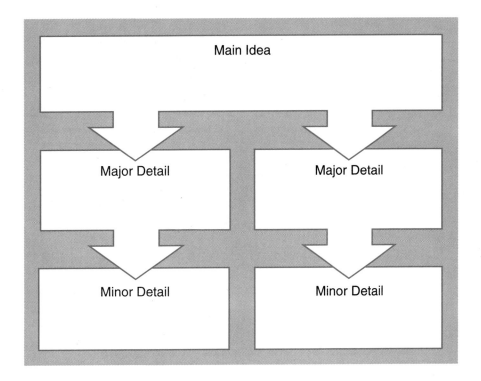

5. Fear plays a role as an internal motivator. The fear of not being accepted by others causes people to take actions they may not have taken on their own. For example, a person may purchase a particular brand of jeans or sneakers to be accepted as part of the group. People are also driven by the fear of being unsuccessful in their career; they may work long hours and take on extra responsibilities to establish their success.

Topic: _____

Main Idea: _____

Major detail: _____

_____

Minor detail: _____

_____

Major detail: _____

_____

Minor detail: _____

_____

6. To consumers, roller coasters and haunted houses are fright fests, but to a proprietor, the fear that these attractions produce can be a profitable business. A dazzling, "scared to death" attraction drives up the season's gate admissions. It creates good word-of-mouth publicity that attracts new customers to come and try out the attraction. It also draws repeat customers who want to relive the thrills and chills.

What is the topic of this paragraph?

_____

What is the main idea of this paragraph?

_____

How does the author support the main idea?

_____

_____

How does the author illustrate the major details?

_____

_____

_____

7. Horror films can give a teenager a temporary feeling of a loss of control that may be healthy. For example, a teenager who goes to a horror movie experiences a safe and sometimes much needed escape. Horror critic, Douglas E. Winter says, "We love to see something so grotesque and unexpected that it makes us scream or laugh . . . secure in the knowledge that in the fun house of fear, such behavior is not only accepted but encouraged." (Adapted from *The Thrill of Chills* by Ellen Blum Barish)

What is the topic of this paragraph?

_____

What is the main idea of this paragraph?

_____

_____

How does the author support the main idea?

_____

_____

How does the author illustrate the major details?

_____

_____

_____

8. Fear has created another valuable use for the technology of virtual reality. Fear has extended virtual reality programs beyond entertainment. Today, virtual reality (VR) programs are used in the psychological treatment of phobic victims. In a therapeutic VR program, an "online shrink" leads the phobics into a controlled VR environment. There they can safely experience what they fear and thereby ease the problem. The fear of flying and the fear of heights are two of the phobias being treated in this manner.

What is the topic of this paragraph?

_____

What is the main idea of this paragraph?

_____

_____

How does the author support the main idea?

_____

_____

How does the author illustrate the major detail?

_____

_____

_____

▩ ▩ ▩ ▩ **Reading Selections**

Selection 1   **Gift of Fear**

FROM GIFT OF FEAR
GAVIN DE BECKER

Before Reading   Before you read "Gift of Fear," predict the topic. After scanning the story, think about your experiences with fear. Is fear a positive or a negative feeling? Set your purpose for reading.

Words to Preview	**vigilance**	*(n.)* alert watchfulness
	intuition	*(n.)* sharp insight
	Klaxon	*(n.)* a trademark for a loud horn formerly used on cars
	emergence	*(n.)* act of becoming evident or obvious
	vulnerable	*(adj.)* susceptible to attack
	kaleidoscope	*(n.)* series of changing phases or events
	profound	*(adj.)* coming from the depths of one's being

During Reading   As you read "Gift of Fear," continue to predict and visualize information and monitor your comprehension. What is the author telling you about fear?

Fears are educated into us, and can, if we wish, be educated out.

KARL A. MENNINGER

We all know there are plenty of reasons to fear people from time to time. The question is, what are those times? Far too many people are walking around in a constant state of vigilance, their intuition misinformed about what really poses danger. It needn't be so. When you honor accurate intuitive signals and evaluate them without denial (believing that either the favorable or the unfavorable outcome is possible), you need not be wary, for you will come to trust that you'll be notified if there is something worthy of your attention. Fear will gain credibility because it won't be applied wastefully. When you accept the survival signal as a welcome message and quickly evaluate the environment or situation, fear stops in an instant. Thus, trusting intuition is the exact opposite of living in fear. In fact, the role of fear in your life lessens as your mind and body come to know that you will listen to the quiet wind chime and have no need for Klaxons.

Real fear is a signal intended to be very brief, a mere servant of intuition. But though few would argue that extended, unanswered fear is destructive, millions choose to stay there. They may have forgotten or never learned that fear is not an emotion like sadness or happiness, either of which might last a long while. It is not a state, like anxiety. True fear is a survival signal that sounds only in the presence of danger, yet unwarranted fear has assumed a power over us that it holds over no other creature on earth. In *The Denial of Death,* Ernest Becker explains that "animals, in order to survive, have had to be protected by fear responses." Some Darwinians believe that the early humans who were most afraid were most likely to survive. The result, says Becker, "is the emergence of man as we know him: a hyperanxious animal who constantly invents reasons for anxiety even when there are none." It need not be this way.

There are two rules about fear that, if you accept them, can improve your use of it, reduce its frequency, and literally transform your experience of life. That's a big claim, I know, but don't be "afraid" to consider it with an open mind.

RULE #1. THE VERY FACT THAT YOU FEAR SOMETHING IS SOLID EVIDENCE THAT IT IS NOT HAPPENING.

Fear summons powerful predictive resources that tell us what might come next. It is that which might come next that we fear—what might happen, not what is happening now. An absurdly literal example helps demonstrate this: As you stand near the edge of a high cliff, you might fear getting too close. If you stand right at the edge, you no longer fear getting too close, you now fear falling. Edward Gorey gives us his dark-humored but accurate take on the fact that if you do fall, you no longer fear falling—you fear landing:

The Suicide, as she is falling,
Illuminated by the moon,
Regrets her act, and finds appalling
The thought she will be dead so soon.

Panic, the great enemy of survival, can be perceived as an unmanageable kaleidoscope of fears. It can be reduced through embracing the second rule:

RULE #2. WHAT YOU FEAR IS RARELY WHAT YOU THINK YOU FEAR—IT IS WHAT YOU *LINK* TO FEAR.

Take anything about which you have ever felt profound fear and link it to each of the possible outcomes. When it is real fear, it will either be in the presence of danger, or it will link to pain or death. When we get a fear signal, our intuition has already made many connections. To best respond, bring the links into consciousness and follow them to their high-stakes destination—if they lead there. When we focus on one link only, say, fear of someone walking toward us on a dark street instead of fear of being harmed by someone walking toward us on a dark street, the fear is wasted. That's because many people will approach us—only a very few might harm us.

Apply these two rules to the fear that a burglar might crash into your living room. First, the fear itself can actually be perceived as good news, because it confirms that the dreaded outcome is not occurring right now. Since life has plenty of hazards that come upon us without warning, we could welcome fear with "Thank you, God, for a signal I can act on." More often, however, we apply denial first, trying to see if perhaps we can just think it away.

Remember, fear says something might happen. If it does happen, we stop fearing it and start to respond to it, manage it, surrender to it; or we start to fear the next outcome we predict might be coming. If a burglar does crash into the living room, we no longer fear that possibility; we now fear what he might do next. Whatever that may be, while we fear it, it is not happening.

After Reading

Word Connections

1. Define *hyperanxious* using your knowledge of word parts.

   _____

2. Create a concept of definition map for *intuition*.

   Diagram:

Connection Meaning

1. The main idea of the selection is that if one feels fear all the time, then fear is no longer a signal of real danger. State one example given by the author that illustrates this idea.

   _____

   _____

   _____

   _____

2. The author provides two rules for dealing with fear. Identify and
   explain each rule.

   _____

   _____

   _____

   _____

   _____

   _____

   _____

Selection 2

Everything You Always Wanted to Know about Fear (But Were Afraid to Ask)

DAVID CORNFIELD

Before Reading

Before you read "Everything You Always Wanted to Know about Fear (But
Were Afraid to Ask)," predict the topic. After scanning the story to see if your
prediction is correct, think about the feeling of fear. How do you deal with
fear? Relate what you know about fear to the author's information.

Words to Preview

untempered	*(adj.)* unaffected
inhibition	*(n.)* act of holding back
impenetrable	*(adj.)* impossible to enter
palpable	*(adj.)* capable of being touched
inarticulate	*(adj.)* unable to speak clearly
paradoxically	*(adj.)* seemingly contradictory statement that may nonetheless be true
repertoire	*(n.)* range or number of skills, aptitudes, or accomplishments
visceral	*(adj.)* relating to or situated in the soft internal organs of the body
pervasive	*(adj.)* being present throughout
embark	*(v.)* to set out on a venture

During Reading

As you read "Everything You Always Wanted to Know about Fear," continue
to predict and visualize the information and monitor your comprehension.
What does the author want you to know or remember about fear?

During the summer of 1983, I created a series of six masks as part of a workshop on clowning. Working the clay with my eyes closed, the masks emerged as powerful expressions of my unconscious mind, untempered by inhibitions from my rational mind.

Each mask was the starting point for the development of a clown personality. Five led quickly and easily to a story and a character. The sixth seemed impenetrable. I left the workshop having found only five of my six clowns, and, on returning to my office, I managed to hang the masks so that the sixth was hidden from view.

I still have that mask. Looking at it now, the fear it expresses is almost palpable. The eyes are wide open and startled, the hair stands on end, the mouth is gasping. Yet at the time, I refused to acknowledge my terrified clown. I wanted him out of sight and out of mind.

Denying fear is not unusual. In our society, to be afraid is considered shameful. Many people hide their fear, from themselves and from others. Yet, fear has survival value. It is there to warn us about danger so that we can take precautions to minimize risk. Ignored, it tries to protect us by finding ways to prevent us from taking risks. It blinds us to an opportunity or makes us arrive late or makes us forget an important detail or makes us inarticulate or . . . the variations are endless.

In my work as a coach for people making the transition to self-employment, the issue of fear is of central concern. An entrepreneur is someone who is able to take risks. If fear prevents you from taking risks, you will not succeed as an entrepreneur. Period. It doesn't matter how marketable your ideas are or how well you understand business concepts. To survive as an entrepreneur, you have to learn how to live with rising levels of fear and not be immobilized.

The best way to deal with fear is to stop pretending to be fearless. Paradoxically, the more you deny fear, the more likely it is to dominate you. Tune into your fear, give it a voice, enter into a dialogue with it, do what you can to reduce the risk, and you will find yourself more able to take risks.

Listening to fear is more easily said than done. We all have a repertoire of defenses that help us deny our emotions. Addictive behaviors are all based in a desire to avoid feeling, and as we know, they are hard to shake. If you avoid feeling your fear by lighting up a cigarette or by getting busy, you have lost the opportunity to respond to your fear. Learning to deal with our fear reduces our need to resort to addictive behaviors.

Fear is visceral. One way we deny our fear is to numb our bodies with muscle tension and shallow breathing. Over time, numbness becomes chronic. In this depressed state, we don't feel fear, but neither do we feel enthusiasm or pleasure. The fear hasn't gone away. We just don't feel it. And if we don't feel it, we can't listen to it. To prevent fear from stopping us in our tracks, we need to learn to relax our bodies, deepen our breathing, open up to feeling. Body-based expressive psychotherapy and relaxation techniques such as massage and yoga are ways to regain lost feeling so that we can be more responsive to our legitimate fears.

Not all fears are legitimate. Legitimate fear is fear that pertains to a real danger in the present. Some fear is an understandable but incorrect response to inadequate information. Ignorance breeds fear. The more informed you are, the easier it is to decide if the danger is real and what precautions you need to take to reduce the risk. If you have a fear about something, get more information.

Some fears belong to unfinished situations from the past. For example, if you were hurt by a man with a beard, you may be triggered into fear every time you see a bearded man. There are a number of ways to deal with old fears. One is to finish the unfinished business in therapy, diminishing its power to distract you from responding to the present. Another is to use meditation to develop your capacity to view your fear with detachment so that you become aware when it is irrational. It also helps to get the perspective of other people—people in a support group or friends whom you really trust.

Some fear is pervasive low-level fear that you carry around with you regardless of present circumstances. If you were abused as a child or overprotected by fearful parents or even if your parents weren't there to back you up, you may feel inadequate and just want to hide away. Again, counseling can be useful to help heal wounds that diminished your self-esteem and hindered your full growth as a human being.

Keep in mind that emotions come in pairs. Hurt and anger go together. So do shame and desire. Behind fear lies excitement. As Sam says to Frodo in *The Lord of the Rings,* the stories that stay in the mind are about ordinary folks who say yes to the adventures that lie in their path, those who go ahead despite the dangers. Risk is a call to adventure. If you listen to your fear and do what needs to be done to avoid unnecessary danger, you enable yourself to embark on the exciting adventure that is your life.

After Reading

Word Connections

1. Define *legitimate fear.* Give one example of a legitimate fear.

   _____

   _____

   _____

2. Using the context of paragraph 5, define *entrepreneur.*

   _____

   _____

3. The prefix *in-* was used several times in the reading, for example, *inadequate*. Create a word map for the prefix *in-*, which means not.

Map:

Connecting Meaning

1. What is the main idea of paragraph 4?

   _____

   _____

2. What is the main idea of paragraph 8?

   _____

   _____

3. Describe what the author thinks is the best way to deal with fear.

   _____

   _____

   _____

4. State at least two ways to deal with old fears.

   _____

   _____

   _____

Selection 3   **Courage and Fear**

CHRISTINE BRUUN

Before Reading   Before you read "Courage and Fear," predict the topic. After scanning the story, think about courage and fear. How would you define courage? What is the connection between courage and fear. Relate what you know about courage and fear to this article.

Words to Preview

banish	*(v.)*	to force to leave a place
intimidate	*(v.)*	to fill with fear
barrage	*(v.)*	overwhelming outpouring
thwart	*(v.)*	to prevent the occurrence of
validate	*(v.)*	justify
invincible	*(adj.)*	incapable of being overcome

During Reading   As you read, continue to predict and visualize the information and monitor your comprehension. What does the author want you to know about courage and fear?

Fear stands in the way of most of our successes. Unfortunately it is left over from the caveman era and serves only as a stumbling block. Fear served its purpose back then. We've all heard of the "flight or fight" syndrome. It has been genetically engineered into all humans to maximize survival at a time when life was very fragile. You either lived or died, so fear served as a gauge by which cavemen chose their daily paths.

Today, however, our very lives seldom hinge on this genetically engineered response. It is baggage left over from a time when it was needed and now, causes us only unnecessary emotional pain. It is wasted emotion that robs us of the joy of creativity and of reaching our goals.

What does courage have to do with this? It takes courage to ignore the fear as we continue a path that leads to our joy. It takes courage to recognize that the fear is blocking our creativity, or blocking our path to a desired goal. It takes great courage to acknowledge the fear, put it in perspective, then banish it to its proper place in our lives. It takes courage to act in spite of the fear. When we find out we have made a mistake, it takes courage to accept responsibility for that error, learn from it, put it behind, then go on as best we can.

There are people who are so intimidated by life in general that they find it impossible to share in the joys and successes of those around them. They give up their dreams of being a doctor, a lawyer, a business tycoon, an artist, or a writer. They do what the world expects of them. This fear of standing up for themselves, of rocking the boat, going against the current, of seeming selfish, of being perceived as odd or different, or of being criticized, so takes over their lives that they become fearful of everything.

A friend related the story of an older woman in her seventies. She had called her to share the excitement of the purchase of some property on a lake where they were having a house built. It was in the country away from the hustle and bustle of the city. She had shared her joy at having crossed paths with a deer and a wild turkey while hiking through the woods behind their home site.

The woman's response was fear and warning. Don't feed the deer or make pets out of them because people get attacked and killed by deer every year. The barrage of negative warnings seemed endless. By the end of the call she had gone from excited and joyous at her life to depressed and empty.

Obviously, fear is here to stay. It is part of us. It takes great courage to accept that part of us as normal. It takes courage to learn to be kind to ourselves and others who are thwarted by it. And it takes even more courage not to let our own fears spill over into other people's lives.

We might think we are helping them by showing them all the possible pitfalls, but what we are doing is sucking the joy from their lives in order to feed our own fears. Instead of trusting that they are capable of taking care of their own lives, we feel the need to rescue them from all the possible bad things of the world. We validate our own fear while we block their joy, their dreams, their possibilities. We place doubt in their minds where once they felt invincible. We become the instrument of fear.

It takes great courage not to be that instrument, but become a support and a foot up for those people who need encouragement. I challenge each and every one of us to become a foothold for those who need our support. I challenge each and every one of us to act even in the face of fear. I made a commitment to myself a long time ago. I vowed never to let fear stop me from reaching my dreams. It has been difficult at times, to fight my demons and face my fears head on. But the rewards have taught me to put my fears behind and go forward toward the life I love. It is worth it!

After Reading

Word Connections

1. What does the phrase *rocking the boat* mean?

_____

_____

2. How can a person *go against the current*?

_____

_____

Connecting Meaning

1. What is the main idea of "Courage and Fear"?

   _____

   _____

2. "It takes courage to ignore fear as we continue a path that leads to our joy." What other actions require courage as stated in the reading?

   _____

   _____

   _____

3. What do you think is the connection between courage and fear?

   _____

   _____

Portfolio Activities

Integrating Ideas

The three readings focus on the value of fear and ways to deal with fear. Do you think that fear is valuable? How do you deal with fear? Relate your ideas in writing or in class discussion.

Extending Concepts

Describe in writing a situation when you or someone you know dealt with true fear. What role did intuition, instinct, and adrenaline play in the response?

Collaborative Activities

How much of fear is a result of media hype? According to Amazon.com, in July 1999 there were 2,998 books with fear and 4,479 with violence in the title. Television news and newspapers report story after story about fearful situations. As a group, decide which medium you wish to research. Explore whether the medium is "creating" fear in society. Present the group's findings to the class.

Additional Portfolio Suggestion

Read *Gift of Fear or Protecting the Gift: Keeping Children and Teenagers Safe (and Parents Sane)* by Gavin De Becker. When you have completed it, write about the book's suggestions for how to deal with fear. Which would you use?

■ ■ ■ ■ Chapter Summary Graphic Organizer

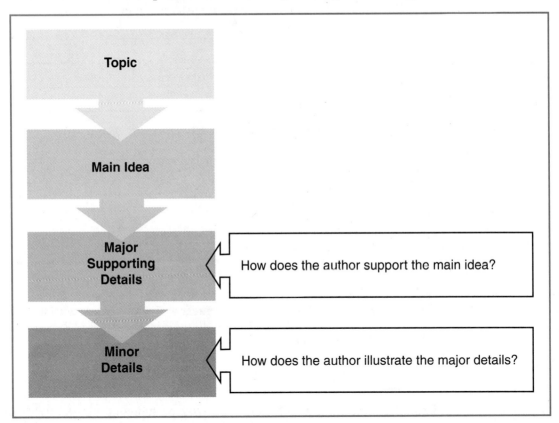

Review

Unit 3

Main Ideas

In this unit, you continued to work with the reading process.

- Before you read, you predicted the topic of the selection by asking: *Who or what is this reading about?*

- As you read, you connected to the topic by asking: *What does the author want me to know or remember about this topic?* This step allowed you to determine the stated or unstated main idea.

- Examples, explanations, or facts support the main idea. To identify these major supporting details ask: *How does the author support the main idea?*

- To illustrate the major details and add more interest, the author provides minor details. To identify the minor details ask: *How does the author illustrate the major details?*

   The answers to these guide questions enhance your comprehension and help you to evaluate your understanding after you read.

Unit Review Graphic Organizer

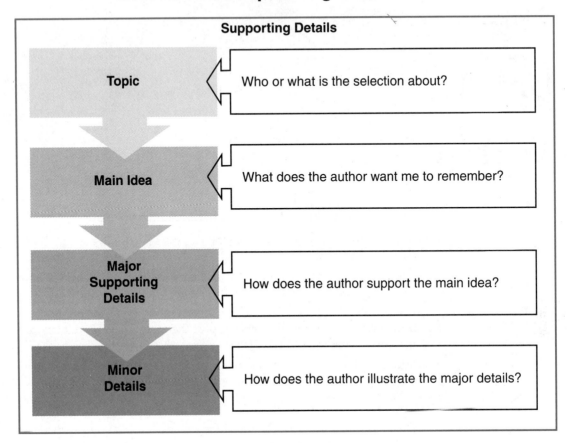

Supporting Details

Topic	Who or what is the selection about?
Main Idea	What does the author want me to remember?
Major Supporting Details	How does the author support the main idea?
Minor Details	How does the author illustrate the major details?

Portfolio Suggestion

To develop lifelong reading habits, it is important for you to read extensively and begin to recognize your reading preferences. A reading log is an excellent place to collect information about your habits and preferences in reading. A chart may be used to keep track of different kinds of information such as date read, title, author, genre, pages, and comments. See Appendix F.

4

Patterns of Organization

Theme of Readings: Social Issues

Fear less, hope more;
Whine less, breathe more;
Talk less, say more;
Hate less, love more;
And all good things are yours.

<small>SWEDISH PROVERB</small>

Social Issues

This unit explores a number of issues and questions that concern us all as members of a society.

- **Career Selection:** What is a good job, and what are some effective ways of finding one? For those with a college education and a resourceful outlook, there are a wealth of fulfilling possibilities. The key to finding "a good fit" is to assess one's skills and strengths, identify potential opportunities, and learn the process of job hunting.

- **Health:** How is lasting health achieved and maintained? Everyone wants to enjoy the best of health at all ages. Educating oneself about both physical and mental health issues is an important step in the process.

- **Censorship:** As a society, how can we balance free speech rights with other rights and responsibilities? An explosion of controversial material on the Internet has raised troubling issues. Many people wonder how best to weigh the First Amendment right for free expression with, for example, the need to guard national security and the need to protect children from obscenity.

- **Violence:** What can best be done about violence in our society? Violence enters our lives through experiences, movies, video games, and television news reports, threatening our sense of security. The quality of life is diminished when homes, streets, schools, and workplaces do not feel safe and may not be safe.

- **Consumer Credit and Indebtedness:** How can we pursue "the good life," and avoid a mountain of debt? Credit cards are easy to obtain and use—so easy, in fact, that unmanageable debt can mount up quickly. Experts can offer helpful tips on managing credit, an important life skill.

Several questions connect these topics. As individuals and as members of a society, we must always ask: *What are my choices and responsibilities? What are the uses and misuses of freedom? What do I want the future to be like, and how can this future come to pass?*

Patterns of Organization

An effective reader makes sense of what is read by being able to identify the topic, main idea, and supporting details. To relate the supporting details to the main idea, authors choose organized patterns. This unit will examine patterns of organization: chronological order and listing, definition and illustration/example, comparison and contrast, cause and effect, and problem and solution.

To assist the reader, authors use words that signal these patterns of organization. Signal words provide clues about the author's choice of organization. Certain signal words are common to several patterns. The author may also apply a combination of patterns within a reading to make the main idea as clear as possible. By recognizing signal words and organizational patterns, it is easier for readers to understand the author's ideas and information.

The following guide questions will help you to analyze and determine the pattern of any paragraph or reading:

What is the main idea of this paragraph or reading?

What are the common signals used in this paragraph or reading?

What details support the main idea?

What is the pattern of organization?

Unit Objectives

After completing this unit, you will be able to

1. **Identify signals for patterns of organization.**
2. **Distinguish between the patterns of organization.**
3. **Identify the supporting details that determine each pattern of organization.**

8

Chronological Order and Listing Patterns

Theme of Readings: Career Exploration

Find a job you like and you add five days to every week.

H. JACKSON BROWNE, JR.

■ ■ ■ ■ Career Exploration

Most people entering the work force today will change careers at least twice during their lifetime. Whether you are looking for your first job or are changing careers, you need to consider your qualifications, research career opportunities, and know the job search process.

Career exploration begins with self-exploration. You need to understand your strengths, weaknesses, interests, habits, and skills. These insights will help guide you in your choice of careers. Finding the right career does not have to be achieved alone, however. Networking with parents, family, and friends can be valuable because of their past and present job experiences. Internships set up by local colleges and businesses can give you a chance to try out a possible field or type of job and see how you like it. Career counselors are good at guiding you to understand the available opportunities and the best choices for you. Books, articles, and Web sites are other helpful sources of information in a job search.

Ultimately, the decision about which career to pursue is yours. Choosing a satisfying career that you enjoy will have a profound impact on your life.

Chapter Objectives

After completing this chapter, you will be able to

1. **Identify the signal words used for the chronological and listing patterns.**
2. **Distinguish between chronological order and listing patterns.**
3. **Identify the major supporting details of the reading that determine the chronological or listing patterns.**

Focus on Chronological Order and Listing Patterns

Authors often choose to relate the supporting details to the main idea by using organized patterns. By recognizing the patterns of organization, it is easier for readers to understand the author's ideas and information.

Chronological Order Pattern

Chronological order organizes information according to the time order in which it occurs. The *order* of events or ideas is important to this pattern. If the events or ideas are taken out of sequence, the reading will no longer make sense. This pattern is often used to tell a story, to relate historic events, or to give directions. For example, the chronological order pattern would be used in a handbook for new employees telling the history of the company, safety procedures, or directions to operate equipment.

Common Signals   Signal words that may provide clues to the chronological order pattern are

first	before	next	when	soon
second	during	then	while	later
third	after	finally	now	until

Dates and **times** may also be used to determine this pattern.

Read the following paragraph. Then read the guide questions and answers that follow. In the future, these guide questions will help you to analyze and determine the pattern of any paragraph or reading.

> Effective job search strategy requires that you set objectives and plan specific times to complete each one. First, schedule planning time. Then, maintain a list of activities. Write up a weekly calendar and enter each item by day or hour. Next, start a notebook with one section for contact names, addresses, and phone numbers and another section for notes about different companies.
>
> —From *Career Fitness Program* by Sukiennik, Bendat, and Raufman

What is the main idea of this paragraph?

The main idea is found in the first sentence: "Effective job search strategy requires that you set objectives and plan specific times to complete each one."

What are the common signals used in this paragraph?

The words *first, then, next,* and *finally* indicate a sequence of activities and identify the major supporting details.

What details support the main idea?

The major supporting details are (1) schedule planning time, (2) maintain a list of activities, (3) start a notebook, and (4) review your progress.

What is the pattern of organization?

This paragraph shows a pattern of chronological order because the order of activities is important.

Listing Pattern

Authors will sometimes use a list of details, reasons, or examples to support the main idea. In contrast to the chronological order pattern, the order in which the details are listed in the reading does not affect the main idea. For instance, an employer may distribute an ad that lists required qualities of prospective employees: "Applicants must be 18 years or older, drive a car, and have a high school diploma." The order in which the requirements are listed does not affect the meaning of the ad.

Common Signals   Signal words that may provide clues to the listing pattern are

first	also	second	many	several
next	another	third	a few	too
finally	in addition	lastly	then	a number of

Details may also be **numbered** or **bulleted** by the author in a listing pattern. Commas, semicolons, or colons may also signal this pattern.

Read the following paragraph. Then read the guide questions and answers that follow. In the future, these guide questions will help you to analyze and determine the pattern of any paragraph or reading.

> Employment will continue to shift from the goods-producing to the service sector of the economy, but the shift will be less pronounced than during past years. The bulk of employment growth will be in three industries: health services; retail trade, including eating and drinking places; and business services, including temporary help services, computer and data processing services, and services to buildings.
>
> —From *1996 Information Please Almanac*

What is the main idea of this paragraph?

The main idea is found in the first sentence: "Employment will continue to shift from the goods-producing to the service sector of the economy . . . "

What are the common signals used in this paragraph?

The use of a colon, semicolons, and commas in the second sentence indicates the listing pattern.

What details support the main idea?

The major supporting detail is that employment growth will be in health services, retail trade, and business services. The minor details are "including eating and drinking places" and "including temporary help services, computer and data processing services, and services to buildings." These phrases illustrate the major detail by providing additional information.

What is the pattern of organization?

This paragraph shows a listing pattern because order is not important to the list of industries.

Determining the Pattern in Longer Selections

It can be helpful when reading longer selections to see if the author uses the chronological order and listing patterns. In longer selections, take note of the headings of the selections that often signal major details. Authors also use or mix several types of organizational patterns within a selection. Look at the entire selection for an overall pattern. Use the same guide questions that you used for single paragraphs.

▪ ▪ ▪ ▪ Short Exercises: Chronological and Listing Patterns

Read each paragraph and complete the questions that follow.

1. Fred DeLuca, president and CEO of Subway, began his entrepreneurial spirit before he was ten years old, picking up two-cent returnable bottles around his Bronx housing project. At seventeen, DeLuca opened his shop, Pete's Super Submarine Sandwiches, with $1000 borrowed from a family friend. By 1982, he owned two hundred stores. In August 1997, there were more than 12,500 Subway stores in over fifty countries. DeLuca's accomplishments over the past thirty years have placed him at the top of a company that now boasts annual sales in excess of three billion dollars. (From "Advice from the Top and How to Get There" by Brian Caruso and Diane P. Licht)

   What is the main idea of this paragraph?

   _____

   _____

   _____

   _____

   _____

What are the common signals used in this paragraph?

_____

_____

What details support the main idea?

_____

_____

_____

What is the pattern of organization?

_____

2. The face of the cable industry changed when Robert L. Johnson launched Black Entertainment Television [BET] back in 1980, and there's been no looking back for him since then. Johnson is the chairman and CEO of BET Holdings, Inc., which is based in Washington, D.C. Now he oversees four major cable channels: Black Entertainment Television; BET On Jazz: The Cable Jazz Channel TM; BET Movies; and BET Action Pay-Per-View, as well as other BET interests outside of the cable industry. (From *Advice from the Top and How to Get There* by Brian Caruso and Diane P. Licht)

   What is the main idea of this paragraph?

_____

_____

_____

What are the common signals used in this paragraph?

_____

_____

What details support the main idea?

_____

_____

_____

What is the pattern of organization?

_____

_____

3. Working out of your home can be a great solution for certain people. You need to ask yourself, "Does this work style fit in with what I want

and how I am most efficient? If you do work out of your home, it is important to remember the following guidelines:

- Maintain a presence at the main office. Report in often, and let your boss know you are alive and productive.
- Treat your study (or wherever you work) like a real office. Close the door at 6:00 P.M., and don't open it until you are beginning work the next morning.
- Get dressed as you would for work, and be consistent with your hours. Act like you are at the office and not at home, and you stand a good chance of actually being productive. (From "Conference Calls in Your Pajamas" by Bradley Richardson)

What is the main idea of this paragraph?

_____

_____

_____

What are the common signals used in this paragraph?

_____

What details support the main idea?

_____

_____

_____

_____

What is the pattern of organization?

_____

4. Opportunities for internships have always existed in fields such as medicine and education; now they are common in the liberal arts as well. Two trends in the past decade have led to this. First, tuition costs have risen fast, and families that might have spent $100,000 or more on an education want to know there's a job at the end of it. Second, corporate downsizing has forced hiring practices that have made internships attractive to many employers. "Internships have become the way to look someone over without making a major investment," says Ann Petelka, senior personnel manager at D'Arcy, Masius, Benton, and Bowles, a New York-based ad conglomerate that offers jobs to more than 70 percent of its interns. (From "Working for Credit: How to Make the Most out of a Semester-long Internship" by Jo Ann Tooley)

What is the main idea of this paragraph?

_____

_____

_____

What common signals are used in this paragraph?

_____

What details support the main idea?

_____

_____

_____

_____

_____

What is the pattern of organization?

_____

5. In August 1977, a young mother with no business experience opened the first Mrs. Fields Cookies store in Palo Alto, California. Debbi Fields, the founder of Mrs. Fields Cookies, has achieved great success through her worldwide chain of cookies and baked goods stores. Her company began franchising in 1990. Today she has over 650 domestic locations and over 65 international locations in 11 different countries. (www.mrsfields.com)

What is the main idea of this paragraph?

_____

_____

_____

What are the common signals used in this paragraph?

_____

What details support the main idea?

_____

_____

_____

_____

_____

What is the pattern of organization?

Reading Selections

Selection 1

For Liberal Arts Majors Only: The Road to Career Success
ROBIN RYAN

Before Reading

Before you read "For Liberal Arts Majors Only: The Road to Career Success," predict the topic, scan the story, and think about your future career choices. If you are pursuing a degree in liberal arts, what kind of job are you preparing for? Do you know how to get the job when you have decided what you want to do? As you read, explore some of the strengths and skills you may not have recognized in yourself.

Words to Preview

networking	*(n.)*	an informal system where people assist each other
predicament	*(n.)*	a situation, especially an unpleasant one
delve	*(v.)*	to search deeply
pursue	*(v.)*	to strive to gain or accomplish

During Reading

As you read "For Liberal Arts Majors Only: The Road to Career Success," continue to predict and visualize the information and monitor your comprehension. Look for signals for the chronological order or listing pattern. What is the author telling you about finding a career for liberal arts majors?

Microsoft. Nike. American Airlines. Nordstrom. Coors. MTV. Magnet companies attracting tens of thousands of resumes. But your degree is in liberal arts—would a magnet company hire you? And an even bigger question—what would you do for them? Important questions. Do you have the answers? Have you begun to consider the endless list of career choices and fields that you could go into? Do you know what steps to take to land that job once you decide exactly what you want to do? Let's begin by exploring your career options and then look at some of the strengths and skills you may not have even recognized you have to offer to an employer.

A World of Opportunity You May Not Have Considered

Some of the liberal arts grads I've worked with over the years were just as confused about their career options as you might be. They just didn't know about all the fields or kinds of jobs that they could investigate.

Dave, for example, had his heart set on working for Nike. He loved sports and had played college baseball. Nike was his place—he just knew it. Problem was, Nike didn't know it. Dave was an English major and never defined what job he could do for them. When a family friend arranged for a meeting with an accountant that worked at Nike, Dave hoped the man would find him a job at the company. Dave never told the man the type of job he could do, never asked questions about Nike's communications department, never inquired about who else he should talk to at the company. The result: Nothing happened after that meeting. It wasn't the Nike employee's job to figure out what career Dave could do, it was Dave's. Not having a clear idea of the types of jobs you can do is a critical error; lots of new college grads are fuzzy about their options because they don't understand their skills and don't know how those skills fit into a variety of careers.

I began to work with Dave shortly after the Nike meeting, focusing him on his stronger skills—writing, editing, and computer skills. He began working temporary jobs and started networking with other alumni. Through networking, he learned about a position at a publishing company. He landed a job as editorial assistant at a company that published comic books and was coming out with a new baseball video game. Dave found a terrific job once he directed his skills to what he could do for an employer instead of what an employer could do for him.

In another instance, Allison, a history major who graduated from one of the West Coast's top colleges, thought that finding a job would be easy. She wanted to work on planning events. Unfortunately, no one would hire her. She sent out hundreds of resumes but got no interviews. When she called employers, everyone said the same thing—experience. Since the only events Allison had every planned were a few sorority functions, I suggested that she volunteer to do an internship for six weeks. There she could learn about the meeting planning business and get some experience for her resume. She persuaded a top events company to take her on by selling them on her good computer skills. Within three weeks, Allison got a job offer from another company after she followed up on a lead from someone in the office. When her internship boss was called for a reference, he offered Allison a paid position. Two years later, she's still there planning large-scale events.

Sometimes, locating a person's special talents takes a bit of digging. Take Sam, for example. He had chosen psychology for a major because it was easier for him than the business courses he'd started out in. He wanted to use his degree and thought he might find a counseling job. The problem was Sam's verbal skills. They were pretty weak, and he recognized that. He was not good at talking to groups and had rather poor grammar skills. We did manage to uncover that Sam had excelled in his job as a pizza delivery man. He'd earned more tips than any driver they had ever hired. He was organized, courteous to customers and efficient. His productivity led to an assistant manager's job where he improved sales by suggesting optional items to customers and ensuring speedy delivery. He quit the job when he left college. I encouraged Sam to explore store management as a career. His organizational skills and ability to think like customers have served him well. He landed a job as a grocery distributor and went on to his second job as a deli manager for a large metropolitan store.

Peggy was in a different predicament. She went back to college after her kids started school and got a degree in sociology. She had never held a paid position. When I first met with her she opened with "Will anybody hire me? I've got no work experience and I'm almost 40." She had discounted her skills that she acquired in school and through volunteer work, important skills that landed her a great job in fundraising.

Heather was a philosophy major and knew nothing about insurance, except that people sold it. Today, she has a good paying job as an underwriter for Prudential Insurance Company. Tanya became a legal assistant; Jason is a probation officer; Steve is a computer communications specialist; Stephanie works as a sales account executive. Eric went into customer service credit. All of these grads—as well as Dave, Allison, Sam, and Peggy—are real people. And, they're all liberal arts grads delving into new fields and new options. You can do it, too.

Where do you start? Start where the grads profiled here started: They evaluated past jobs, volunteer work, activities, and academic projects to identify the skills they had developed. They found that they had a lot of skills that matter to employers—and you will too. Start by completing the checklist provided to identify your skills.

Where Are the HOT Opportunities?

Pursue a field where you have a lot of interest—broadcasting, computers, fashion—and it can lead to greater lifetime satisfaction. If you have a practical way to mix interests with work, follow your dreams. Dave was discouraged that Nike didn't hire him, yet he now loves his job at the publishing company. The greatest number of opportunities lie within small companies, so look for small organizations—those employing fewer than 100 people. Typically, you'll find you have more responsibility in a small office than you would in a large one; that level of responsibility can propel your career along into future jobs. You'll find such employers in the yellow pages and in want ads and by asking family and friends for leads. Remember, too, that many good jobs are available with nonprofit organizations such as the American Lung Association, which has offices across the country and hires fundraisers, events planners, and communications people. And, consider state and local government jobs, not just those with the federal government.

The environmental, high-tech, service, telecommunications, and retail industries—as well as certain areas of healthcare—will remain strong. But racing after a job simply because it is in a hot field is like racing after a magnet company—your future job and happiness may not lie there. It's better to combine your interests and your abilities when you're looking for career sat-

---

Skills You've Acquired
(Check all that apply)

___ Administering programs
___ Advising people
___ Analyzing data
___ Budgeting
___ Calculating numerical data
___ Collecting money
___ Compiling statistics
___ Conducting experiments
___ Coordinating events
___ Dealing with customers
___ Designing ads
___ Drawing charts/graphs
___ Editing
___ Evaluating programs/
　　products
___ Fundraising
___ Generating ideas
___ Handling complaints
___ Implementing ideas
___ Inspecting physical objects
___ Interpreting languages
___ Interviewing people
___ Investigating problems
___ Making presentations
___ Mediating between people
___ Negotiating contracts
___ Operating equipment
___ Organizing people/projects/
　　tasks
___ Persuading others

___ Planning programs/projects
___ Problem solving
___ Programming computers
___ Promoting events
___ Public speaking
___ Recordkeeping
___ Rehabilitating others
___ Repairing mechanical devices
___ Researching
___ Running meetings
___ Scheduling
___ Selling products/services
___ Supervising others
___ Teaching others
___ Updating files
　　Using a computer:
　　　___ IBM
　　　___ Macintosh
　　　___ Mainframe
　　　___ Other(s)
　　Using software:
　　　___ Word
　　　___ WordPerfect
　　　___ Windows
　　　___ Lotus
　　　___ Excel
　　　___ PageMaker
　　　___ QuarkXPress
　　　___ Other(s)
___ Writing articles/reports

---

isfaction. Spend time investigating career options. Career centers and libraries have extensive resources available. The *Occupational Outlook Handbook* is a good place to start researching potential career areas.

Finding the Job

Job hunting is challenging, so learn the process. Visit your career center. Read books. Attend workshops and seminars on the job search, resume writing, and interviewing. Volunteering, doing internships, and working at temporary jobs can all give you valuable experience and often lead to that first paid position. Network—and start with your college's alumni. Many will be happy to clue you in on their job, field, and/or company.

Remember that careers are built one step at a time. The market is competitive, but *you are unique.* Always remember you have a lot to offer. Do what you like best, in organizations whose products and services you find interesting. You'll find more satisfaction and reward this way. Finding the right career opportunities becomes easier when you view this process as an exciting adventure and realize you can be anything you choose to be. So explore, and you'll discover opportunities you didn't know existed and talents you didn't know you had. Your future is what you make it.

After Reading

Word Connections

1. "Racing after a job simply because it is in a hot field is like racing after a magnet company—your future job and happiness may not lie there."

   Give a definition and example of a *magnet company* from the context of the reading.

   _____

   _____

   _____

   _____

2. Create a concept of definition map for *networking* as it relates to the job market.

   Diagram:

Connecting Meaning

1. What is the main idea of this selection?

   _____

   _____

   _____

   _____

2. Identify any common signals used in this selection.

   _____

   _____

   _____

   _____

3. Identify the major supporting details.

   _____

   _____

   _____

   _____

   _____

4. Determine the overall pattern of organization.

   _____

   _____

5. Give two examples of liberal arts majors who had difficulty finding a
   job after graduation. How did their skills relate to the position for
   which they were hired?

   _____

   _____

   _____

   _____

   _____

   _____

   _____

Selection 2

Making a Job-Search Plan

BOB ADAMS

Before Reading Before you read "Making a Job-Search Plan," predict the topic, scan the reading, and think about your job hunting techniques. Do you have a plan or strategy, or do you search for a job in a haphazard way? Relate your experience to the plan given by the author.

Words to Preview

vigorous	*(adj).* strong, energetic, active
dismay	*(v.)* to disillusion; to deprive of courage
vary	*(v.)* to make changes
tedious	*(adj.)* boring
fine-tune	*(v.)* to adjust for the best performance or effectiveness
initiative	*(n.)* the ability to begin or follow through on a task
ethic	*(n.)* a set of standards governing the conduct of a person or members of a profession

During Reading As you read "Making a Job-Search Plan," continue to predict and visualize ideas and monitor your comprehension. Look for signals for chronological order or listing pattern. What does the author want you to know about conducting a job search?

It's vitally important to have a job-search plan so that you can pace yourself and monitor your progress against predetermined goals. Having a plan will also help you to keep up the vigorous pace of the job-search process and help keep you from becoming frustrated or unmotivated. If your plan is not an effective one, you will be able to see problems more clearly and tackle them head-on by changing direction or using different techniques.

Choose a Career Path

As I noted earlier, you must select an industry and job category as your first step. If you have trouble deciding on just one career path, you should do more research on the fields you are most interested in. Try your local library and your college's career center—they're both great sources of information about different professional occupations. Speak with people who work in the different industries you are interested in. If, after all of this, you still can't decide which is best for you, a good option is simply to pick one field from the group and focus your job-search efforts on it exclusively. If you don't find any job leads after an appropriate interval of time, then you can look into a different field or a different position.

Develop a Strategy

Your job search plan should take into consideration many different job-finding strategies. Decide whom you plan to get in touch with initially for networking; find out which sources of company listings will best suit your needs; decide whether or not you will participate in on-campus recruiting; decide which newspapers are worth monitoring. Then predict how much time you are going to spend pursuing these different avenues and set up a schedule for yourself. It's very important to plan out your job search in this way; you'll be less likely to fall behind. You'll also find that it's easier to put that extra effort and energy into job hunting if you can actually see the progress you're making as you go along.

A Job-Hunting Plan for Your Senior Year

If it's at all possible, begin your job search campaign early in your senior year—it will give you an edge over the competition. Here is a general outline for a job-hunting plan for your senior year:

September/October   Decide on which industry or job function you are interested in. . . . Put your resume together and practice writing cover letters. Buy any stationery that you will need (including paper and envelopes for your resume and cover letters).

November   Develop a comprehensive job-search plan. If you decide that on-campus recruiting is a good option for you, decide which on-campus recruiters you'd like to talk to. Express your interest in those companies you choose with a letter and perhaps a follow-up phone call as well.

December   Start to contact those companies who *won't* be coming to your campus, beginning with those companies who expressed interest through your school in receiving applications from college students. Then start contacting other companies that you learned about through other resources such as library listings and the *JobBank* series of local employment guides.

January   Start networking.

February   Set aside time for interviewing, both on and off campus.

March   Begin to review help-wanted advertisements in newspapers.

April   Start to focus your efforts on the job-search method that has been most productive for you so far. If you are not sure of which technique to use, I would suggest either contacting companies on your own or networking. These are probably the two most dependable methods for finding a job.

How Many Students Land a Job before They Graduate?

Most students won't have jobs by the time they graduate. So if you fall into this category, don't be dismayed—you're not alone! Don't sell yourself short, you went to school to get an education—and you did. But finding a job is a completely separate endeavor.

A Job-Hunting Plan for after Graduation

Ideally, for the first few months after graduation, you should try to look for a job full-time. If you're able to do this, be sure to work from a vigorous, intense job-search plan that allows you to invest about forty hours per week.

Vary your activities a little bit from day to day—otherwise it will quickly become very tedious. For example, every Sunday you can look through the classified ads and determine which jobs are appropriate for you. On Monday, follow up on these ads by sending out your resume and cover letter and perhaps making some phone calls as well. For the rest of the week I would suggest that you spend your time doing other things besides following up specific job openings. On Tuesday, for instance, you might decide to focus on contacting companies directly. On Wednesday, you can do more research to find listings of other companies you can contact. Thursday and Friday might be spent networking, as you try to set up appointments to meet with people and develop more contacts.

Every few weeks, you should evaluate your progress and fine-tune your search accordingly. If you find that, after putting in a great deal of effort over a period of several months, you aren't even close to getting a job, then it's probably time to reconsider your options. Is the job you want realistic for you? Are the opportunities for getting this position greater in another city?

At this point you should probably think about changing your job-search techniques, moving to another city, or focusing on a different job or industry—but there is always the possibility that you need to be more aggressive in your job-search efforts. The key is knowing when to persist in the current direction that your job hunt is taking and when to give up what you're doing and start anew. It isn't easy. Often, talking with other job hunters and knowing the current state of the job market in your industry of interest will help you to draw this fine line.

How Much Effort and Energy Should a Job Search Take?

Finding a job is not easy. It takes a lot of energy and a tremendous amount of effort. If you are looking for a job full-time after graduation, your job search will probably last from three to six months. If the economy is in particularly bad shape, however, you should be prepared to search for a year or more.

Note: If you still don't seem close to finding a job after two or three months of searching full-time, you should consider finding a part-time position. (Financially, this will probably be something of a necessity at this point.) With a part-time job, you will earn some money and gain a valuable sense of personal accomplishment. After several months of tedious searching, you will probably have dealt with your share of stress; a part-time job will help to break up your routine a bit and help keep you motivated and enthusiastic about your job-search campaign. Working part-time also displays initiative and a good work ethic, which is something that recruiters always like to see.

If you think that you might be having trouble finding a job because you have no experience in a particular field, consider doing an internship while you are job hunting. Although internships are often unpaid, they can, as we have seen, provide valuable experience, numerous business contacts, and sometimes even job opportunities.

After Reading

Word Connections

1. What does the phrase *tackle them head on* mean in the first paragraph?

   _____

   _____

2. List examples of a *good work ethic,* such as punctuality.

   _____

   _____

   _____

3. Create a concept of definition map for *strategy.*

   Diagram:

Connecting Meaning

1. What is the main idea of this selection?

   _____

   _____

   _____

2. Identify any common signals used in this selection.

   _____

   _____

3. Identify the major supporting details.

   _____

   _____

   _____

   _____

4. Determine the overall pattern of organization.

   _____

   _____

5. Describe the monthly suggestions for job hunting during your senior year.

   _____

   _____

   _____

   _____

   _____

   _____

   _____

   _____

   _____

   _____

Selection 3

Contemplating a Career Change? Think before You Leap!

STEVEN WARREN

Before Reading

Before you read "Contemplating a Career Change? Think before You Leap!" predict the topic, scan the reading, and think about changing careers. Are you in college to begin a new career? Are you changing the type of employment you currently have? Relate what you know to the author's suggestions for career changes.

Words to Preview

lament	*(v.)*	to wail
quagmire	*(n.)*	a difficult situation
ponder	*(v.)*	to consider carefully
validate	*(v.)*	to establish the soundness of
aspiration	*(n.)*	a desire for high achievement
plethora	*(n.)*	a superabundance

During Reading

As you read "Contemplating a Career Change? Think before You Leap!" continue to predict and visualize ideas and monitor your comprehension. Look for signals for chronological order or listing pattern. What does the author want you to know or remember about career changes?

Okay, it's another Monday morning. You're standing in front of the bathroom mirror, putting on your work face, wolfing down your bagel, and taking that last gulp of coffee before you run out the door. But somehow this morning is different. Something is nagging at you. You glare at your reflection, observing the new lines above your brow and the puffiness under your eyes. You squint at the image in front of you, not really sure who that person is staring back at you. Then it hits you, and you groan, "I don't even know why I'm doing this anymore!"

If you've ever had this dialogue with yourself, then you could be suffering the career-changer's blues! You know it's happening when you sense yourself coming down with the Gump Syndrome—you know, the scene where Forrest Gump is just running. He doesn't know why he's running or to where he's running. He's just running. Sometimes work feels the same way. You get up, get dressed, go to work, come home, go to bed, get up, go to work . . . day after day, after day. Then, one Monday morning, you discover that it's you staring back from that bathroom mirror, lamenting, "There's got to be more to life than this!"

Maybe the time has come to have a more in-depth conversation with yourself. If you are beginning to believe that the only difference between a rut and a grave is the dimensions, then maybe you need to re-examine your career needs. Ruts, however, do come in all shapes and sizes. It may not even be your job that's put you in this quagmire, but rather some other aspect of your life. Once you've had that serious talk with yourself and definitively conclude that your job is the source of your discontent, then ponder the following:

1. Since you don't wish to repeat past mistakes, analyze your true feelings. Specifically determine what is wrong with your current career situation. Are you just bored? Is it your boss's attitude? Do you need a vacation? Is money the issue? Are you insufficiently challenged and need more responsibility? Confirm what it is about you (and maybe not your job) creating the need for a change. The key is this: Remember that all change must begin with yourself.

2. While it sounds simplistic, getting what you want means you must first decide what it is that you want. That is, before you leap from the bed that you already lie in, you have to validate your real motives. Perhaps, you want to be in sales, interacting with customers every day. Maybe your dream is to be entrepreneurial, starting your own business. Or you may decide that more education or training is the real missing link to your career satisfaction. Whatever it is, be sure of your aspirations before doing anything radical.

3. After concluding what you don't want and then deciding what you do want, investigate the possibilities of achieving it within your present company. After exploring what's in your own back yard, you might be surprised that the solution is right under your nose. Progressive companies recognize that motivated employees are critical to their success. They may bend over backwards to assist you once they know your real interests and desires.

4. If you still believe a career change is in order, then give yourself time to work things out. The process has many intimidating steps and options to contemplate. Jumping to another job simply to avoid what you have now may put you in a more stressful situation than the one you left behind. There's a plethora of sad tales about job changers that found the grass was not greener in their next work life. Take a few deep breaths and read Richard Bolles' *What Color Is Your Parachute* before you take that leap.

In the final analysis, career changing can be an exciting and rewarding adventure. The key to making a successful transition is to know your motives, take action for the right reasons, explore all alternatives, and go slowly! By doing your homework and developing the right plan, your possibilities for career fulfillment are unlimited. The ultimate satisfaction is looking into the mirror and discovering that big smile belongs to you!

After Reading   **Word Connections**

1. The author refers to the "Gump Syndrome." How would you define this syndrome? How does it relate to this article?

_____

_____

_____

_____

_____

2. "The only difference between a rut and a grave is the dimensions." Explain this statement.

_____

_____

3. Define *entrepreneurial* from its context in the reading.

_____

_____

4. Create a concept of definition map for *plethora*.

Diagram:

Connecting Meaning

1. What is the main idea of this selection?

_____

_____

_____

2. Identify any common signals used in this selection.

_____

3. Identify the major supporting details.

_____

_____

_____

_____

4. Determine the overall pattern of organization.

_____

5. "All change must begin with yourself." Do you agree or disagree with this statement? Explain your answer.

_____

_____

_____

Portfolio Activities

Integrating Ideas

Use the checklist provided in the article "For Liberal Arts Majors Only: The Road to Career Success" to examine the skills you have acquired. In writing or in class discussion, relate these skills to potential career opportunities.

Extending Concepts

Conduct an interview with someone who has been employed in a career you are interested in pursuing. Write a summary of your interview.

Collaborative Activities

Design a job search plan. Consider how the Internet and e-mail may figure in a job search.

Additional Portfolio Suggestion

Explore internship or cooperative education opportunities available on your campus or in your community.

■ ■ ■ ■ Chapter Summary Graphic Organizer

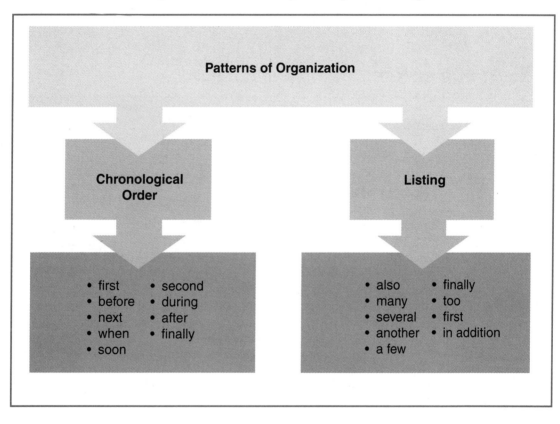

Patterns of Organization

Chronological Order

- first
- before
- next
- when
- soon
- second
- during
- after
- finally

Listing

- also
- many
- several
- another
- a few
- finally
- too
- first
- in addition

9

Definition and Illustration/ Example Patterns

Theme of Readings: Health Issues

Learn from yesterday, live for today, hope for tomorrow.
ANONYMOUS

Health Issues

Open a magazine or newspaper, turn on the local or national news, or get together with friends, and you will find that one issue—health—is frequently being discussed. As a society, we are curious and concerned about all aspects of health. We want to know how to feel good and how to prevent or cure illness. Collectively the federal government, medical industry, and individual consumers spend billions of dollars on health-related issues.

With research being done in many areas, we face an avalanche of information. Cholesterol counts, weight-reduction programs, the effects of secondhand smoke and air pollution, herbal supplements, and gene therapy are just a few areas being studied and debated. In the past, mental health issues were generally less publicized than those relating to physical health. Today, information is readily available on depression, eating and anxiety disorders, and other mental health topics.

The readings for this chapter focus on the area of mental health. Being aware of these topics may help you or someone you know or may encourage you to read further in the important area of health.

Chapter Objectives

After completing this chapter, you will be able to

1. **Identify the signal words used for the definition and illustration/example patterns.**
2. **Distinguish between definition and illustration/example supporting details.**
3. **Identify the supporting details that determine the definition and illustration/example patterns.**

Focus on Definition and Illustration/Example Patterns

Definition Pattern

When authors want to give the precise meaning of something and convey its distinct characteristics or features, they use a definition pattern of writing. A definition pattern answers the question *What is it?* This pattern is often used in textbooks and academic journals, where understanding exact meanings of words and ideas is important to understanding a subject area. For instance, in an article about blood cholesterol, an author may begin with a definition: "Cholesterol is a waxy substance made by the liver and used to build cell membranes and brain and nerve tissues."

Common Signals   Signal words that may provide clues to the definition pattern are

means   is   defines   consists of

Definitions may also be set apart by punctuation such as commas, parentheses, and dashes. For example, Prozac—a specific serotonin inhibitor—has become a widely used drug in the treatment of depression.

Read the following paragraph. Then read the guide questions and answers that follow. In the future, these guide questions will help you to analyze and determine the pattern of any paragraph or reading.

> Anorexia nervosa is a state of starvation and emaciation brought about by severe dieting or by purging. People with anorexia nervosa become emaciated to the point of actual starvation, losing at least 15 percent to as much as 60 percent of normal body weight. Half of these patients, anorexic bulimic patients, maintain emaciation by purging. This behavior imposes additional stress on an undernourished body. Anorexia nervosa is a serious eating disorder that can be fatal.
>
> —Adapted from www.noah.cuny.edu/wellconn/eatdisorders.html

What is the main idea?

The main idea is found in the first sentence: "Anorexia nervosa is a state of starvation and emaciation brought about by severe dieting or by purging."

What are the common signals used in this paragraph?

Anorexia nervosa is being defined. The word *is* helps to indicate the pattern of definition.

What details support the main idea?

All of the sentences that follow the definition of anorexia nervosa continue to describe the illness. Patients lose 15 to 60 percent of normal body weight by starvation. Half of these patients maintain emaciation by purging. Purging imposes additional stress on an undernourished body. Anorexia nervosa can be fatal.

What is the pattern of organization?

This paragraph shows a pattern of definition because the term anorexia nervosa is defined. All other sentences expand the definition by providing the characteristics and features of this eating disorder.

Illustration/Example Pattern

Illustrations or examples are often given when an author wants to create a clearer picture of the main idea. These examples help to make difficult or confusing topics easier to understand. Relating the main idea to actual situations allows the reader to visualize the information. For example, in an article about cardiovascular disease, an author may write: "To illustrate the blood flow of arteries blocked by cholesterol, visualize the movement of water through a clogged sink pipe."

Common Signals   Signal words that may provide clues to the illustration/example pattern are

for example   for instance   to illustrate   including   such as

Examples may also be set apart by punctuation such as semicolons and commas.

Read the following paragraph. Then read the guide questions and answers that follow. In the future, these guide questions will help you to analyze and determine the pattern of any paragraph or reading.

During the twentieth century, the medical milestones have been mind boggling. For example, antibiotics, a new class of medicines appropriately labeled "miracle drugs," were created in the 1930s and 1940s. Imaging technology such as x-rays, ultrasound, CT scans, PET scans, and MRIs has provided an internal view of the body without actually invading it. Another example of medical milestones is organ transplants, which became routine in the late 1970s due to the drug cyclosporine, which suppresses the body's tendency to attack a new organ.

—Adapted from www.healthcentral.com/News

What is the main idea?

The main idea is found in the first sentence: "During the twentieth century, the medical milestones have been mind boggling."

What are the common signals used in this paragraph?

The words *for example, such as,* and *another example* indicate the pattern of example.

What details support the main idea?

The major supporting details are that antibiotics, imaging technology, and organ transplants are all medical milestones.

What is the pattern of organization?

This paragraph shows a pattern of illustration/example because of the illustrations given to clarify the main idea.

Determining the Pattern in Longer Selections

To find the definition or illustration/example patterns in longer selections, use the same guide questions that you use for single paragraphs. In longer selections, authors often combine the definition and illustration/example patterns by first defining a word or idea and then providing illustrations or examples for the reader. Look at the entire selection for the overall pattern.

Short Exercises: Definition and Illustration/Example Patterns

Read each paragraph and complete the questions that follow.

1. Prozac is an antidepressant medication that was introduced for use in the United States in December 1987. Since that time, Prozac has become the most widely prescribed antidepressant in America. Prozac is FDA approved for the treatment of depression and has been found useful in the treatment of obsessive compulsive disorder, bulimia, panic disorder, and other conditions. (From www.psych.helsinki.fi/~janne/mood/prozac)

   What is the main idea of the paragraph?

   _____

   _____

   _____

   What are the common signals used in this paragraph?

   _____

What details support the main idea?

_____

_____

_____

_____

What is the pattern of organization?

_____

2. You can take a huge step in reducing your fat intake at breakfast by making simple substitutions. For instance, replace pork bacon with turkey bacon, use one-percent milk in your coffee instead of half and half, and try egg substitutes. Other breakfast alternatives such as low-fat spreads on toast in place of butter and fat-free pound cake with fresh fruit rather than donuts and pastries can lessen your fat intake even more. (Adapted from Tom Ney, "Satisfying, Low-Fat Breakfasts," *Prevention* Home Page <http://healthyideas.com> (April 9, 1999))

What is the main idea of the paragraph?

_____

_____

_____

_____

What are the common signals used in this paragraph?

_____

What details support the main idea?

_____

_____

_____

_____

What is the pattern of organization?

_____

3. Anorexia nervosa is an illness that mainly affects adolescent girls. The most common features are loss of weight and a change in behavior. The weight loss may become severe and life threatening. The personality

changes will be those of increasing seriousness and introversion and an increasing tendency to become obsessional. She will usually begin to lose contact with her friends. She will regress and appear to lose confidence. She may become less assertive, less argumentative, and more dependent. (From www.priority-hospital.co.uk/atm/anorex.htm)

What is the main idea of the paragraph?

_____

_____

_____

_____

What are the common signals used in this paragraph?

_____

What details support the main idea?

_____

_____

_____

_____

What is the pattern of organization?

_____

4. Bulimia is an eating disorder in which a person repeatedly binge eats, then uses self-induced vomiting, diuretics, laxatives, fasting, or excessive exercising to prevent weight gain. Symptoms of bulimia always include recurrent episodes of binge eating (defined as rapid consumption of a large amount of food in a brief period of time); a feeling of lack of control over eating during the binges; regular vomiting; use of laxatives or diuretics; strict dieting, fasting or vigorous exercise to prevent weight gain; a minimum of two binge eating episodes a week for at least three months; and a self-evaluation that is unduly influenced by body shape or weight. (From www.noah.cuny.edu/illness/mentalhealth/cornell/conditions/bulimia.html)

What is the main idea of the paragraph?

_____

_____

_____

_____

What are the common signals used in this paragraph?

_____

_____

_____

What details support the main idea?

_____

_____

_____

_____

_____

What is the pattern of organization?

_____

_____

5. Herbal remedies have become very popular over the last several years as an alternative to conventional prescription medications. For example, kava is used to reduce anxiety, ginkgo biloba has been shown to provide cognitive benefits, valerian root is used to treat insomnia, and St. John's wort improves mild to moderate depression. For upset stomachs, indigestion, and nausea, some feel that herbs such as ginger and chamomile are known to be of help. (Adapted from "A List of Common Herbal Medications," by K.B. Schomberg-Klaiss, D.O.)

What is the main idea of the paragraph?

_____

_____

_____

_____

What are the common signals used in this paragraph?

_____

_____

_____

What details support the main idea?

_____

_____

_____

_____

What is the pattern of organization?

_____

_____

■ ■ ■ ■   **Reading Selections**

Selection 1

Forever Frazzled?

MAYA BOLTON

Before Reading

Before you read "Forever Frazzled?" predict the topic, scan the story, and think about your attention span. Have you ever had problems paying attention for more than a few minutes? Do you know anyone who has been diagnosed with attention-deficit disorder? Relate what you know to the author's experiences with ADD.

Words to Preview

lapse	*(n.)* a failure; a slip
pathological	*(adj.)* relating to disease
hypothesis	*(n.)* uncertain explanation; a theory
predominantly	*(adv.)* having greatest importance or influence
skepticism	*(n.)* a doubting state of mind
du jour	*(adj.)* of the day
positron-emission tomography	*(n.)* test that produces computer-generated images of activity within the body
rigorous	*(adj.)* very accurate; precise
capper	*(n.)* the finale
pseudonym	*(n.)* a pen name
liberate	*(v.)* to set free

During Reading

As you read "Forever Frazzled?" continue to predict and visualize the information and monitor your comprehension. Look for signals for the definition and illustration/example patterns. What does the author want you to know about attention-deficit disorder, ADD?

After years of feeling torn in a million directions, I finally got a diagnosis. And it wasn't stress.

Recently I had to cut short a telephone call to handle some urgent business. The distraction lasted only a few minutes, but by the time it was over I'd forgotten about the call. By chance something jogged my memory, and I called my friend back—but not until the following day.

Unfortunately, that kind of disconnect is not unusual for me. Walking around my house in the morning, I find myself narrating reminders: "Turn off the iron," or, with a slap to my forehead as I'm heading out the door, "Keys!" Shortly after arriving at the office I often have to return home to retrieve a notebook or a file.

For years friends, family members, and colleagues kindly chalked up these lapses to my being a little "spacey." I have, they would tell me, plenty of charming qualities to compensate. But lately it seemed my absent-mindedness had gone out of control.

More and more people were getting insulted by those neglected phone calls. My tendency to procrastinate was reaching pathological proportions. And in the office, where I edit documents, my "eye" was becoming remarkably inconsistent. Even my boss had noticed. Eventually, at wit's end, I sought the advice of a psychologist.

After a lengthy conversation about my personal history, he offered a surprising hypothesis: Perhaps I had the adult version of attention-deficit disorder, or ADD. "But aren't people with ADD hyperactive?" I asked. The official name of the condition is, after all, attention-deficit/hyperactivity disorder, and as anyone who knows me will attest, I operate in anything but high gear. Even when the brain is working fast and furious, this body barely budges. That was even more true of me during childhood, when ADD is generally diagnosed.

It seems, however, that there are two distinct types of the condition: the more familiar one, called predominantly hyperactive, and the one that's gaining recognition, predominantly inattentive. People with the latter variety are notably absentminded, the day-dreamy types who quietly tune out at meetings or in class. Often they go undiagnosed because their symptoms are so subtle. The majority are female.

Perhaps, the psychologist suggested, I was suffering from ADD number two.

Over the next few weeks as I talked to people I knew about ADD, I heard skepticism and even contempt. "You can focus," one colleague told me. "ADD people can't focus." (She was wrong. ADDers can focus—just not consistently.)

"You've simply got too much on your plate," a friend said. (She had a point. I was working on many projects at once. Was I merely overextended?)

"Oh, ADD," moaned someone else. "Isn't that the disorder du jour?"

It seems that it is. Since 1990 diagnoses of ADD have more than doubled, and the curve seems to be getting steeper. Books on the topic are selling briskly. At conferences with themes like "Living the ADDventure," vendors hawk ADD-pride paraphernalia, special ADD date books, and coaching services for the terminally scattered. In some places high school and college students who have ADD can get extra time on standardized tests because of their disability.

The boom in part reflects a rise in diagnoses among children. But a portion of the newly diagnosed are adults. In 1990 Alan Zametkin, a psychiatrist at the National Institutes of Health, published evidence from positron-emission tomography scans that ADD was associated with at least one physical marker in the brain: lower levels of activity in the prefrontal cortex, from which planning and self-control proceed. Other researchers have suggested the condition tends to run in families.

The findings haven't settled a raging debate about how common adult ADD really is. Some critics charge that psychologists are too quick to diagnose it without the proper testing. But even skeptics agree that at least some of the newly identified are the personality type described by the psychologist I saw and could benefit from treatment.

So I decided to go for the more rigorous evaluation. During the three-hour session, I took numerous tests of comprehension, memory, and problem-solving skills. The capper was a particularly frustrating one called the TOVA (Test of Variability of Attention), which consists of watching an orange square appear and disappear on a computer screen. When the square appears below the screen's center, you do nothing. When it appears above, you hit a button. Simple, right? Wrong. Despite humming and even biting my lip to stay focused, I ended up making an incredible number of errors.

It turns out my childhood history was also riddled with signs of the disorder. I recalled that often when I asked my mother a question, she'd first want to know precisely how long she had to answer. She knew at some point I would get that glazed look—distracted by other concerns, impatient to move on. At school I was a classic underachiever; lost in my thoughts, I had difficulty concentrating on the subject at hand.

Looking at the overwhelming evidence, both the doctor and I ended up convinced that mine was a classic case of attention-deficit/hyperactivity disorder, inattentive type. My reaction when she told me her opinion further convinced me: I cried, both fearful of the implications of the diagnosis and relieved to find an explanation for the problems that have plagued me all these years.

And what next? There are any number of behavioral approaches to treating ADD, such as workbooks and coaching programs designed to help people focus. But for the underlying attention problem, particularly for someone like me who does detail-oriented work, the doctor favored a low dose of Ritalin, the chief medication used to treat ADD.

Though I can't begin to address the controversy surrounding this drug, particularly about its use on children, I can testify that a minimal dose works wonders for me. It keeps my editorial eye focused for three to four hours at a stretch. I feel less scattered, and I've noticed a definite improvement in my moment-to-moment memory. (And all these benefits come to me without side effects.) When I went back to take the TOVA on medication, I got a perfect score.

Still, even though my behavior has improved, I worry. If people, particularly coworkers, knew about my diagnosis, might they consider me one of the shirkers, someone who just wants an excuse for flaky behavior? That fear is why I've used a pseudonym for this story.

And I can't say ADD isn't a fad diagnosis. But to tell you the truth, in my case the treatment was so liberating that I don't really care.

After Reading

Word Connections

1. "By chance something jogged my memory . . ." Define *jogged* as used in this sentence.

   _____

   _____

2. "For years friends, family members, and colleagues kindly chalked up these lapses to my being a little 'spacey.'" What does the phrase *chalked up* mean in this context?

   _____

   _____

3. "The findings haven't settled a raging debate about how common adult ADD really is." What is a *raging debate*?

   _____

   _____

   _____

Connecting Meaning

1. What is the main idea of this selection?

   _____

   _____

   _____

2. What are two types of attention-deficit disorder?

_____

_____

3. Give at least three examples of the author's behavior that provide evidence of ADD.

_____

_____

_____

_____

4. Why did the author choose to use a pseudonym for this story?

_____

_____

_____

_____

Selection 2	**Understanding Obsessive-Compulsive Disorder**

CATHERINE WEISKOPF

Before Reading   Before you read "Understanding Obsessive-Compulsive Disorder," predict the topic, scan the story, and think about obsessive-compulsive behavior (OCD). Have you ever been obsessed with anything or anyone? Do you have to repeat actions over and over without reason? As you read, relate what you know about everyday obsessions or compulsions to those seriously afflicted with OCD.

Words to Preview

ritualistic	_(adj.)_ practicing a ritual or ceremonial act
neurotransmitter	_(n.)_ a chemical substance that transmits nerve impulses
serotonin	_(n.)_ a chemical that transmits nerve impulses

During Reading   As you read "Understanding Obsessive-Compulsive Disorder," continue to predict and visualize the information and monitor your comprehension. Look for signals for the definition and illustration/example patterns. What does the author want you to learn about OCD?

W hat's it like to have obsessive-compulsive disorder (OCD)? Stephanie, age eighteen, knows all about how OCD can turn a life upside down.

Stephanie had trouble with math when her OCD was in high gear. "If I got to number 17 on the math test, I would have to tap my pencil seventeen times."

Like any major illness, OCD affects everyone in the family. "My parents have gone through so much because of me," says Stephanie. It's often difficult for family members to accept that a person with OCD cannot stop his or her ritualistic behavior. This can cause anger and resentment. On the other hand, the family may end up assisting in the rituals to keep peace.

It can affect every aspect of life: school, family, and friends. Although Stephanie has lost some friends because of it, most people have been very supportive. "My friends have known me all my life, and OCD is just part of who I am," she says.

A Painful Disorder

Obsessive-compulsive disorder, as the name implies, consists of obsessions and/or compulsions. Have you ever spent hours daydreaming about a movie star? While we may call these thoughts obsessions, they are not OCD because they involve pleasurable thoughts. Maybe you can't stop thinking about your math test next Friday, or you wonder if you remembered to shut your locker. If you have OCD, these thoughts could take over your day. OCD obsessions are unwanted, recurrent, and unpleasant thoughts that cause anxiety. A person with OCD may continue to worry about his or her locker, even after checking it ten times. People with OCD can become obsessed with anything, but some of the most common obsessions are about contamination, lucky and unlucky numbers, fear of intruders, and an intense need for order.

Compulsions, the second part of OCD, are repetitive ritualistic behaviors that the person feels driven to perform to relieve the anxiety caused by the obsessions. A person with OCD feels driven to perform these rituals according to some self-prescribed rules. For example, if a person with OCD is worried about safety, his or her compulsion may be to lock and relock each door fifteen times. Following such a routine may make the person feel less anxious, but the relief is often incomplete and short-lived. Although their behavior sounds "crazy," people with OCD are not crazy. They describe their actions as "silly" and "dumb" but still find they have little or no control over them.

We witnessed how difficult OCD is to live with when it hit the big screen recently with Jack Nicholson's Oscar-winning performance in *As Good As It Gets*. We watched him twist and turn to avoid cracks, scare customers away from his table, and go through multiple bars of soap washing his hands.

Good News and Bad News About Treatment

Living with OCD is difficult, but it is a treatable disease. The bad news, however, is that people often spend years suffering before they get help. Many factors stand in their way:

1. People with OCD know something is wrong, but they commonly don't know what it's called and that it's treatable. It took Marc Summers, an OCD sufferer and the host of "Double Dare," twenty-five years to learn that his symptoms had a name and could be treated.

2. People also often hide their symptoms because they are embarrassed by them. They know their compulsions appear "crazy," so they don't tell anyone and perform their rituals in secret.

3. When people with OCD finally do seek help, they are frequently misdiagnosed. People with OCD typically see three or four doctors before a correct diagnosis is made.

All these factors have led to inaccurate statistics about OCD. Researchers once thought OCD was rare, but now they think between 2 and 3 percent of the population will suffer from it during their lifetime.

The good news about treatment is that there have been major breakthroughs over the last few years. The two main avenues of treatment are medication and behavioral therapy, which are often used in combination for the best results.

"Clinical trials in recent years have shown that drugs that affect the neurotransmitter serotonin can significantly decrease the symptoms of OCD," says the National Institute of Mental Health. These drugs are called serotonin reuptake inhibitors (SRIs) and also are used to treat depression and other anxiety disorders. Because OCD patients respond well to this treatment, scientists have abandoned the theory that OCD is caused by a parent's rigid rules. They now believe it's caused by abnormal chemical activity in the brain.

While traditional psychotherapy is generally not helpful in relieving OCD, behavioral therapy can be. Behavioral therapy involves exposing patients to whatever triggers their compulsive behavior. For example, a person who has a contamination obsession and a washing compulsion may be asked to remain in contact with a "germy" object and not be allowed to wash his or her hands for gradually lengthening time periods. Through this repetition, the person's anxiety about germs can be reduced.

But the advancements of recent years do no good if people don't ask for help. What should you do if you are suffering from OCD? Stephanie says: "Don't be ashamed of it. I was ashamed for many years. I tried to hide it and make up excuses. One day I didn't care anymore, and I became more open." Stephanie is a straight A student this year because of the person she has become and the help she has received.

After Reading

Word Connections

1. Create a concept of definition map for *rituals*.

   Diagram:

2. Distinguish between an *obsession* and a *compulsion*.

   _____

   _____

   _____

   _____

   _____

Connecting Meaning

1. What is the main idea of this selection?

   _____

   _____

   _____

   _____

   _____

2. Define obsessive-compulsive disorder.

   _____

   _____

   _____

3. Give examples of obsessive and compulsive behaviors.

_____

_____

_____

_____

4. "People often spend years suffering before they get help." List three factors that stand in the way of treatment.

_____

_____

_____

_____

_____

_____

Selection 3   # An Armful of Agony

CLAUDIA KALB

Before Reading   Before you read "An Armful of Agony," predict the topic, scan the story, and think about painful experiences. Have you ever had a deep or bloody cut? What was your reaction? Read about people who cut themselves intentionally.

Words to Preview

articulate	_(v.)_ to give words to
incarnation	_(n.)_ bodily form
outed	_(v.)_ spoke out
dissociate	_(v.)_ to separate
impose	_(v.)_ to force on another
demean	_(v.)_ to degrade or put down
loathe	_(v.)_ to dislike greatly
quell	_(v.)_ to quiet
dialectical	_(adj.)_ arriving at the truth by using conversation involving question and answer
devise	_(v.)_ to form a plan

Copyright © by Houghton Mifflin Company. All rights reserved.

During Reading   As you read "An Armful of Agony," continue to predict and visualize the information and monitor your comprehension. Look for signals for the definition and illustration/example patterns. What does the author want you to know about self-mutilation?

D rugs and therapy offer new hope for "cutters."

Stacy is a churchgoing midwesterner, a twenty-five-year-old sec-retary who wears cardigan sweaters and wire-rimmed glasses. She's the blond, blue-eyed girl next door—seemingly about as wholesome as they come. But for more than ten years, Stacy secretly indulged in a passion fit for B-grade horror movies: She scratched at her skin, burned it with hot knives, and sliced it repeatedly with razor blades and shards of glass. To-day Stacy's arms are a jumbled mess of thin white lines from elbow to wrist. They are not just physical wounds, but emotional battle scars. The cutting wasn't gruesome or even painful, Stacy says. It was soothing, a re-lease for inner turmoil she could not articulate. "Once I did it," she says, "I felt better."

Self-mutilation—also called self-injury and, in its most basic incar-nation, cutting—is alarming and unfathomable even to many therapists. For decades, patients like Stacy have been mental health's untouchables, bounced from emergency rooms to institutions. "They've been ignored, they've been shunned," says Dr. Armando Favazza, a psychiatrist at the University of Missouri-Columbia Medical School, who has written exten-sively on self-mutilation. But three years ago, Princess Diana outed cutting on a global scale when she admitted in a television interview that she had intentionally injured her arms and legs. "You have so much pain inside yourself that you try to hurt yourself on the outside because you want help," she said. There are two new books on the topic, *Bodily Harm* and *A Bright Red Scream*. And though research is still in its infancy, therapists say there are now promising treatments—from medications to intensive psychotherapy—for the estimated 2 million self-mutilators in this country.

The vast majority are women who started cutting as teenagers. Stacy recalls picking up a piece of broken glass in a parking lot when she was thirteen, but she can't remember why or how she decided to slash herself. Some self-mutilators are suicidal as well, although most cut themselves not to die, but to cope with the pressures of staying alive. Experts say that at least half were sexually abused as children. Many learned to shield themselves from horror in their lives by dissociating from their emotions. They say cutting snaps them back into consciousness. "It proves 'I'm alive, I'm human, I have blood coursing through my veins,'" says Marilee Strong, author of *A Bright Red Scream*. Others, many of whom also suffer from anorexia or bulimia, self-mutilate to gain control over their bodies or to express their feelings about being abused. "They're wearing a visible symbol of the violation imposed on them," says Dr. Joseph Shrand, director of the Child and Adolescent Outpatient Clinic at McLean Hospital in Belmont, Mass.

Cutters come from less tormented backgrounds, too. As children, some endured their parents' bitter divorces or may have been verbally abused—demeaned as too fat or lazy. Others were told never to cry. Whatever the trauma, experts say almost all grew up in homes with poor communication between parent and child. They suffer not just low self-esteem, but absolute self-loathing. "Cutting is literally like letting out bad blood," says Strong. Many are high achievers, even perfectionists, but they are failures when it comes to emotions. "They have no language for their own feelings," says Steven Levenkron, a psychotherapist and author of the book *Cutting* . . . "Cutting is the replacement for the absent language." Experts say they can help. Self-mutilators often suffer from related conditions like depression, anxiety, eating disorders, and posttraumatic stress syndrome. Treatment varies accordingly. Some patients benefit from antidepressants. In certain cases, the cutting impulse can be quelled by the drug Naltrexone, commonly used to treat heroin addicts. Medication alone, though, is unlikely to be enough. Cutters are often unreceptive to traditional talk therapy, but some psychologists are finding success with dialectical behavior therapy, devised in the 1980s by University of Washington psychologist Marsha Linehan. The treatment teaches patients skills for tolerating distress and controlling behavior.

Intensive inpatient therapy can work, too. Karen Conterio and Wendy Lader, authors of *Bodily Harm,* run a thirty-day clinic for self-mutilators outside Chicago. Stacy is one of their successes. A year after entering the program, she's stopped cutting. "It just seems so absurd," she says. Experts hope that through compassionate counseling, other cutters will one day be able to say the very same thing.

After Reading **Word Connections**

1. In the reading, find the synonym for *self-mutilation*.

2. Define the word *shunned* as given in the context of the story.

3. Define *demean* in your own words.

Connecting Meaning

1. What is the main idea of this selection?

_____

_____

2. Give examples of the behavior of a self-mutilator.

_____

_____

_____

3. What are some of the causes of self-mutilation?

_____

_____

_____

_____

Portfolio Activities

Integrating Ideas

Each of the readings deals with a health issue. What other health issue interests you? Is your interest based on personal experience? What sources can you use to increase your knowledge about the subject? Reflect on these ideas in writing or in class discussion.

Extending Concepts

In every decade the younger generation seems to engage in activities that meet with the disapproval of older generations. Today tattooing and body piercings are in vogue. Why do you think some people object to these activities? Is there a point where you find these activities excessive or unacceptable? Write your opinions about and experiences with tattooing and body piercing.

Collaborative Activity

As a group, research an area related to health. Give a short oral presentation to the class. It should include definitions, causes, treatments, and other interesting facts.

Additional Portfolio Suggestion

Health products are advertised in a variety of ways. Find two full-page print advertisements. For each, define the product being advertised. Give examples of its claims. Do you think these claims are true? What documentation does the product give for its claims? Would you use this product?

■ ■ ■ ■ ■ Chapter Summary Graphic Organizer

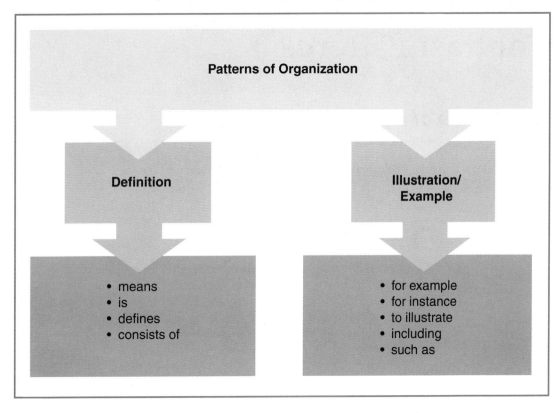

Patterns of Organization

Definition

- means
- is
- defines
- consists of

Illustration/ Example

- for example
- for instance
- to illustrate
- including
- such as

10

Comparison and Contrast Patterns

Theme of Readings: *Censorship*

The worst thing about censorship is [deleted by the censorship bureau].

ANONYMOUS

■ ■ ■ ■ Censorship

"Congress shall make no law respecting an establishment of religion, or prohibiting the free exercise thereof; or abridging the freedom of speech, or of the press; or the right of the people peaceably to assemble, and to petition the Government for a redress of grievances." The First Amendment to the Constitution of the United States was written to ensure that Americans would enjoy a free exchange of ideas. While essential in a democratic society, this right is not absolute. From the start of this nation, Americans have struggled to find a balance between the freedom and the limits of expression.

When the Bill of Rights was written in 1791, people did not have as much access to mass media as they do today. Now newspapers, magazines, books, radio, television, movies, music, and the Internet are all avenues of expression. With the increase in mass communication has come an increase in questions about censorship: What constitutes obscenity? What secrets can a government hide in the interest of national security? What books are suitable for children to read? What words are offensive to others? How can the right to free speech be balanced with the right for freedom from discrimination? Do any ideas undermine democracy? Should television, movies, or song lyrics be censored? How would you feel if you went to the store and were unable to purchase your favorite CD because it had obscene lyrics? Who should set guidelines for what is acceptable or not acceptable to the general public?

The debate over these questions and over what is acceptable or unacceptable will always be complex and ongoing. The right to debate these issues is, in itself, an expression of the freedom of speech.

Chapter Objectives

After completing this chapter, you will be able to

1. **Identify the signal words used for the comparison and contrast patterns.**
2. **Distinguish between comparison supporting details and contrast supporting details.**
3. **Identify the supporting details that determine the comparison and contrast patterns.**

Focus on Comparison and Contrast Patterns

Comparison Pattern

Authors use a comparison pattern when they want to stress similarities between two or more people, places, things, or ideas. The comparison pattern gives readers information and shows connections and likenesses. For example, someone comparing two newspapers could discuss similarities in the feature stories, editorials, and level of vocabulary. A reviewer writing about a movie and its sequel could comment on the sameness of the plots, characters, and special effects in each. This pattern may also be used to clarify a difficult concept by comparing it to something familiar to the reader. A chemistry teacher may explain the chemist's unit of amount, a mole, as being like a dozen or a gross, common units of amount.

Common Signals   Signal words that may provide clues to the comparison pattern are

like	likewise	just like	just as	both
similarly	same	alike	same as	in the same way
in comparison	similarities	resembles	compare	

Read the following paragraph. Then read the guide questions and answers that follow. In the future, these guide questions will help to analyze and determine the pattern of any paragraph or reading.

Some parents feel that two best-selling books by Judy Blume are not appropriate for children for similar reasons. *Are You There God? It's Me, Margaret* and *Superfudge* both contain profane language. In addition, the books are alike in their use of offensive and immoral material. In *Superfudge*, references to bodily functions and toilet humor were found to be offensive. In *Are You There God? It's Me,*

Margaret, the idea that Margaret is without religious background and yet speaks to God about nonreligious, adolescent issues is objectionable to some.

What is the main idea?

The main idea is found in the first sentence. Some parents think the two Judy Blume books mentioned are inappropriate for children.

What are the common signals used in this paragraph?

The words *similar, both,* and *alike* indicate a comparison pattern.

What details support the main idea?

The books are inappropriate because of their profane, offensive, and immoral material. Examples of offensive material are given.

What is the pattern of organization?

This paragraph shows a pattern of comparison because it shows similar reasons why two books are thought to be inappropriate for children.

Contrast Pattern

Authors use the contrast pattern to describe differences between two or more people, places, things, or ideas. This pattern helps readers evaluate and organize information and see the differences. For example, a writer may contrast a politician's view on a subject expressed several years ago and in the present.

Common Signals   Signal words that may provide clues to the contrast pattern are

in contrast	but	yet	although
while	instead	on the other hand	rather
however	than	on the contrary	differs from
unlike	nevertheless	different	in spite of
as opposed to			

Read the following paragraph. Then read the guide questions and answers that follow. In the future, these guide questions will help you to analyze and determine the pattern of any paragraph or reading.

In 1998, the United States Supreme Court decision in *National Endowment for the Arts v. Finley* stated government officials who administer the National Endowment for the Arts (NEA) can be required to take into account common standards of decency, respect for diversity, and American values when they award grants to artists and organizations. In the opinion of the NEA chairman, this ruling would not affect the day-to-day operations of the organization. Many artists and art supporters hold a contrasting opinion. Unlike the chairman, artists feel NEA choices for funding will be affected because the standards of decency are vague and leave no artistic avenue for controversial protest or political art.

What is the main idea of this paragraph?

Government officials and artists hold contrasting opinions about the *NEA v. Finley* decision.

What are the common signals used in this paragraph?

The words *in contrast* and *unlike* indicate a contrast pattern.

What details support the main idea?

The chairman feels operation of the NEA will not be affected, while artists and art supporters feel funding will be affected.

What is the pattern of organization?

This paragraph shows a contrast pattern because it describes differences between two opinions.

Comparison/Contrast

An author will often combine the comparison and contrast patterns and state both similarities and differences. The signal words will help to identify whether two or more people, places, things, or ideas are being compared and/or contrasted.

Short Exercises: Comparison and Contrast Patterns

Read each of the following paragraphs and complete the questions that follow.

1. The freedom of speech that was possible on the Internet could now be subjected to governmental approvals. For example, China is attempting to restrict political expression, in the name of security and social stability. It requires users of the Internet and electronic mail (e-mail) to register, so that it may monitor their activities. Similarly, in the United Kingdom freedom of speech on the Internet is restricted as state secrets and personal attacks are off-limits. Laws are strict, and the government is extremely interested in regulating the Internet with respect to these issues. (Craig Atkinson)

   What is the main idea of this paragraph?

   _____

   _____

   _____

   _____

What are the common signals used in this paragraph?

_____

What details support the main idea?

_____

_____

_____

_____

Determine the pattern of organization.

_____

2. The books *Flowers in the Attic, Garden of Shadows, Petals in the Wind,* and *Seeds of Yesterday* were written by V.C. Andrews. Besides the author, these titles have other similarities. Each book was removed from the Oconee County, Georgia, school libraries in 1994. The reason stated for their removal was also the same—"due to the filthiness of the material." (*Banned Books 1999 Resource Guide*)

What is the main idea of this paragraph?

_____

_____

What are the common signals used in this paragraph?

_____

What details support the main idea?

_____

_____

_____

_____

Determine the pattern of organization.

_____

3. Television censorship of musicians has a long history. However, the reasons behind the censorship differ. In the 1950s, Elvis Presley was shown only from the waist up. His gyrating hips were considered too sexually suggestive to be shown on television. In the 1960s, the Beatles' views on religion were not aired as they might offend mainstream

beliefs. In the 1990s, MTV censored a KISS video featuring a fire-breathing scene because of the fear it would be imitated by children. (Adapted from "MTV Censors KISS Video")

What is the main idea of this paragraph?

_____

_____

_____

What are the common signals used in this paragraph?

_____

What details support the main idea?

_____

_____

_____

_____

Determine the pattern of organization.

_____

4. Stealth censorship, the unofficial censoring of a book collection, cannot be compared to the outright banning of books. Yet the results are the same—fewer books are available for the public to read. Instead of the formal removal of a book, a book may quietly disappear from a library shelf after a parent complains. With ever tightening budgets, both librarians and school administrators are cautious about their purchases. Publishers, with economic pressures, reject many manuscripts that contain problematic language or stories on tough subjects like sexual abuse. These quiet book bannings affect the book world just as the officially banned books do. (Adapted from "What Johnny Can't Read—Censorship in American Libraries")

What is the main idea of this paragraph?

_____

_____

_____

What are the common signals used in this paragraph?

_____

What details support the main idea?

_____

_____

_____

_____

_____

Determine the pattern of organization.

_____

5. Almost six score years ago, a poor white boy known as Huckleberry
   Finn rafted down the Mississippi River and into the American
   imagination. For the better part of the following century, his story, as
   told by Mr. Mark Twain, has been regarded as a classic work of
   American fiction. Poet T.S. Eliot is said to have read the book at least
   once each year throughout his life, and novelist Ernest Hemingway
   declared, "All American literature comes from one book by Mark Twain
   called *Huckleberry Finn*. . . . It's the best book we've had." Twain's book
   even provided one of the formative themes for James Joyce's difficult
   Irish masterpiece, *Finnegan's Wake*.
       During the same century, *Huckleberry Finn* has repeatedly been
   banned from library shelves, removed from classrooms, and challenged
   by censorious voices for promoting improper or indecent conduct and
   for being insensitive to matters of race. As early as 1885, the book was
   banned in Concord, Massachusetts, as "trash and suitable only for the
   slums." In 1905, the book was taken from the children's room of the
   Brooklyn Public Library because "Huck not only itches but scratches";
   and in 1969, it was deleted from the required reading list at Miami-Dade
   Junior College in Florida, because it "inhibits learning" by black
   students. During the first week of 1989, newspapers reported that author
   Alex Haley was defending the book against would-be censors in
   Knoxville, Tennessee. (Frances Leonard)

What is the main idea of this paragraph?

_____

_____

_____

_____

What are the common signals used in this paragraph?

_____

_____

What details support the main idea?

_____

_____

_____

_____

Determine the pattern of organization.

_____

Reading Selections

Selection 1

Free Speech: Lyrics, Liberty, and License

SAM BROWNBACK

Before Reading

Before you read "Free Speech: Lyrics, Liberty, and License," predict the topic, scan the story, and think about free speech and music lyrics. Have you ever found music lyrics to be offensive? Do you think they should be censored? Relate your knowledge and opinion about music censorship to the author's view of the subject.

Words to Preview

discourse	*(n.)* speech; conversation
pervasive	*(adj.)* having the tendency to spread throughout
debase	*(v.)* to lower in value; to degrade
perverse	*(adj.)* directed away from what is right and good
bigotry	*(n.)* intolerance of those who differ
latitude	*(n.)* a range of values or conditions
immunity	*(adj.)* not subject to an obligation; freedom or exemption
predisposition	*(n.)* tendency
bulwark	*(n.)* defense
discern	*(v.)* to recognize or comprehend mentally
edify	*(v.)* to instruct, especially so as to encourage intellectual, moral, or spiritual improvement
refute	*(v.)* to prove false

During Reading   As you read "Free Speech: Lyrics, Liberty, and License," continue to predict and visualize the ideas and monitor your comprehension. Look for signals for the comparison and contrast patterns. What does the author want you to understand about censorship of music lyrics?

The following is an excerpt from a speech given by Sam Brownback, United States Senator from Kansas, on March 23, 1998.

I want to talk with you today about music and freedom about lyrics, liberty, and license. This is an issue that is important to me—as it is, I suspect, important to you. I can't think of a more fitting place for this discussion than here, at a forum dedicated to upholding the principle of free speech, in Cleveland, the home of the Rock and Roll Hall of Fame.

As many of you know, I recently held a Senate hearing on the impact of violent music lyrics on young people. During this hearing, we heard a variety of witnesses testify on the effects of music lyrics that glorified rape, sexual torture, violence, and murder. Some of these lyrics are almost unbelievably awful, but they are backed by huge, powerful, prestigious corporations. I have grown more and more concerned about the content and the impact of these lyrics. And I have publicly criticized the entertainment executives who produce, promote, and profit from such music.

I am also the only Senator on the Commerce Committee to vote against a very popular bill that would coerce TV stations into labeling their programs. I publicly opposed V-chip legislation. I have consistently voted against any sort of government involvement in regulating or rating music or television. Some people don't think the two go together. They think that if you talk about some music lyrics being degrading and violent, then you must be in favor of censorship. Others think that if you vote against various government restrictions on television programs, or music content, you must approve of those programs and songs. Both views are mistaken.

And today, I'd like to talk about legislating in a way to maximize freedom, and agitating for civility and decency, and why the two not only can go together, but should—and indeed, if we are to preserve freedom, they must.

Most of you here have strong ideas about music. As indeed, you should. Music is powerful. It changes our mood, shapes our experience, affects our thoughts, alters our pulse, touches our lives. The rhythm, the beat, and the lyrics all impress us with their message. Thousands of years ago, the great philosopher Plato stated, "Musical training is a more potent instrument than any other, because rhythm and harmony find their way into the inward places of the soul, on which they mightily fasten."

As such, music lyrics have profound public consequences. In many ways, the music industry is more influential than anything that happens in Washington. After all, most people spend a lot more time listening to music than watching C-Span or reading the newspaper. They're more likely to recognize musicians than Supreme Court justices. Most of us spend more time thinking about music than laws, bills, and policies. And that's probably a good thing.

And as many of you know, no one spends more time listening to music than young people. In fact, one recent study conducted by the Carnegie Foundation concluded that the average teenager listens to music around four hours a day. In contrast, less than an hour is spent on homework or reading, less than 20 minutes a day is spent talking with Mom, and less than five minutes is spent talking with Dad. If this is true, there are a lot of people who spend more time listening to shock-rock artist Marilyn Manson or Snoop Doggy Dogg than Mom or Dad. In fact, Marilyn Manson himself said: "Music is such a powerful medium now. The kids don't even know who the President is, but they know what's on MTV. I think if anyone like Hitler or Mussolini were alive now, they [sic] would have to be rock stars."

In short, because of the power of music, the time we spend listening to it, and the potency of its messages, music has a powerful public impact. It affects us, not only privately, but publicly. It helps shape our attitudes and assumptions, and thus, our decisions and behavior—all of which has [sic] a public dimension, and merits public debate.

Frankly, I believe there needs to be more public discourse over music. It is too important to ignore. Its influence reaches around the world. American rock and rap are popular exports. They are listened to by billions, in virtually every nation on earth. And for good or bad, our music shapes the way in which many people around the world view the United States—American music is the most pervasive (and loudest) ambassador we have. Unfortunately, its message is too often a destructive one.

Many of you may already know the kind of lyrics I am talking about. If not, it is useful to read some of them—they won't be hard to find; they are quite popular. Then ask yourself: What are the real-world effects of these lyrics? What do these lyrics celebrate, and what do they ridicule or denounce? What are the consequences of glorifying violence and glamorizing rape? Have record companies behaved responsibly when they produce music that debases women? You and your friends may come up with different answers. But they are good questions to think about. And I hope recording industry executives think about them as well.

There are no easy answers to those questions. It is impossible to quantify the ways in which such lyrics affect us. But it is equally impossible to believe they have no effect at all. Of course, most rock and rap do not have hyperviolent or perverse lyrics. In the grand scale of things, it is a small number of songs from an even smaller number of bands that produces these sorts of lyrics. They are the exception, not the rule.

It is also true that people will disagree over which music is offensive. Some people thought the Beach Boys were a problem, and some think the Spice Girls are. I do not happen to be one of them. There will always be songs about which reasonable people with good judgement will disagree.

But there should also be some things that we can all agree on. And one of those things is that music that glorifies rape, violence, and bigotry is wrong. It may be constitutionally protected. The huge entertainment corporations that produce, promote, and profit from this sort of record may have a right to do so. But it is not the right thing to do.

For free societies to endure, there must be a distinction between what is allowed and what is honored. I believe that the First Amendment assures the widest possible latitude in allowing various forms of speech—including offensive, obnoxious speech. But the fact that certain forms of speech should be allowed does not mean that they should be honored, or given respectability. There are many forms of speech that should be thoroughly criticized, even as they are protected. Freedom of expression is not immunity from criticism.

The proper response to offensive speech is criticism— not censorship, and not apathy. Vigorous criticism of the perverse, hateful, and violent reflects a willingness on the part of citizens to take ideas seriously, evaluate them accordingly, and engage them directly. A cultural predisposition to care about ideas and to judge between them—while protecting the liberty of others, is the best bulwark of a free society. A citizenry that evaluates ideas, that discerns the true from the false, that values reason over reaction, that affirms that which is edifying, and that refutes that which is wrong—is exactly the society most likely to value, to have, and to keep free speech.

After Reading

Word Connections

1. From the context of the second paragraph, define *prestigious*.

   _____ _____

2. "Most rock and rap do not have hyperviolent or perverse lyrics." What do you think *hyperviolent* means?

   _____

3. Give at least two examples of *apathy*.

   _____

   _____

Connecting Meaning

1. What is the main idea of this selection?

   _____

   _____

   _____

   _____

2. More time is spent listening to music than a variety of other activities—for example, listening to music rather than watching C-Span or reading the newspaper. What other activities listed in the reading contrast to the listening of music?

_____

_____

3. Senator Brownback described two kinds of responses to offensive lyrics or speech. What are these two responses? Which does the senator feel is more effective?

_____

_____

_____

4. Do you think music lyrics should be censored? If so, by whom and for what reasons? If not, give reasons to support your opinion.

_____

_____

Selection 2

Textbooks and Fairy Tales: The Value of Classic Myths

BARBARA KEELER

Before Reading

Before reading "Textbooks and Fairy Tales: The Value of Classic Myths," predict the topic, scan the story, and think about the fairy tales you have heard or read. Did you enjoy them? Have you ever thought of fairy tales as being violent, sexist, or gruesome? Relate your experiences with fairy tales to their use in modern textbooks.

Words to Preview

recoil	(v.) to shrink back, as in fear
fundamentalism	(n.) a movement or point of view characterized by rigid support of basic principles
incompatible	(adj.) not capable of blending
embrace	(v.) to take up willingly or eagerly
embody	(v.) to represent
betroth	(v.) to promise to marry
morbidity	(n.) the quality of being unwholesome, gruesome
inherent	(adj.) an essential characteristic
imprudent	(adj.) unwise
behoove	(v.) to be necessary

During Reading

As you read "Textbooks and Fairy Tales: The Value of Classic Myths," continue to predict and visualize the information and monitor your comprehension. Look for signals for the comparison and contrast patterns. What does the author want you to know about the use of fairy tales in textbooks?

Parents in La Puente (California) recoiled recently at what they found in their children's elementary-school reading books: monsters that cut children's heads off, pigs that live on body wastes, witches that cast spells. Their objections, spread through a national Christian group called Citizens for Excellence in Education, has resulted in several school districts dropping the nationally used texts.

In targeting the series called "Impressions" and its publisher, Harcourt Brace Jovanovich, the complaining parents seem unaware that what offends them arises from the nature of many literary classics themselves, and that such elements abound in classic literature. The decision to base reading texts on classics—getting away from Dick-and-Jane style readers—was made by the creators of the English-Language Arts Framework of the state of California, not by textbook publishers.

The new texts have been praised by educators for stimulating children's imaginations, but Citizens for Excellence in Education and other fundamentalist Christian groups have mounted a growing attack on such books as inappropriate for young children, claiming the books attack values that parents try to inculcate in the home.

California-approved school texts are now required to draw selections from literary classics. Such classics have retained their popularity over time and are valued by educators for richness of language, appeal to universal feelings and needs, and a "capacity to move the human spirit in any age," as the state guidelines put it.

But a decision to choose classics as sources of reading material is a decision to accept elements that would not be acceptable in material written in 1990 for today's educational market. Any reading series adopted in California, therefore, is likely to contain some such elements.

A story that has been around long enough to become classic has necessarily originated at times when different values dominated—some of which are incompatible with those embraced by today's educational system. Therefore publishers who would write textbooks for the state of California face contradictory mandates. Any original material they write must be free not only of gruesome elements, but of sexism, racism, and ageism.

Text material must deal sensitively with disabilities and deformities. Yet textbooks are required to include classics written in a setting where sexism and racial stereotyping are a fact of life; good parents and teachers beat children; elderly or deformed characters are often cast as villains; witches cast evil spells, to be countered by benevolent spells, and a happy tale ends with the cruel and unusual punishment of the guilty.

The elements probably most at odds with today's values are to be found in fairy tales, traditionally read to young children.

"I would suggest that parents who are concerned about these stories take a look at the Brothers Grimm," said Thomas Williamson, director of the school textbook division of Harcourt Brace Jovanovich.

The Brothers Grimm—Jakob and Wilhelm, 19th-Century German philologists—created early written versions of the oral tales from which many of today's popular fairy tales are derived.

Let's look at the Grimm fairy tales, which children have loved for years—they offer magic and enchantment, triumphs of good over evil, wishes fulfilled under impossible odds. They are tales in which the small, young, or weak can vanquish a monster or powerful villain, giving children hope. Long before they can evaluate more complex issues, children can appreciate the stark contrasts of absolutes: good versus evil, greed versus generosity, industry versus laziness, beauty versus ugliness, cleverness versus stupidity.

On the other hand, Grimm's and other fairy tales embody many elements that would seem grotesque or perverted even in today's adult literature. Characters are threatened or devoured by cannibals or human-eating animals and monsters. In "Robber Bridegroom," for example, a betrothed maiden discovers that her intended plans to cook and eat her. Hansel is fattened up by the witch and checked daily for weight gain. In early versions of "Little Red Riding Hood," the heroine is eaten alive as a fitting punishment for her disobedience. In the later Grimm version, she is unappetizingly rescued through an incision in the wolf's belly, which is subsequently filled with rocks.

The wolf's punishment is mild compared with that inflicted on many fairy-tale villains. Children demand justice in a story, but justice hardly requires the brutal, inhuman penalties imposed on villains in Grimm's fairy tales. In "The Goose Girl," for example, a treacherous maid is "put stark naked into a barrel stuck with nails, and dragged along by two white horses . . . until dead." In Grimm's version of "Snow White," the stepmother is forced to dance in red-hot iron shoes until she dies. In the Grimm version of Cinderella, the stepsisters' eyes are pecked out by doves—this after they have mutilated their feet in attempts to fit the glass slipper. In "The Pink," a villain is forced to eat live coals and is then torn into quarters.

Hans Christian Andersen's fairy tales also contain material that seems sick by today's standards. In "The Wild Swans," for example, witches dance naked in the cemetery, dig up dead bodies, and eat them. In "The Rose Elf," a young girl visits her decapitated lover's grave, digs up his body, retrieves his head, kisses it, takes it home with her, and buries it in a flowerpot.

Karen Stone, El Segundo children's librarian and instructor of literature for adolescents and children at Loyola Marymount University, points out that ancient tales were not originally created for children. "The concept of childhood as we see it is a recent invention—children were once viewed as small adults. They were dressed as adults, educated as adults, and worked with adults. Issues in these tales were addressed to adults and children alike."

In other words, cautionary tales required penalties more significant than being grounded or standing in the corner. Many traditional tales were written to influence the behavior of the audience, and storytellers who would discourage given behavior were challenged to devise deterrents more severe than the hardships and brutal conditions of the historical period.

Not that the behavior rewarded in fairy tales is always exemplary. For example, the "villain" who tears himself in two at the end of "Rumpelstiltskin" is the only character who has told the truth, kept his word, and showed compassion. The miller who lies about his daughter, a wife who deceives her husband, and a husband who threatens to kill his wife live happily ever after.

Disney versions of fairy tales omit the most gruesome elements. Snow White's stepmother does not eat the heart she believes to be Snow White's. Commercial producers are free to adapt these tales at will. The Disney versions of "The Little Mermaid" and "Peter Pan," for example, depart radically from the story lines of the original classics. Textbook publishers, however, can be penalized for taking such liberties. In many districts, adoption committees rate programs by a system that penalizes them for any editing, abridgement, or adaptation of a classic, regardless of the reason.

Publishers can choose from many classic versions of fairy tales, and they choose versions containing the least violence and morbidity. However, they cannot get around the fact that these tales themselves came from times and cultures whose values clashed with our own. Many elements considered objectionable today are inherent in such tales. Can publishers be blamed for that?

Apart from violence, the sexism that pervades fairy tales could never be smuggled past adoption committees if it were written today. In many fairy tales, the heroine is valued primarily as a sexual prize. She need only be young and beautiful to attract countless suitors, often despite appalling behavior and character traits. For example, in Andersen's "The Traveling Companions," Hans tours the garden of the princess and finds it decorated by the bones and skulls of the imprudent suitors who have courted her. She had agreed to marry any man who could guess her thoughts, but the penalty for error was a cruel death. Nevertheless, Hans falls in love at first sight.

Fairy tales and other classics are well-crafted works of literature with enduring appeal. As such, they are worth teaching. It behooves parents and teachers, however, to discuss classics in light of the way values have changed.

After Reading

Word Connections

1. "Classics have retained their popularity over time and are valued by educators for several common elements." Identify the elements of a *literary classic*.

_____

_____

_____

_____

2. Textbooks must be free of *sexism*, *racism*, and *ageism*. Define each term.

_____

_____

Connecting Meaning

1. What is the main idea of this selection?

_____

_____

_____

_____

_____

2. Identify three examples of elements of fairy tales that would probably not be published if written today.

_____

_____

_____

_____

3. How do the elements of fairy tales differ from today's values?

_____

_____

_____

4. Name some elements of Grimm's fairy tales that the author feels are positive.

_____

_____

_____

_____

Selection 3

Stuff a Gag in the V-chip

Art Hilgart

Before Reading

Before you read "Stuff a Gag In the V-chip," predict the topic, scan the reading, and think about censorship of television programs. As a child, were you ever forbidden to watch a particular television show? Do you think television should be censored for children? Relate your experiences to the views of the author.

Words to Preview

V-chip	*(n.)* computer chip that receives encoded information as part of the television broadcast. It may be programmed to block violent or offensive programming.
perpetrate	*(v.)* to commit
ethnocentrism	*(n.)* belief in the superiority of one's own race

During Reading

As you read "Stuff a Gag in the V-chip," continue to predict and visualize the information and monitor your comprehension. Look for signals of the comparison and contrast patterns. What does the author want you to understand about the V-chip and television censorship for children?

Of all the crybabies demanding government protection from their own free will, the parents wanting ratings of television programs deserve to spend hell watching "The Jetsons." By their standards, Americans are utterly irresponsible parents.

When our elder son was five, we took him to a production of *The Three-Penny Opera*, about a bigamist throat cutter and a prostitute. His younger brother, when he was five, was treated to *West Side Story*, which includes rape and murder. We didn't lock up our bookshelves, and the boys skipped kiddie lit and went straight from Dr. Seuss and Maurice Sendak to the great books. They didn't seem interested in Henry Miller, though, preferring H. P.

Lovecraft and H. G. Wells. They could see any movie to which they could manage admittance and, as for television, our only warning was that commercials are cleverly produced lies, especially those for toys and breakfast food. We're proud that they ignored the made-for-television cartoons and searched out pre-World War II Warner Brothers material, and that one of them played the Monty Python transvestite lumberjack in his high school variety show. Both boys are grown now, and neither has a criminal record—one is an English professor, and the other studied political economy at Oxford.

What do the censors find acceptable for children? Violence is okay if it is "clean." In the movie *GoldenEye,* James Bond machine guns several hundred innocent people, but they die bloodlessly, so it received a PG rating. In the *Home Alone* films, a sadistic kid gleefully and repeatedly tortures some bumbling burglars, but the villains survive dozens of seemingly lethal encounters, and it's all in good fun, so the films are rated G. Violence perpetrated by "good guys"—like John Wayne—seems to be an acceptable moral lesson. The only problem is that each of us, however monstrous, believes him- or herself to be the good guy.

I might approve of video censorship were I the censor. I'd have a truth-chip block news stories presenting as fact the press releases of corporations or politicians. There would be a taste-chip to block any program interrupted with commercials. An ethnocentric-chip would block fiction and nonfiction that implies it's okay for us to kill them but not for them to kill us. And there would be a biology/religion-chip to block any suggestion that humans are not members of the animal kingdom. But if I had the power, I wouldn't use it. Even idiots and advertisers have the right to freedom of speech.

After Reading

Word Connections

1. What does the phrase "own free will" mean to you?

_____

_____

2. "Violence is okay if it is 'clean.'" What does the term *clean* mean in this context?

_____

Connecting Meaning

1. What is the main idea of the selection?

_____

_____

_____

2. What do the censors find acceptable for children?

_____

_____

_____

_____

3. How does what the censors find acceptable contrast to reality?

_____

_____

_____

_____

4. What does the author see as the problem with ratings and censorship?

_____

_____

_____

_____

■ ■ ■ ■ Portfolio Activities

Integrating Ideas

Do you think censorship is necessary for any facet of the media or for a particular age group? Who should set censorship guidelines? Does your view of censorship differ for obscenity, national security, racism, or sexism? Reflect on these ideas in writing or in class discussion.

Extending Concepts

Write an evaluation of the rating given to a movie of your choice. State whether you agree with the rating. Support your opinion with specific examples from the movie.

Collaborative Activity

Choose a fairy tale and rewrite it to avoid any elements that might be inappropriate for children by today's standards. You may also want to use politically correct terminology. Compare your version to the original story. Is it as captivating and powerful?

Additional Portfolio Suggestion

Read a book that has been challenged or banned in the United States within the last ten years. The American Library Association provides lists of these books. Ask your local librarian for information. After reading the book, do you feel it should be banned from library shelves?

Chapter Summary Graphic Organizer

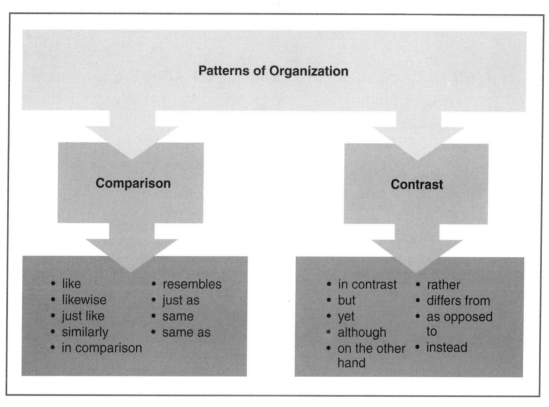

Patterns of Organization

Comparison

- like
- likewise
- just like
- similarly
- in comparison
- resembles
- just as
- same
- same as

Contrast

- in contrast
- but
- yet
- although
- on the other hand
- rather
- differs from
- as opposed to
- instead

11

Cause and Effect Pattern

Theme of Readings: Violence in America

You cannot shake hands with a clenched fist.

INDIRA GANDHI

■ ■ ■ ■ Violence

The news media reports on shootings, bombings, hijackings, crimes, and acts of war on a daily basis. Do we notice these violent images and stories? Are we shocked by them? To some degree, we have become desensitized. Violence tends to become real only when we are somehow directly involved—as victims or witnesses.

Still, our lives have been affected by violence. Children are taught to be wary of strangers. Schools have programs to help children guard their personal safety and learn conflict resolution techniques. Many young men and women attend self-defense classes. Homeowners purchase burglar alarms, heavy-duty locks, and in some cases, guns to protect themselves and their families. Business owners purchase alarms, surveillance equipment, and guard dogs. Through these means, people hope to prevent violence and crime from intruding into their daily existence.

What causes violent behavior? No one knows for sure. Research has suggested that contributing factors may be drug use, physical abuse, easy access to guns, and perhaps even the high number of violent scenes shown in the popular media. The causes are complex and debatable, but the effects are undeniable. The question remains—when, if ever, will the violence stop?

Chapter Objectives

After completing this chapter, you will be able to

1. **Identify the signal words used for the cause and effect pattern.**
2. **Distinguish between cause and effect supporting details.**
3. **Identify the supporting details that determine the cause and effect pattern.**

Focus on Cause and Effect Pattern

Cause and Effect Pattern

Authors use a cause and effect pattern to discuss the reasons why something has happened or will happen in the future. This pattern answers the questions *Why?* (to establish a cause) and *What resulted?* (to establish the effect or effects). An author may use this pattern to explain, for example, how Rosa Parks' nonviolent action in 1955 (her refusal to give her bus seat to a white male passenger) resulted in her arrest, which led to the boycott of the bus company, and eventually resulted in an end to "Jim Crow" laws.

Common Signals   Signal words that may provide clues to the cause and effect pattern are

because	because of	caused by	since
reason	leads to	effects	as a result
if . . . then	therefore	consequences	due to
outcomes	thus	results	results in

These words may indicate either cause or effect, so it is important to look for answers to the questions of *Why?* (cause) and *What resulted?* (effect).

Read the following paragraph. Then read the guide questions and answers that follow. In the future, these guide questions will help you to analyze and determine the pattern of any paragraph or reading.

> Family violence can have serious long-term effects on children who live in the home. Difficulties in school such as poor grades or discipline problems are often a result of living in violent homes. Living with family violence may also cause low self-esteem. In addition, it may result in children imitating the violent behavior they have seen.

What is the main idea of this paragraph?

The main idea is found in the first sentence: Family violence can have serious long-term effects on children who live in the home.

What are the common signals used in this paragraph?

The words *effects, result of, cause,* and *result in* indicate the cause and effect pattern.

What details support the main idea?

The major supporting details are difficulties in school, low self-esteem, and imitation of violent behavior.

What is the pattern of organization?

This paragraph shows a cause and effect pattern because it states the effects caused by family violence in the home.

Determining the Cause and Effect Pattern in Longer Selections

In longer selections, authors rarely use the cause and effect pattern to describe one cause and one effect. There may be several causes for one effect, several effects for one cause, or a chain of events—one event being caused by the previous one. For example, in an article about the effects of a gun control law, an author may discuss the impact on crime rates, the impact on the legal system, and the impact on the illegal sale of firearms.

Short Exercises: Cause and Effect Pattern

Read each of the following paragraphs and complete the questions that follow.

The paragraphs were chosen from "The Man Who Counts the Killings" by Scott Stossel.

1. In 1977, Ronny Zamora, a fifteen-year-old, shot and killed the eighty-two-year-old woman who lived next door to him in Florida. Not guilty, pleaded his lawyer, Ellis Rubin, by reason of the boy's having watched too much television. From watching television, Ronny had become dangerously accustomed to violence. Suffering from what Rubin called "television intoxication," he could no longer tell right from wrong. "If you judge Ronny Zamora guilty," Rubin argued, "television will be an accessory." The jury disagreed: Ronny was convicted of first-degree murder.

   What is the main idea of the paragraph?

   _____

   _____

   _____

   What are the common signals used in this paragraph?

   _____

   _____

What details support the main idea?

_____

_____

_____

_____

2. A 1956 study investigated a cause of violent behavior in children by comparing the behavior of twelve four-year-olds who watched a Woody Woodpecker cartoon containing many violent episodes with that of twelve other four-year-olds who watched "The Little Red Hen," a nonviolent cartoon. Due to the watching of violent cartoons, the Woody Woodpecker watchers were much more likely than the Red Hen watchers to hit other children, break toys, and be generally destructive during playtime.

What is the main idea of this paragraph?

_____

_____

_____

_____

What are the common signals used in this paragraph?

_____

What details support the main idea?

_____

_____

_____

_____

_____

3. In 1960, Leonard Eron, a professor of psychology at the University of Michigan's Institute for Social Research, studied third graders in Colombia County in semirural New York. He observed that the more violent the television these eight-year-olds watched at home, the more aggressive they were in school. Eron returned to Colombia County in 1971, when the children from his sample were nineteen. He found that the boys who had watched a lot of violent television when they were eight were more likely to get into trouble with the law when older. Eron returned to Colombia County a third time, in 1982, when his subjects

were thirty. He discovered that those who had watched the most television violence at age eight inflicted more violent punishments on their children, were convicted of more serious crimes, and were reported more aggressive by their spouses than those who had watched less violent television.

What is the main idea of this paragraph?

_____

_____

_____

_____

What are the common signals used in this paragraph?

_____

_____

What details support the main idea?

_____

_____

_____

_____

_____

_____

_____

_____

4. The latest burst of activity around the issue of television violence, ending in the legislating of the V-chip, can trace its initial cause to a night in the mid-1980s when a weary Senator Paul Simon of Illinois, lying in his motel bed, flipped on the television and saw, in graphic detail, a man being sliced in half with a chain saw—a victim, Simon's staff later figured, of Colombian drug dealers in the movie, *Scarface.* Upset that there was nothing to prevent a child from witnessing such grisliness, Simon urged the passage of a law reducing gore on television. The result, the 1990 Television Violence Act, was a compromise between the broadcasting industry and those who, like Simon, wanted somehow to reduce the violence on shows that children might be watching.

What is the main idea of this paragraph?

_____

_____

_____

What are the common signals used in this paragraph?

_____

What details support the main idea?

_____

_____

_____

_____

5. There are several reasons for the prevalence of violence on television news. Watch your local newscast tonight: it is not unlikely that the majority of news stories will be about crime or disaster—and it may well be that all six stories will be outside your state, especially if you live far from any major metropolis. Fires and shootings are much cheaper and easier to cover than politics or community events. Violent news also generates higher ratings, and since the standards for television news are set by market researchers, what we get is lots of conformity, lots of violence.

What is the main idea of this paragraph?

_____

_____

_____

What are the common signals used in this paragraph?

_____

What details support the main idea?

_____

_____

_____

_____

■ ■ ■ ■ Reading Selections

Selection 1 **Does TV Affect Your Psyche?**
JAY KIST

Before Reading Before you read "Does TV Affect Your Psyche?" predict the topic, scan the story, and think about how television affects you. Do you think television violence encourages violent behavior in viewers? Relate your knowledge and your opinion about television violence to the author's view.

Words to Preview

psyche	*(n.)*	the mind
compelling	*(adj.)*	urgently requiring attention
spectrum	*(n.)*	a range of ideas
mayhem	*(n.)*	state of riotous confusion
suppress	*(v.)*	to put an end to

During Reading As you read "Does TV Affect Your Psyche?" continue to predict and visualize the ideas and monitor your comprehension. Look for signals for the cause and effect pattern. What does the author want you to understand about television violence?

Surrounded by bowls of popcorn and cans of cola, you and your three best friends are watching a violent TV movie. Shortly after the movie, one friend makes a comment you really take offense at—and a heated argument follows. Is there a connection?

Jan's favorite show has lots of jokes about drinking, drug use, and smoking. She gets a kick out of watching the characters on the show interact with each other in such a natural way. Jan's invited to a party over the weekend where there are lots of booze and other drugs. Although she has never been tempted before, she decides to try a couple of beers that night. Is there a connection?

Perhaps you're thinking "That's ridiculous! Those TV programs or movies have nothing to do with real life. Can anyone really imagine having this type of response to something that's just meant to entertain?" Most people would say the only effect television has on them is a compelling urge to get up and look in the refrigerator.

Leave it to Beaver or Beavis?

Yet a national debate rages over television's effect on young people. The American Psychological Association published a study that concluded the average child between ages three and twelve who watches 27 hours of TV a week (that's just under four hours a day) will watch 8,000 murders and 100,000 violent acts. More than 1,000 studies have found a connection between violence on TV and people's real-life behavior. Statistics like these are one reason why Congress wants to pass a law that requires new TV sets to have a built-in "V-chip." Parents could use this technology to bar violent programs from their home.

All along the political spectrum, leaders are calling for a return to "family values," accusing Hollywood of being out of touch with the values of the American people. Part of the problem is the creeping erosion of what used to be called the "family hour"—that period between 8 P.M. and 9 P.M. when the major networks used to air programs that the family could watch together. Now they have to compete with cable TV, which offers more violent programming.

Money is the bottom line, so they gear their programs to appeal to the young urban adults (ages 18 to 49) that advertisers target. Shows with high ratings bring in more advertising dollars. This is also true of television news shows, which typically lead with stories of murder and mayhem.

Shakespeare Rated X?

Violence and sex in entertainment are nothing new. Shakespeare and Homer were often quite graphic in treating these themes. Some paintings that hang in famous museums are pretty rough viewing. So why does the behavior we see on TV bother us so much? Part of it is the sheer amount that's there, but just as important is something that's not there. What's often missing is the context and reality that help us understand a violent act and what it means to the victim and to our society. Casual violence is mindless and teaches nothing. There's no point.

What TV does teach is sometimes wrong. Young people look to peers and role models to help them figure out their feelings and how to behave. They also can be influenced by characters on the small screen. A University of Rochester School of Medicine study of nearly 3,000 adolescents looked at the relationship between the media and risky behaviors such as drinking, smoking cigarettes and marijuana, sexual activity, stealing, cheating, cutting school, and driving a car without permission. The greater risk takers were those who watched music videos and television movies more frequently.

No Bad-Hair Days on TV

Another pitfall in using television as a role model is the gap between real life and what is seen onscreen. Most people, including teens, are not as beautiful, handsome, or witty as television actors and actresses who have the benefit of writers, directors, hairstylists, makeup artists, and cinematographers to help them look and sound their best. Most people can't solve their problems neatly in half-hour segments of life. But if that's what you are led to believe is normal, your own real life and the people in it are going to give you fits.

Finally, what about your real life? You know, the one that goes on hold while you watch the fake ones taking place onscreen. Even if watching TV doesn't encourage some risky behaviors, it surely can suppress some good ones: talking, exercising, playing games, eating together, going places—doing real things, with real people. Joan Wilking, who wrote *Breaking the TV Habit*, says that young people "must learn to live their own lives before they learn TV lives."

It's more interesting . . . plus there are no commercials!

After Reading

Word Connections

1. "Part of the problem is the creeping erosion of what used to be called the 'family hour.'" What does *creeping erosion* mean?

   _____

2. Create a concept of definition map for *role model*.

   Diagram:

Connecting Meaning

1. What is the main idea of this selection?

   _____

   _____

   _____

   _____

2. What caused the erosion of the "family hour"?

   _____

   _____

   _____

3. What type of behavior resulted from watching music videos and television movies frequently?

_____

_____

_____

4. Do you agree or disagree with Joan Wilking who says that young people "must learn to live their own lives before they learn TV lives"? Explain your answer.

_____

_____

Selection 2

'Roofies': Horror Drug of the '90s

JUDY MONROE

Before Reading

Before you read "'Roofies': Horror Drug of the '90s," predict the topic, scan the story, and think about the drug Rohypnol. What do you know about the drug? Do you know anyone who has been a victim of this drug? Relate your knowledge about Rohypnol to the author's information.

Words to Preview

Rohypnol   *(n.)* a tasteless, odorless, and colorless sedative that can be easily added to a beverage

anonymity   *(n.)* the state of being unknown

During Reading

As you read "'Roofies': Horror Drug of the '90s," continue to predict and visualize the ideas and monitor your comprehension. Look for signals for the cause and effect pattern. What does the author want you to know about the drug Rohypnol?

"Thanks for offering to drive me home."

Barney grinned. "No prob-lem-o. I'll get us a drink to go."

Amy smiled as she thought about her luck in meeting Barney at her first party in college. He was funny and cute and interested in her!

When Barney returned, he handed her a plastic cup filled with beer, and the two pushed their way through the crowd. They talked as Barney drove Amy home.

Barney refused to drink while he drove, and Amy mentally added another point to his appeal rating. About fifteen minutes later, Barney pulled up to Amy's house. She complained she was sleepy and dropped her house key several times. Barney opened the front door, guided Amy inside, then told her he'd put her to bed since her roommates weren't home. Amy remembered nothing after that.

Early the next morning Amy woke feeling shaky and sore. Stumbling out of bed, she saw that she was half naked and bruised. She had been raped. Crying, she phoned the number Barney had given her.

The sleepy voice at the other end said no Barney lived there. Amy realized she didn't even know Barney's last name.

Across the United States, sexual assaults like Amy's are being connected to Rohypnol, a sedative drug often called the "date-rape drug." That's what happened to Amy. Barney had slipped Rohypnol, a white pill that quickly dissolves, into Amy's beer. It left no odor, color, or taste. The powerful drug made Amy sleepy and wiped out her memory for six to eight hours.

It's hard to catch people who use drugs such as Rohypnol to commit crimes, particularly in rape cases. That's because, when someone slips Rohypnol into a drink, the victim seldom remembers any details of the rape. About ten to twenty minutes after ingesting the drug, many victims feel dizzy and disoriented, hot or cold, and nauseated. Some have trouble speaking and moving. Most pass out and have no memory of what happened while under the drug's influence.

An Illegal Depressant

Rohypnol ranks as the most widely prescribed sedative or sleeping pill in Europe, but it is not approved for sale in the United States. Most Rohypnol in the United States is imported from Mexico and South America, where it is sold legally.

Rohypnol often is sold in the manufacturer's bubble packaging, which looks like a package for cold pills. The tablets are white and are single- or cross-scored on one side with "ROCHE" and "1" or "2" encircled on the other. It is cheap—users can get it for as little as $1 to $1.50 per tablet. Some users believe it is a "safe" drug because it looks legal. However, Rohypnol is illegal in the United States—and it is not safe.

On October 13, 1996, President Bill Clinton signed into law the "Drug-Induced Rape Prevention and Punishment Act of 1996." This law makes it a felony to distribute Rohypnol or similar substances to someone without that person's knowledge and with the intent to commit violence against that person, including rape. If Barney were tried and convicted for raping Amy, he could be sentenced to 20 years in prison.

Rohypnol is a central-nervous-system depressant like Valium, but it is ten times stronger. Larger than aspirin but smaller than an antacid tablet, the pills are taken by mouth or crushed and inhaled through the nose.

The drug's effects begin within thirty minutes, peak within two hours, and may persist for up to eight hours or more. When used illegally, adverse effects include decreased blood pressure, memory impairment, drowsiness, vision problems, dizziness, confusion, nausea, and inability to urinate. Repeated Rohypnol use can lead to dependence. If a user tries to stop taking the drug, withdrawal symptoms result, including headache, muscle pain, extreme anxiety, tension, restlessness, confusion, and irritability. Numbness, tingling, convulsions, shock, and collapse also may occur.

Horror Stories

In the 1970s, Rohypnol was introduced in Europe and South America. Beginning in the '80s, drug users in Europe started using it to come down from a cocaine or methamphetamine (speed) high. Americans discovered the drug in the '90s.

Although small in size, these pills have powerful effects. Early in 1994, the late grunge rock star Kurt Cobain fell into a coma after taking Rohypnol and drinking champagne while on tour in Italy. After his stomach was pumped, he revived, only to commit suicide under the influence of drugs shortly afterward. Like Cobain, some teens take Rohypnol with alcohol. The combination greatly impairs a person's motor ability and memory and can be deadly.

Sometimes Rohypnol causes aggression, rage, or hallucinations. More often it causes short-term amnesia for six to eight hours. It also reduces inhibitions and makes users feel fearless. In 1995, Rob, age 19, lived in Houston, Texas, and often used Rohypnol. He explained, "You take it—you black out. The next day people tell you what you did, and you're like, 'Wha-a-a-a-t?'"

In 1995, Annette*, age 16, was buying Rohypnol regularly in Austin, Texas. Less than a year later she entered Odyssey House, a teen treatment facility in Houston. "I'm the kind of person who wouldn't take one or two. I would take three or four and drink at the same time. We used to call them 'run-trip-and-falls.' . . . I would black out for days."

Tim's* story is another common one. A couple of years ago, while on a business trip in Florida, he stopped at a bar for a drink. After twenty minutes or so, he felt sleepy and had trouble sitting upright. Hours later, he woke up in an alley, bleeding and bruised with torn clothing. His wallet was gone, and he had no memory of what had happened. When Tim told his story to the police, they said that someone had probably slipped Rohypnol in his drink, and when he blacked out, he was taken outside, beaten, and robbed.

Be Aware

To protect yourself from drugs like Rohypnol, watch what you drink at parties or when you're out on dates. Do not take any drinks (soda, coffee, as well as alcohol) from someone you do not know well and trust. Refuse open-container drinks. If you think you were drugged, call 911 right away or get to an emergency room. If possible, try to keep a sample of the beverage.

*Annette and Tim are not their real names. Both have requested anonymity.

After Reading

Word Connections

1. "When used illegally, adverse effects include decreased blood pressure, memory impairment, drowsiness, vision problems, dizziness, confusion, nausea, and inability to urinate." Define *adverse* from context.

_____

_____

2. "It also reduces inhibitions and makes users feel fearless." What does *inhibition* mean?

_____

_____

3. Annette called her combination of drugs and alcohol "run-trip-and-falls." What do you think this phrase means?

_____

_____

_____

_____

Connecting Meaning

1. What is the main idea of this selection?

_____

_____

_____

_____

2. What crimes are committed with the help of Rohypnol?

_____

_____

_____

3. When used illegally, what are some of the adverse effects of Rohynpol?

_____

_____

_____

4. Why is it difficult to prosecute a crime in which Rohynpnol was used?

_____

_____

_____

_____

Selection 3   **They Each Had a Gun**

Ted Gottfried

Before Reading   Before you read "They Each Had a Gun," predict the topic, scan the story, and think about gun control. Do you think everyone has the right to own a gun? Would you feel safer if you owned one? Why or why not? Relate your knowledge and opinion about gun control to the author's view.

Words to Preview

lurch	*(v.)* to roll or pitch forward abruptly
advocate	*(n.)* supporter
cite	*(v.)* to mention as example or proof
negligent	*(adj.)* paying little attention to
interloper	*(n.)* one who interferes with the affairs of others
crucial	*(adj.)* extremely significant or important

During Reading   As you read "They Each Had a Gun," continue to predict and visualize the ideas and monitor your comprehension. Look for signals for the cause and effect pattern. What does the author want you to understand about gun control?

Although Hannah LaMarca and Arthur Strang* both lived in the same middle-class midwestern suburb, they did not know each other. It was by chance that they acquired their handguns on the same day. But it was something more than chance that pushed them into getting their firearms.

Arthur Strang had become alarmed by a rash of robberies on his block. In one case a neighbor was pistol-whipped by two of the burglars. In another, a watchdog, a family pet, was killed. Arthur Strang thought about it

---

*Hannah LaMarca and Arthur Strang are composites of case histories compiled by the National Rifle Association in *The Armed Citizen* (1989), and of examples cited by the Center to Prevent Handgun Violence, Handgun Control Inc., and various law enforcement agencies.

and decided he and his wife and two children needed protection. He applied for a gun license, and when it came through, he bought a .38 caliber Smith & Wesson revolver.

Hannah LaMarca was a single woman who shared an apartment in a two-family house with two other women. One night, after dinner and a movie with an office friend, Hannah was returning home alone when a man emerged from the shadows of the tree-lined street on which she lived and demanded that she hand over her pocketbook. He was a small man and didn't seem to be armed, and so she hesitated. Should she scream, run, or do what he demanded?

She never had a chance to decide. She never saw what hit her. When she regained consciousness a while later in the arms of the neighbor who found her, Hannah's cheekbone was shattered and her jaw fractured. From the bruise marks, it was later determined that she had been struck three times by brass knuckles. Her pocketbook, and the small amount of money in it, was gone.

"It wasn't just the money," Hannah said. "Or even being beaten up. I'd been violated in a much worse way. You see, I'd never given much thought to my safety. Now I would never feel safe again."

She applied for a license to carry a small pistol, a so-called "lady's revolver," which fit into her handbag. Then she joined a gun club and went through an intensive course on target shooting. She learned to hit what she aimed at from various distances and under pressure.

Hannah LaMarca's ownership of a firearm was a reaction to being a victim. Arthur Strang's purchase of a revolver was his response to the fear of becoming one. Perhaps his fear was less immediate, and that is why, once he had the gun, he never even fired it.

He showed it to his wife and to their children. Arthur and Charlotte Strang had two children—Michelle, age fourteen, and Neil, who was eleven. After he showed it to them, Arthur put the .38 in a drawer of the night table beside his bed, where it would be handy if needed to repel an intruder. Everybody in the family knew where the gun was kept in case it was ever needed for protection.

The situation that Arthur Strang feared never occurred. A similar situation, however, did present itself to Hannah LaMarca. She was home alone one night, dozing over a book she'd been reading in bed, when she heard noises coming from the bedroom of one of her housemates. Hannah took out her pistol and went to investigate.

A man she had never seen before was coming through the window as she opened the door to the bedroom. He landed on his feet and lurched forward. Hannah LaMarca fired three times. All three bullets hit the intruder in the chest, killing him.

Some weeks later, Arthur Strang's eleven-year-old son Neil told his friend Bruce Kammerer about the .38 his father kept in the night table. Bruce was interested and asked to see it. Neil took Bruce up to his parents' bedroom and started to remove the pistol from the drawer.

"Is it loaded?" Bruce Kammerer asked.

Before Neil could answer that he wasn't sure, the gun slipped from his hand, hit the baseboard and the floor simultaneously, and fired. The bullet struck Bruce Kammerer in the side of the skull. He died instantly.

Neil Strang, like Hannah LaMarca, had killed a fellow human being with a firearm. He had done so accidentally, she deliberately. A gun had slain a child. A gun had stopped a crime. Two people were dead: an innocent boy, and a criminal who, as it turned out, had a prior record of burglary arrests. As different as the circumstances were, each of these cases provokes opposite reactions from those who are for gun control and those who are against it.

In Hannah LaMarca's case, those who think citizens should arm themselves are satisfied that their point has been proven. A woman successfully protected her property and herself against a potentially dangerous criminal. A victim struck back. There is one less lawbreaker to threaten society, and we are all the better for it. The weapon Hannah LaMarca used is a tool that, to some small extent, has shaped a more decent and law-abiding world for all of us. The gun is an instrument to ensure our quality of life.

With equally strong conviction, gun-control advocates view the tragic shooting of eleven-year-old Bruce Kammerer as grim proof of the rightness of their position. Some (but not all) believe that Arthur Strang should never have had a gun in his home in the first place. There were other measures he could have taken to protect his property and his family. He could have installed safety locks and an alarm system. He could have gotten a watchdog. (Police interviews reveal that most professional thieves will not target a home where a watchdog is present.) They say the gun posed more of a threat to Arthur Strang and his family than to any robber. (They cite cases in which the sight of a gun in the hands of a homeowner provoked an armed intruder to shoot first.) Strang's gun was one more addition to the mounting violence of our world, they conclude, and Bruce Kammerer's death demonstrates the truth of that judgment.

They also challenge the conclusions drawn by their opponents regarding Hannah LaMarca's slaying of the housebreaker. If robbery is not legally punishable by a death sentence, then what right does a private citizen have to shoot and kill a burglar? they ask. Was Hannah LaMarca's fear—stemming from her previous experience—a justification? Was her fear realistic? Was her life in danger, or were only her possessions at risk?

Despite his previous criminal record, the second-story man was unarmed. Nor had he been armed when committing the crimes for which he had previously been arrested. Just how much force is justified—legally or morally—to protect property? Is killing an appropriate response? If lethal punishment is to be the answer to every crime, gun-control advocates insist, then the climate of violence that results will undermine the moral fiber of our society.

But it is that very moral fiber that concerns those who champion a citizen's right to be armed. In their view, if criminals have guns and decent people do not, then that aspect of society we call "civilized" will surely be destroyed. To fight for what is right is an individual obligation, and to be armed is to see to it that one is at least on equal terms with those criminal elements we all must oppose.

Yes, they concede, the shooting of eleven-year-old Bruce Kammerer was a tragedy. Terrible accidents do happen to children. But, they remind us, most such accidents do not involve firearms. The right to self-protection cannot be set aside because there are unfortunate incidents. More children by far die by fire than are slain by guns, but we do not license or limit the sale of matches.

Arthur Strang should not be criticized for having bought a gun, they say, but rather for treating it negligently. He had an obligation to familiarize himself with its use. He had an obligation to see that it was properly secured where neither children nor interlopers could get at it. Above all, he had an obligation to see that it was not loaded.

Firearms advocates like to stress the need for such safety precautions. But their demand that a gun be treated with respect does not answer the concerns of their opponents, who find inconsistencies in the position.

If a gun is secured out of the reach of others, they point out, then it will not be easily accessible when needed. If it is not loaded, then of what use is it as protection? Is the housebreaker going to stand by idly while the homeowner puts bullets in the chambers? Yes, if there are to be guns, then safety precautions are crucial. But if observing them cancels out the purpose of the firearm, then why have it in the first place?

Back and forth the argument goes. A gun stopped a crime; a gun killed a child. Guns are protection. Guns are dangerous.

Who is right?

After Reading   **Word Connections**

1. "Arthur Strang had become alarmed by a rash of robberies." What is meant by *a rash of robberies*?

   _____

2. Explain the phrase *climate of violence*.

   _____

   _____

3. The author refers to the moral fiber of society. What is meant by *moral fiber*?

   _____

   _____

   _____

Connecting Meaning

1. What is the main idea of the selection?

    _____

    _____

2. What caused Hannah La Marca to purchase a hand gun? What caused
    Arthur Strang to do the same?

    _____

    _____

    _____

    _____

    _____

3. What were the results of gun ownership by Hannah and Arthur?

    _____

    _____

    _____

4. Firearms advocates stress the need for safety precautions. How was
    Arthur Strang negligent as a gun owner?

    _____

    _____

    _____

Portfolio Suggestions

Integrating Ideas

What do you think causes violent behavior? Has violence in society increased or decreased? How do you think violence has affected you personally? Reflect on these ideas in writing or in class discussion.

Extending Concepts

Make a guess as to how many times physical violence occurs on television
each hour in the evening. Then actually count the number of violent acts you
see. Write about your observations and give your opinion.

Collaborative Activity

Examine violence in the newspapers. Bring several newspapers to class. Note photographs, words, and articles that show or describe violence. Discuss with the group the impact of the photos and print on the reader.

Additional Portfolio Suggestion

Investigate one recent federal or state law, such as the Brady Bill or Megan's Law, that has been passed to curb violence. Discuss the pros and cons of the bill.

▪ ▪ ▪ ▪ Chapter Summary Graphic Organizer

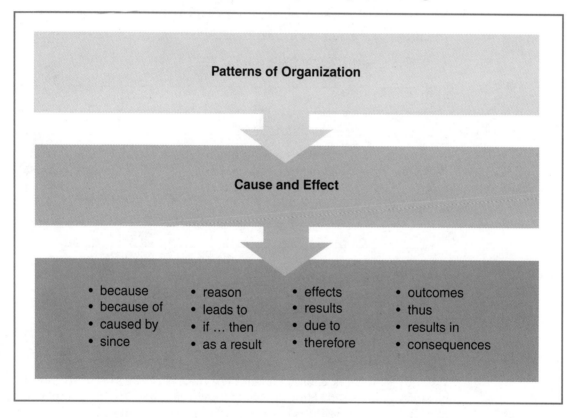

Patterns of Organization

Cause and Effect

- because
- because of
- caused by
- since

- reason
- leads to
- if … then
- as a result

- effects
- results
- due to
- therefore

- outcomes
- thus
- results in
- consequences

12

Problem and Solution Pattern

Theme of Readings:
Consumer Credit and Indebtedness

There's no such thing as a free lunch.

   MILTON FRIEDMAN

■ ■ ■ ■ Consumer Credit and Indebtedness

Traditionally, the rite of passage into adulthood means the completion of a series of survival tests. Today a young person's rite of passage into adulthood may be marked by acquiring a driver's license and obtaining a first credit card. To get a driver's license, one has to practice driving and pass a written exam and a road test. To obtain a credit card, one just has to fill out a form and sign on the dotted line. The credit card arrives in the mail, ready to use. Because credit card companies profit from the interest they charge on unpaid balances, they don't necessarily stress caution and restraint in the use of credit cards. Young people in particular often find themselves unable to repay mounting debt.

   The February 1998 issue of *Consumers' Research Magazine* reported that credit card debt amounted to $528 billion in the United States alone. Because of the size of consumer debt, an entire industry has arisen to deal with credit-related problems. Do-it-yourself money management books, television and radio talk shows, money management workshops, and individual credit counselors all focus on the problems people have managing finances. As with the cards themselves, solutions are made to seem easy and readily available: "Just sign here and your debt will be consolidated or eliminated," the ads say. But it is rarely that easy. If one needs these services, one should do research, use caution, and determine which alternative will offer the best solution to credit problems. Ideally, one will not need these services—the best approach is to avoid credit card problems in the first place.

Chapter Objectives

After completing this chapter, you will be able to

1. **Identify the problem in a problem and solution pattern.**
2. **Determine the facts that explain the problem.**
3. **Identify the solution, if any, offered by the author.**

Focus on Problem and Solution Pattern

Authors use a problem and solution pattern to present a problem to be identified, considered, explained, or solved. A solution may be offered, or it may be left to the reader to think further about the problem. The problem and solution pattern differs from the other patterns in that there are no specific signals.

Read the following paragraph. Then read the guide questions and answers that follow. In the future, these guide questions will help you to analyze the pattern of any paragraph or reading.

> It is easy for anyone to overspend when the overspending is done in small increments. Ten dollars for greeting cards and magazines, fifteen dollars for a meal, twenty dollars at the clothing or hardware shop—keep charging and soon these small amounts add up to a large credit debt. The thought of being free of debt seems impossible. It is, however, possible to get out of debt by using the same pattern you used to get into debt. By making small but frequent payments that are larger than the monthly minimum payments, you may rid yourself of debt.

What is the main idea?

The main idea is stated in the first and last sentences. It is easy for anyone to overspend when overspending is done in small increments, but by making small, frequent payments, you may rid yourself of debt.

What are the common signals used in this paragraph?

There are no common signals.

What details support the main idea?

Small amounts of money are frequently charged at various shops and restaurants. The small amounts quickly add up to large debt.

What is the pattern of organization?

This paragraph shows a pattern of problem and solution. After the problem of overspending is identified, the solution offered is to make frequent payments larger than the monthly minimum.

■ ■ ■ ■ **Short Exercises: Problem and Solution Pattern**

The first selection is excerpted from "Card Tricks," by Carrie Coolidge, and the second from "10 Things You Should Know before Filing Bankruptcy," by Kelly Beamon. Read each selection and complete the questions that follow.

1. When Walter Dodge received his Direct Merchants Bank Visa statement in September, he was baffled by a $60 charge for something called Purchase Shield Membership. Dodge, a technology consultant who lives in New York City, called Phoenix, Arizona-based Direct Merchants and learned the charge was the annual fee for its extended warranty program for goods purchased with the card—which he didn't want. Direct Merchants automatically signs up many of its holders for the overpriced warranty unless they think to object. After some hassle, Dodge got the charge removed.

    The charge at least was easy for Dodge to spot. Card issuers are sneaking more and more charges into monthly bills lately by increasing little-noticed existing fees or inventing new ones. So you have to watch your monthly statement more than ever. While we're hardly talking about bankrupting sums, you shouldn't pay extra if you can avoid it.

    What is the main idea of this selection?

    _____

    _____

    _____

    What are the common signals used in this selection?

    _____

    What details support the main idea?

    _____

    _____

    _____

    _____

2. Could it be that in ten short years, the ultimate financial taboo has become just another trend? One million people declared bankruptcy last year, twice the number of a decade earlier, and that figure is not inflated by business filings. Of the 300,000 bankruptcy petitions filed in U.S. courts during the 1996 fiscal third quarter, all but 14,000 were personal.

Experts in the field say bankruptcy filings are growing so fast, it's almost as if the average debtor now sees bankruptcy as a financial panacea—a carte blanche debt-free card.

Yet, for all the widespread publicity and the dozens of do-it-yourself manuals, misconceptions about personal bankruptcy still cloud this serious matter. For instance, Keith, a twenty-nine-year-old computer operator from New York City, thought it was his only salvation three years ago when he graduated from college and found a tighter job market than he expected. Out of work and strapped with $12,000 in credit card debt and student loans, he decided to go ahead and start anew by filing for Chapter 13 bankruptcy protection. "Since I wanted to wipe out the entire debt at that point, I was convinced an extreme solution would be best," he recalls.

Finding a lawyer in the yellow pages was easy, and legal fees amounted to no more than $700. "I'd already made the decision to file after reading books and talking to other folks who had done it," says Keith. So why is he haunted by hindsight even though he's squarely on his feet? For starters, he's barred from any line of credit for another four years. When he and his wife went looking for their new home two years ago, Keith knew his name couldn't appear on the mortgage, even though he can well afford the couple's monthly payment on his own. However, what really hurt was the realization that with his sterling credit record prior to bankruptcy proceedings—Keith never once missed a bill payment—he might have had the opportunity to cut a payment deal with his creditors.

He now regrets not having looked at other options, especially since he found a new job just a month after filing. Looking back, he says his situation was not as urgent as he had thought: He wasn't behind on any payments and now realizes that his $12,000 credit card debt pales in comparison with the burden carried by many. Keith's story underscores the importance of knowing what bankruptcy is and how to file properly.

What is the main idea in this selection?

_____

_____

_____

_____

What are the common signals used in this selection?

_____

_____

What details support the main idea?

_____

_____

_____

_____

_____

▪ ▪ ▪ ▪ Reading Selections

Selection 1

In Debt All the Way Up to Their Nose Rings

JOSHUA WOLF SHENK

Before Reading   Before you read "In Debt All the Way Up to Their Nose Rings," predict the topic, scan the story, and think about your credit history. Is credit too easy to obtain? Do you think Generation X is accumulating excessive debt? Relate your experiences with debt to the author's view of the problem with credit.

Words to Preview

disaffection	*(n.)* loss of loyalty or affection
proliferation	*(n.)* the act of increasing rapidly
qualm	*(n.)* an uneasy feeling about the rightness of a course of action
imperative	*(n.)* a command or order
scrimp	*(v.)* to economize severely
lure	*(n.)* something that tempts or attracts
emulate	*(v.)* to strive to equal or excel
exacerbate	*(v.)* to increase the severity of
incur	*(v.)* to acquire
aspiration	*(n.)* a desire for high achievement

During Reading   As you read "In Debt All the Way Up to Their Nose Rings," continue to predict and visualize the ideas and monitor your comprehension. What is the problem the author is explaining? What facts are given about Generation X debt? Is a solution offered?

It's not just a figure of speech to say credit cards these days are being passed out on college campuses like candy. Monet Martin discovered this her freshman year at the University of Texas–Austin when someone offered her a pack of Twizzlers and a Discover Card application. Soon, she was $2,800 in the hole.

Martin hasn't yet tried the debt-management technique of her friend Yashika Gomes, another student at UT. After charging her way through Europe last summer—and doubling her credit card balances to $4,500—Gomes immersed her three cards in a mug of water and put it in the freezer, a trick learned from Oprah. It actually worked, until a fire ripped through her room and she had to thaw the cards to buy new clothes and furniture. Now she owes $7,000. Both Martin and Gomes are also borrowing their way through college—they owe about $17,000 and $22,000, respectively.

Generation X may be best known for political disaffection and a tiny attention span, but its most defining characteristic may be debt. Two trends—the growth in student loan volume and the proliferation of credit cards—have combined to alter the behavior of young adults profoundly. Required to borrow in order to finance their education, members of this generation have no qualms about using credit to pay for comfort or even luxury. The moral imperative of living within one's means seems as distant as the Great Depression.

Consider that between 1990 and 1995, the average outstanding credit card balance of households headed by someone under 25 grew from $885 to $1,721. Carrying plastic is the norm for young people—65 percent of college students have cards, for example—and they are more prone than those in

Credit cards and the Internet have combined to make spending money a quick and easy task. (Bob Daemmrich/Stock Boston)

other age groups to get in over their heads. Of the debtors seeking professional help at the National Consumer Counseling Service, more than half are between 18 and 32.

The bucks start here.   Meanwhile, the past two decades have seen not only explosive growth in the cost of college but a dramatic change in who pays. From 1974 to 1994, the average cost of four years of tuition, room, board, and fees at public universities rose from $11,032 to $25,785. Private school costs went from $25,514 to $64,410.

Reacting to growing costs, Congress through the '80s and '90s expanded the student loan program, while scrimping on no-strings-attached grants. Undergraduates can now borrow up to $46,000, and graduate students, $138,500, in federally guaranteed loans—and many approach these high limits. So far this decade, students have borrowed at least $140 billion—more than total student borrowing over the past three decades combined. Since 1977, median student loan debt has leapt from $2,000 to about $15,000.

At the same time, parents have been bearing less of the burden. In interviews with *U.S. News,* financial aid administrators at a dozen different schools agreed that parents' contributions haven't nearly kept up with college costs. "Rather than pay out of their pocket," many parents expect their children to borrow, says Lawrence Burt, director of UT–Austin's financial aid office—"even if they can afford to pay tuition." In the only national survey on this question, taken in 1991, just 26 percent of student borrowers said their parents paid for more than one fifth of college costs. Studies have shown that typical parents pick up about 10 percent of their kids' student loans.

Consider Jenn Sanchez and Leslie Garza, roommates and sophomores at Texas's Austin campus. According to the federal financial aid guidelines, Sanchez's parents are supposed to contribute $5,000 a year. "I'm lucky if they give me $5 to go to McDonald's," she says. Garza receives $3,800 in loans and grants per semester, about half of which she sends to her mother who, Garza says, "is in extreme debt herself." Despite working between twenty-five and thirty hours a week, both Sanchez and Garza expect to owe more than $20,000 in student loans by graduation.

But if college costs put Sanchez and Garza in a bind, so does their own behavior. Though they could eat more cheaply at home, they often dine out. They could resist the lure of Austin's many clubs and bars, but they don't. "I guess I use cards to get stuff I want but don't need—or can't afford," Sanchez says. She has eighteen credit cards and a balance of $12,000.

For many students, it starts in their freshman year. "You've got all this freedom," says Tara Copp, editor of the school newspaper, the *Daily Texan.* "And then you have all these credit card companies saying, 'Look, we're going to extend you a thousand dollars in credit.'" Her freshman year, Copp charged about $2,000 on six credit cards, even though her father gave her tuition money plus $600 a month for expenses. Spending the $2,000 was easy, Copp says: two trips to New Orleans, new outfits for sorority parties, and a good many pitchers of beer. Lawrence Burt, UT's financial aid chief, remembers an even more vivid example of lifestyle debt: He once saw a student in the financial aid line talking on a cellular phone.

Keeping up with the Coxes.   One explanation for such debt, argues economist Juliet Schor, is the widening gap between the wealthy—who dominate popular culture—and the rest of the country. More image conscious than other age groups, young people are especially prone to thinking they need to emulate the "normal" lifestyle of, say, Courteney Cox's character on TV's "Friends." But this fictional world is pretty cushy. For many, the only way to afford to live so well is through the magic of plastic.

Basic ignorance exacerbates the problem. In a recent survey by the Consumer Federation of America, 78 percent of college juniors and seniors didn't know that the best way to figure out the cost of a loan was to look at the interest rate. Card companies take advantage of the confusion. "Congratulations!" one company informed a debtor. "You have qualified to skip this month's [minimum] payment." But skipped payments benefit only the lenders, who are charging sky-high interest.

Debt is shaping the career aspirations of a generation. Desiree Saylor, a senior at the University of Texas, says she had hoped to work in academia as a physical anthropologist. "If I didn't have this debt, I'd go for it," she says. But she has $16,000 in debt and has decided on the higher-paying career of occupational therapy. Even the children of the wealthy find career options affected by their debt. The two sons of Joseph Biden, who makes six figures as a U.S. senator, have amassed $196,000 in student debt between them. The younger worked at a homeless shelter between college and graduate school, Senator Biden says, but "with his debt, there's no possibility he could take a job there." With a third of all medical school graduates owing more than $75,000, few can work in low-paying health clinics.

Of course, given the long-term benefits [of a college degree], the vast majority of college students are investing very wisely. And young Austinites know well the inspiring story of Richard Linklater, who filmed the acclaimed movie *Slacker* there by charging $23,000 on credit cards.

On the other hand, many incur college debt and never get a degree. Among the quarter of students with the least money, only about 1 in 5 will get a bachelor's degree within six years of entering. And Linklater's success is hardly the norm. Linklater says aspiring filmmakers regularly approach him, stacks of credit cards in hand, with "nothing now, or probably ever, to show for it."

After Reading

Word Connections

1. "Reacting to growing costs, Congress through the '80s and '90s expanded the student loan program, while scrimping on no-strings-attached grants." Explain the phrase *no strings attached.*

_____

_____

2. In the reading, Generation X is described as more image conscious. What is meant by *image conscious*? Give an example.

_____

_____

_____

3. Give an example of how someone can be *lured* into spending money.

_____

_____

_____

Connecting Meaning

1. According to the author, what is the financial problem of Generation X?

_____

_____

_____

_____

2. What are the facts that explain why this is a problem for Generation X?

_____

_____

_____

_____

_____

_____

3. What solution is offered by the author? If none is offered, what do you think is a possible solution?

_____

_____

_____

_____

4. Explain what the author means by "debt is shaping the career aspirations of a generation."

_____

_____

_____

_____

Selection 2

Downsize Your Debt: Is Credit-Card Debt Cramping Your Cash Flow?

GLINDA BRIDGEFORTH

Before Reading

Before you read "Downsize Your Debt: Is Credit-Card Debt Cramping Your Cash Flow?" predict the topic, scan the story, and think about your cash flow. Are you aware of your spending patterns? Do they need to be changed? Relate your experiences with debt to the author's suggestions to solve debt problems.

Words to Preview

deprivation	*(n.)* the act of taking something away, loss
holistic	*(adj.)* concerned with wholes rather than separation of parts
sabotage	*(v.)* to destroy
affirmation	*(n.)* a positive statement
constitute	*(v.)* to amount to, equal
solvency	*(n.)* state of being able to meet financial obligations
prioritize	*(v.)* to arrange or deal with in order of importance

During Reading

As you read "Downsize Your Debt: Is Credit-Card Debt Cramping Your Cash Flow?" continue to predict and visualize the ideas and monitor your comprehension. What is the problem the author is explaining? What facts are given about downsizing your debt? What solution, if any, is offered by the author?

I s credit-card debt cramping your cash flow? By raising your prosperity consciousness, you can ease the money squeeze and get on the path to financial freedom.

Mention the word downsizing and what usually comes to mind are negative images of job loss and financial deprivation. But downsizing can be viewed another way—as a carefully structured plan to reduce and even eliminate your debt.

There's no special secret to achieving effective debt reduction, but there is a path you should follow. As a financial counselor, I guide my clients in moving beyond practical skills, like checkbook balancing and budgeting, to exploring the emotional and spiritual traits that subconsciously affect their spending habits. Identifying and understanding your belief systems and attitudes about money and the core issues of why you create so much debt are essential to putting a successful debt-reduction plan in place.

I recall one client who had purchased a fur coat she could ill afford. At the time of her "retail therapy," she was angry and depressed because her husband was out of town on their wedding anniversary. After reviewing her spending patterns and leveling with herself, she finally acknowledged that many of her impulse-shopping binges were efforts to make herself feel better about voids caused by unmet emotional needs.

If you're tired of being overwhelmed by debt, living from paycheck to paycheck, and wondering why you can't get ahead, there is a way out. When practiced consistently, these five simple steps are guaranteed to bring down the size of your debt.

1. Think Holistically. If you want to change your spending patterns, you'll have to change your thought patterns.

   - Work on developing a more positive belief system about money. Because our beliefs are typically formed in childhood, we tend to either emulate or go 180 degrees from what we have seen, heard, or absorbed from family members, friends, and others close to us. What childhood experiences regarding money are you re-creating as an adult? What effects are they having on your current financial life? For instance, if you were raised with the message "Money is the root of all evil," you could subconsciously believe that money is bad. This could explain why you quickly get rid of money by spending it or giving it away. Or you may believe "I just don't understand money," when in fact, it's high finance that you don't understand. Join the club! To understand your finances better, you don't need a Ph.D. in economics. Some simple arithmetic will do. Get clear about how much money comes in and goes out monthly. Balance that checkbook. These very basic measures can help keep you "in the light" about your money and make you feel more financially empowered.

- Boost your self-esteem. The way we handle money is a direct reflection of how we feel about ourselves. Dr. Brenda Wade, a San Francisco psychologist, recalls working with a millionaire client who wouldn't pay her Neiman Marcus bill. This particular woman's inner critic was constantly telling her that she wasn't good enough, smart enough, or successful enough. Her sense of self-worth was so low that she always found ways to sabotage herself. One way was by not paying her bills, which created unnecessary drama and chaos in her life. For women who chronically need to raise their self-esteem, Wade suggests sitting quietly and affirming to yourself "I am enough; I have enough; I know enough; I do enough." Repetition is a powerful way to reprogram your subconscious to accept these ideas as reality.

- Develop a prosperity consciousness. Meditate on positive affirmations that can help you envision a life of abundance. . . . Visualize prosperity and success. Use your imagination to see your life as you would like it to be. Hold the vision of yourself being surrounded by loving, supportive, and nurturing family and friends. See yourself living in your dream home and having an emergency savings account that will tide you over in case of need. Let your imagination expand as you consider all your heart's desires and see yourself with all your needs and wants met.

2. Stop Creating New Debt. Debt puts you in a rut, so stop digging! Make a personal commitment to yourself each morning: I will not create debt today. Reward yourself with something small at the end of the month when you've kept your promise. What constitutes "small" depends, of course, on your cash flow. It could be a new compact disc or taking a ninety-minute, uninterrupted bubble bath! These strategies will help you cut down on your debting:

- Don't play games with yourself. Just because it's on sale doesn't mean you should buy it. Ask yourself, "Do I really need another pair of leopard stretch pants?"

- Close extra charge accounts. Don't use them to fall back on credit; leap forward to solvency! You need only one or two credit cards.

- Leave your credit cards at home. Put them in the freezer, a safe-deposit box, or the kitty-litter box—anywhere that makes it inconvenient to get to them. Don't memorize or carry the account number with you, either. That information could provide unbearable temptation during one your momentary "slips."

3. Set a Goal and a Target Date. You need a good reason to be debt-free. What do you keep postponing because you don't have the money? Maybe it's purchasing a new home, taking a Caribbean vacation, or

starting an investment portfolio. Whatever creates a burning desire and motivates you to remain disciplined is the perfect goal. And when do you want it? In the year 2010? Be specific. Pick a target date, a time to shoot for. Make sure that at the end of each day you've done something to advance toward your objective. For example, did you take your lunch to work instead of eating out with coworkers? Did you resist the temptation to make an impulse purchase? Acknowledge all these small victories as stepping stones to your ultimate success.

4. Make a Plan. A spending plan or a budget is the road map for your journey to financial freedom. How do you chart your course? First, identify in detail all the areas where you expect to spend money in the upcoming month. Place a picture of your goal in front of you as you create the plan. It will help you prioritize and make choices as you determine how to spend next month's income. Keep in mind that the spending plan is not cast in stone. It should be specific, yet flexible. Your plan must include a record of every cent you spend, especially the "easy" money you withdraw from the ATM. Get receipts for everything. Track your spending by category. For example, "food" would include meals eaten out for breakfast, lunch, or dinner; groceries; even snacks. Total and analyze all your spending for the month. Remember, it doesn't count if you don't add it up! Consider using a budgeting software program like Quicken. Evaluate each category to determine whether you were on target, you overspent, or you deprived yourself.

5. Get Support. Seek financial counseling. There are several types to consider. Debtors Anonymous, based on the twelve-step principles used in Alcoholics Anonymous, is a national support group for anyone with compulsive debt and spending problems (check the white pages of the telephone directory in your area). The Consumer Credit Counseling Service is a nonprofit organization that strives to educate, counsel, and promote the prudent use of credit as a tool for financial planning. A financial consultant can provide one-on-one cash-flow management and debt-management coaching and counseling services. Or ask friends for a referral. All of these are good choices to provide direction, guidance, and encouragement. You'll see that you're not alone. You'll no longer use the excuse that your debt was really caused by aliens who turned out to be your parents who never taught you how to manage money.

Remember, it's important to live a balanced life, so don't be too hard on yourself for the wreckage created in the past. Forgive yourself and love yourself. Now, go clean out the freezer and make room for those credit cards, because you're on your way to solvency!

After Reading

Word Connections

1. What two meanings for *downsizing* are given in the selection?

   _____

   _____

   _____

   _____

2. Define *retail therapy*.

   _____

   _____

3. What does *prosperity consciousness* mean?

   _____

   _____

   _____

   _____

Connecting Meaning

1. What is the problem stated in the selection?

   _____

   _____

   _____

   _____

   _____

2. What are the five steps presented as a solution to this problem?

   _____

   _____

   _____

   _____

   _____

3. How does the way you handle money reflect how you feel about yourself?

_____

_____

_____

_____

Selection 3   ## Choose a Debt Consolidator Carefully
VALERIE LYNN GRAY

Before Reading   Before you read, "Choose a Debt Consolidator Carefully," predict the topic, scan the story, and think about how to find a way out of debt. Do you think you would use a credit counselor if you were in serious debt? Relate your knowledge and opinion about ending debt to the author's information.

Words to Preview

consolidate	(v.)	to combine
prestigious	(adj.)	having the high regard of others
taint	(v.)	to spoil
disperse	(v.)	to scatter in different directions
tag line	(n.)	often-repeated phrase
haste	(n.)	rapid action or motion
clarification	(n.)	act of making easier to understand
affiliate	(v.)	to associate as a member or employee

During Reading   As you read "Choose a Debt Consolidator Carefully," continue to predict and visualize the ideas and monitor your comprehension. What problem is the author explaining? What facts are given about choosing a debt consolidator? What tips on evaluating a credit counseling service are presented?

Y ou've probably seen the ads that claim to consolidate your credit-card debt with no upfront fees. Some say they'll reduce interest rates and give you lower monthly payments. If you're in a rut, this may seem like an easy alternative—better than dealing with banks or credit card companies. But if you don't do your research and rush into signing your debt over to a third party, you could end up ruining your credit.

That's what happened to fifty-eight-year-old Jacqueline Brown*, a professor of philosophy in Atlanta. Brown, a single parent, found herself $35,000 in debt with eight credit cards after sending her daughter to a prestigious law school. Her $73,000 a year salary wasn't enough to handle the $161,000 in tuition plus expenses. When she saw a classified ad offering to make her payments easier, she thought she'd found a quick-fix answer to her problems.

"It wasn't that I was behind in my bills, [but] I was looking for the lower interest rates that would help me lower my monthly payments," Brown explains. Her interest rates averaged about 19 percent for each card. She called an 800 number and was put in touch with a representative who explained how the service worked. Brown would make one payment to the service which, in turn, would negotiate lower interest rates and make monthly payments on her behalf to the creditors. To Brown, it seemed less costly than dealing with a bank or taking out a loan. She received a contract in the mail, quickly signed it, faxed it back, and mailed her first payment of $800.

"I sent payments ahead of time to make sure all accounts were paid," she recalls. A few months later, she became concerned by late-bill notices and called one of her credit card companies, who revealed that it was reluctant to do business with the service, since it was for-profit. She later found the contract to be misleading; she was told that no upfront fees would be charged, yet her first payment was actually held for fees. That made payments to her creditors late and tainted her credit record.

"I called the Better Business Bureau to report the company, and in the meantime, I started making payments myself to get my accounts caught up," she says. The company did not give her a good reason for the late payments but said that since they processed thousands of accounts, a few may have slipped through the cracks. The Better Business Bureau had received dozens of complaints against the company and gave it an unsatisfactory rating. Brown wrote to each of her creditors, explaining that she dropped the service and asked that her credit be restored while she made payments directly.

What Brown experienced is not unusual, says Bud Hibbs, a consumer credit expert and author of *The American Credit System: Guilty until Proven Innocent*. "Usually when people go to these services, they are already in trouble," he says. "What most credit counseling services do is collect your money and discount it back to the creditors usually at a rate that averages 12–15 percent. To me, that says collection agency—someone is getting paid a commission to collect money and disperse it to the creditors. They are really looking after the creditors' best interest, not the consumer's," Hibbs notes, adding that in most cases, credit counseling services are doing what consumers can really do on their own.

*Jacqueline Brown is a pseudonym.

"I tell consumers to stay away from these services because if you owe X amount of dollars and the counselor sets you up on a repayment program, there is no incentive to get you in and out of the program in a hurry," counsels Hibbs. "They will try to keep you in for an average of three to five years because they are collecting a commission." Consumers also need to be aware that a tag line will be put on the credit report that states "account in credit counseling," which is seen as a negative factor.

Hibbs conducted a survey of major lenders in the country, including major banks and auto lenders, who admitted that such a tag line would keep them from loaning money to that individual. "When you're dealing with independent services, you really don't have any idea what they're doing with your money, how they're handling it, or even if they're paying your debt. There's nothing that guarantees you anything, so my advice is to stay away from them," Hibbs warns.

Brown has learned her lesson after losing her initial payment and trying to reestablish her credit. "I signed the contract in haste. In my need to satisfy an immediate desire, I didn't make an intelligent decision. A five-year-old would have known better," she admits. Brown advises consumers to take their time, never to sign and send a contract within the same day of receiving it, and not to send it back by fax or overnight delivery. "Take the time to understand what you are signing," she says.

Before signing away your debt to a credit service, consider these suggestions from Janice Grassi, executive director of the Better Business Bureau in Long Island, New York:

- Find out if the service is truly trying to consolidate your debt or if they are actually trying to offer you a loan. A loan could get you even deeper in debt if the interest rate is higher than what you were paying.

- A good service should offer budget counseling and debt repayment as part of the package. Get names, titles, and phone numbers of everyone who is supposed to work with you, and ask specific questions.

- Watch out for advance and up-front fees, and look for hidden charges within the contract. Review the contract carefully, and if you don't understand the language, ask for clarification—in writing, if possible.

- In many states, the service should have a nonprofit status. Your creditors may not deal with the service otherwise, and they may not be looking out for your interest.

- Check out the company with the attorney general's office and the Better Business Bureau to find out if any complaints have been filed. Don't confuse the BBB with Better Businesses of America. The two are not affiliated.

- Ask the service what companies they deal with, and call those companies to see how satisfactory their performance has been.

- Best yet, call your creditors yourself. Explain your circumstances and ask for lower payments. Most will try to help.

After Reading

Word Connections

1. What is a *collection agency*?

    _____

    _____

    _____

    _____

    _____

2. What is meant by *nonprofit status*?

    _____

    _____

    _____

    _____

Connecting Meaning

1. What is the problem stated in the selection?

    _____

    _____

    _____

    _____

2. What are the facts to explain why this is a problem?

    _____

    _____

    _____

    _____

    _____

    _____

3. What are some of the tips that help you to avoid the problem?

_____

_____

_____

_____

_____

_____

_____

_____

_____

Portfolio Suggestions

Integrating Ideas

What does it mean to live within your means? Do you think people today are willing to live within their means? If not, why? Reflect on these ideas in writing or in class discussion.

Extending Concepts

You may not realize exactly how you spend your money. Keep track of your spending for a week. Analyze your spending, and develop a personal budget for the next three months.

Collaborative Activity

Research various credit cards from different banks. Gather information on the interest rates, late charges, minimum payments, cash advances, credit limit, and any other consumer advantages. Choose the credit card you feel is the best, and explain why.

Additional Portfolio Suggestion

Develop an essay discussing the problems of television and Internet shopping. What solutions would you propose to eliminate these problems?

▪ ▪ ▪ ▪ Chapter Summary Graphic Organizer

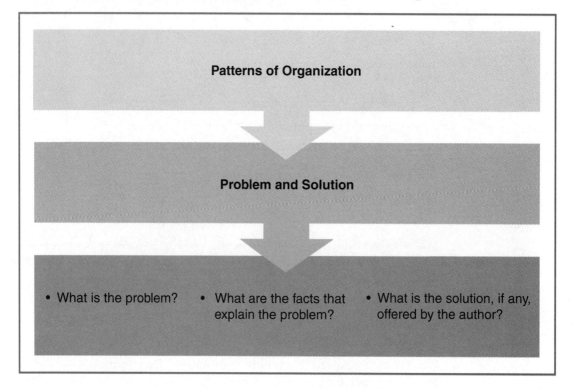

Patterns of Organization

Problem and Solution

- What is the problem?
- What are the facts that explain the problem?
- What is the solution, if any, offered by the author?

Review

Unit 4
Patterns of Organization

In this unit, you examined several patterns of organization used by authors and the signals associated with them. In each pattern, the main idea is supported by major and minor supporting details. These patterns of organization helped you to make sense of the readings. Authors may choose one pattern or a combination of patterns to explain the main idea:

- Chronological Order and Listing
  - Chronological order organizes information according to the time order in which it occurs.
  - Listing is used by authors to give details that support the main idea.

- Definition and Illustration/Example
  - A definition pattern answers the question *what is it*? by giving the precise meaning of words and ideas.
  - Illustrations or examples are often given when an author wants to create a clearer picture of the main idea.

- Comparison and Contrast
  - The comparison pattern connects two or more people, places, things, or ideas by describing how they are alike.
  - The contrast pattern examines two or more people, places, things, or ideas by describing the differences between them.

- Cause and Effect
  - The cause and effect pattern is used by authors to discuss the reasons why something has happened or will happen in the future.

- Problem and Solution
  - The problem and solution pattern presents a problem to be identified, considered, explained, or solved. The solution may be offered, or it may be left to the reader to think further about the problem.

Unit Review Graphic Organizer

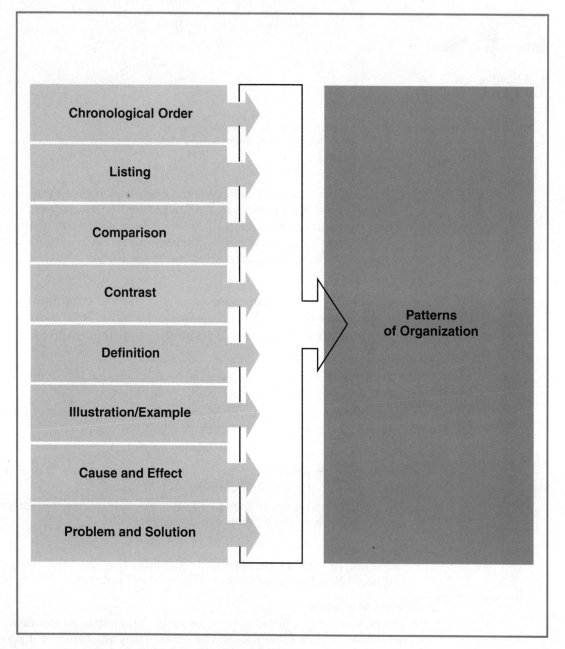

Chronological Order

Listing

Comparison

Contrast

Definition

Illustration/Example

Cause and Effect

Problem and Solution

Patterns
of Organization

Portfolio Suggestion

In your outside reading, find one example of each pattern of organization presented in Unit 4.

5

Reading Critically

Theme of Readings: *Search for Truth*

Truth comes only to a prepared mind.

<small>UNKNOWN</small>

■■■■■ Search for Truth

What is truth? Truth is defined not only as what is proven but also as what is accepted. Before the 1500s, for example, it was a generally accepted truth that the earth was flat. Christopher Columbus helped to prove this accepted statement incorrect, and the earth's true shape was redefined as round. When people search for the truth, they sort fact from opinion, inferring ideas from accurate information and observations.

For many people, seeking the truth is a lifelong pursuit, performed on a daily basis. Philosophers, theologians, and journalists explore and study the truth about life, love, and death. Judges, lawyers, and juries seek to uncover the truth about crime or injustice. Scientists seek truth through research and experimentation. Insurance companies seek the truth about clients' claims and liabilities. Journalists and scholars work to discover and write about the truth.

When we read, we, too, need to sort out what is fact and what is opinion, speculation, or fictional invention. We need to question and evaluate critically the truth of what we read, not automatically to accept all statements. Consider, for example, reports of paranormal phenomena, such as UFO sightings, ghostly encounters, ESP, and psychic predictions. These reports are plentiful, but are they true? How trustworthy are the facts presented, and how reliable are the author and his or her sources?

Advertising also can be an attractive blend of fact and opinion, truth and fantasy. Every day we are bombarded with carefully crafted messages that try to persuade us to buy certain products and services. We as consumers must seek the truth in advertisements, sorting facts from opinions.

Reading Critically

As a critical reader, you must look beyond the printed word to the information given, the sources used, and the evidence provided. Reading critically involves sorting facts from opinions. The ability to identify the facts presented by an author will help you to make inferences. These facts, combined with your knowledge and experience, will allow you to interpret, or infer, the author's message.

A fact is something that can be proven as true by observation or written records. Statements of fact do not reflect personal feelings or attitudes. Facts are often reported using dates, numbers, statistics, and measurements: "In 1961, Yuri Gargarin became the world's first spaceman as he orbited the earth once, remaining in space for one hour, forty-eight minutes."

In contrast, an opinion cannot be proven as true. Statements of opinion give a person's view of an idea and reflect personal feelings, attitudes, or beliefs. For example, "John believes there are extraterrestrial beings living on earth" is a statement of opinion. An opinion may be labeled as informed or uninformed. An informed opinion is based on knowledge or experience with the subject and provides supporting details. An uninformed opinion lacks the knowledge, experience, or details to support it.

By providing facts, details, or opinions, an author supports the main idea. However, not everything an author wants you to understand is directly stated. You need to read between the lines by using clues, knowledge, and experience to make an inference about the author's unstated points. An inference is an educated guess based on the information presented.

Having the ability to distinguish between fact and opinion and to infer information will help you to read critically and effectively.

Unit Objectives

After completing the unit, you will be able to

1. **Distinguish between a fact and an opinion.**

2. **Construct an inference from information given.**

13

Fact and Opinion

Theme of Readings: *Strange but True?*

There's a little truth in all jive, and a little jive in all truth.

LEONARD BARNES

■ ■ ■ ■ Strange but True?

Do you believe in paranormal phenomena? Events that go beyond the normal experience or have no scientific explanation are considered paranormal. ESP, ghostly sightings, UFOs, or psychic abilities are among a wide variety of phenomena that fascinate people from all walks of life. These strange experiences are sometimes blindly accepted as true. They are also examined for facts that explain the phenomena as a natural occurrence or a hoax. A few strange happenings remain unexplained.

Some strange things are known to be true because they have been clearly documented and observed. *The Guinness Book of World Records* or *Ripley's Believe It or Not* give examples of oddities such as thirty-inch fingernails or two-headed goats. Other strange occurrences are not as clearly documented. Questions arise, for example, about crop circles, spontaneous human combustion, or skyfalls—questions about the nature of these phenomena and their causes. Personal beliefs, attitudes, and the quality of the evidence affect how unusual claims are evaluated.

Many people note the wide variety of paranormal experiences reported and believe that these phenomena point to larger truths beyond our everyday experience. In the end, we often listen to fascinating, interesting, and strange stories and are left wondering, are they true?

Chapter Objective

After completing this chapter you will be able to distinguish between a fact and an opinion.

■ ■ ■ ■ Focus on Fact and Opinion

In the information age, text is presented in books, magazines, journals, or online. Boldly presented, well-written, and visually pleasing information catches your attention, but a critical reader must look beyond the presentation to determine whether any particular piece of information is fact or opinion.

Fact

A fact is a statement that can be proven as true by observation or written records. Direct observation may provide evidence of truth. "The sky looks blue today," is an example of an observable fact. A writer may present statements as fact, but these claims may not be true. It is up to the reader to decide if the facts presented can be verified. Facts may be verified through written records such as dictionaries or reference books. They are often reported using dates, numbers, statistics, and measurements. For example, the statement, "A spider never gets stuck on the sticky threads of its own web because it keeps its own body constantly oiled," may be checked for accuracy by looking in an encyclopedia or a book about spiders.

Reading critically does not mean that you must necessarily prove every fact that you read. It is enough to keep a critical eye open and question whether the statement can be determined to be true or false. A factual statement does not reflect the author's personal feelings or attitudes. In addition, it is important to note the author's qualifications in the subject area. For instance, many medical doctors are expert sources on their particular specialty in medicine, and professional athletes are expert authorities on their particular sport. By critically reviewing for feelings and attitudes and checking the sources, you can determine whether a statement is fact.

Opinion

In contrast to a fact, an opinion cannot be proven as true or false. An opinion states a writer's personal feelings, attitudes, or beliefs about a subject. Words used when stating opinions mean different things to different people. Individual definitions of words such as beautiful, good, bad, or ugly vary. For example, "Using alternative medicine is bad for your health," is a statement of opinion. People would agree or disagree with this statement depending upon their belief in alternative medicine. Because of the differences in beliefs, this statement cannot be proven as true or false.

Opinions fall into two categories—informed or uninformed. A person with an informed opinion has some experience or knowledge with the topic and provides evidence in support of his or her opinion. An uninformed opinion is a statement made without any background knowledge or experience. It may also be based on someone else's statements that may not be accurate or reliable. When a writer discusses a subject or presents an argument, an informed opinion carries more weight than an uninformed opinion. To be a critical and effective reader, you must be able to distinguish between a fact and an opinion.

Short Exercises: Fact and Opinion

Read each paragraph and complete the questions that follow.

1. You've told this story a million times, and everybody still thinks you're nuts. "There I was, minding my own business, leaning against the bar at La Casa de los Marinos on Decatur one night, when there he was: the ghost of James Dean. He gave that famous goofy little giggle, and then he lit up a cigarette and bought us each a beer. Swear on my Aunt Lizzie's grave it happened . . . "

   Larry Montz doesn't think you're nuts. In fact, Montz says that a majority of the buildings in the Quarter—not to mention a fair number around other parts of town—are laden with spirits from beyond the grave.

   Montz is New Orleans' bona fide ghostbuster, whose "Hauntings Today" business consists of twice-daily "ghost expedition" tours, a bimonthly newsletter, and a cadre of specialists who answer anywhere from eight to ten calls a week to investigate things that go bump in the kitchen. (George Gurtner)

   Why would Larry Montz accept the story about James Dean as true?

   _____

   _____

   _____

   What factual information is given about Larry Montz?

   _____

   _____

   _____

   _____

2. Prior to a Los Angeles earthquake in 1990, I was in graduate school working in the Learning and Memory Lab on the fifth floor of the USC Neuroscience Building with several other students and three calm rabbits. Suddenly the rabbits became noticeably agitated. They started hopping around in their cages wildly for around five minutes, right before a 5.2 earthquake sent the whole building rolling and swaying.

   After my experience with the anxious rabbits, I learned that, since the beginning of recorded history, virtually every culture in the world has reported observations of unusual animal behavior prior to earthquakes (and—to a lesser extent—volcanic eruptions), but conventional science has never been able to explain the phenomenon adequately. Nonetheless, the Chinese and Japanese have employed such sightings for hundreds of years as an important part of a nationally orchestrated earthquake warning system, with some success. (David Jay Brown)

   State the facts of David Brown's experience with animal behavior.

   _____

   _____

   _____

   _____

   _____

   What is the Chinese and Japanese opinion of the usefulness of animal behavior as a predictor of earthquakes?

   _____

   _____

   _____

   _____

3. Arthritis "cures" range from the venom of snakes and ants to honey, liver, and herbs. Arthritics have been advised to bury themselves in uranium-bearing soil, to sit in abandoned mine shafts, and to stand naked under 1,000 watt light bulbs during a full moon—and pay for the privilege! They have been wrapped in manure, soaked in mud, and bathed in cod liver oil, kerosene, peppermint oil, and even WD-40. Others have suggested splitting open a frog and rubbing it on the skin or sprinkling the afflicted area with "moon dust."

   Medical quackery is no joke. It affects all of us and exists in every area of health care. Tragedy arises every year because quack practitioners have caused adults and children to turn away from proper medical treatment for countless treatable diseases like Hodgkin's disease, diabetes, leukemia, and meningitis. (Al Seckel and Pat Linse)

What are some remedies believed to cure arthritis?

_____

_____

_____

What opinion do the authors hold about these types of medical treatments?

_____

_____

_____

4. The ritual of firewalking is an ancient one that can be categorized as a wonderous performance with a powerful effect on believers. Being able to walk on fire unharmed is seen by some as an act of faith; by others as the power of positive thinking; and by still others as the power of the mind over matter.

Firewalking is an ancient religious ritual that is still practiced in present times. Corbis/ Bettmann Archive)

However, David G. Willey, an instructor of physics at the University of Pittsburgh, is a veteran firewalker. His explanation for how walkers like himself avoid painful burns relies on physics. "A firewalk of short length is something any physically fit person could do. It does not need a particular state of mind. Rather, it is the short time of contact and the low thermal capacity and conductivity of the coals that are important." While the coal bed may reach extremely high temperatures, it still takes time for heat to flow from the coals to the flesh. (Dan Noelle)

What facts does David G. Willey use to explain the ability to firewalk?

_____

_____

_____

_____

Some people have an opinion differing from Willey's explanation about the ability to firewalk. What is their explanation?

_____

_____

_____

_____

5. In 1982, a professor at a Vietnamese university was exploring the slopes of Mom Ray Mountain near the Cambodian border when he stumbled upon a strange footprint. Measuring ten-by-six inches, it was wider than any human foot and had longer toes. Some speculated that the footprint might belong to a legendary creature called Ngoing Rung, or "Wildman."

To this day, no one knows for certain who—or what—made the footprint. Is "Wildman" an ape? Or more tantalizing, could it be a human ancestor still hiding in Asian forests? (Leslie Alan Horwitz)

State the facts about the discovery made on the slopes of Mom Ray Mountain.

_____

_____

_____

_____

What opinions do people have about the origin of the footprint?

_____

_____

_____

■ ■ ■ ■ Reading Selections

Selection 1

Crop Circles and Aliens: What's the Evidence?

CARL SAGAN

Before Reading

Before you read, "Crop Circles and Aliens: What's the Evidence?" predict the topic, scan the story, and think about the possibility of the existence of aliens. What have you read or heard about UFOs? Do you believe in extraterrestrial beings? Relate your opinion about alien beings to that of Carl Sagan, a noted author and professor of astronomy and space sciences.

Words to Preview

languish	(v.) to become weak
lenticular	(adj.) shaped like a double-convex lens
garish	(adj.) loud and flashy
anomalous propagation	(n.) radio traveling curved paths
rogue	(n.) unreliable person
charlatan	(n.) quack or fraud
shoddy	(adj.) of poor quality
saga	(n.) a long, detailed report
tangent	(adj.) touching but not intersecting
symmetry	(n.) balanced or mirrored images
depredation	(n.) damage or loss
dowser	(n.) a person who uses a divining rod to search for underground water
orgone	(n.) an energy found in nature that can be captured by a boothlike device
inept	(adj.) not appropriate; incompetent
doggerel	(n.) clumsy verse
meticulous	(adj.) extremely careful or precise

During Reading

As you read "Crop Circles and Aliens: What's the Evidence?" continue to predict and visualize the ideas and monitor your comprehension. How does the author explain the existence of crop circles and UFOs? Think about the facts Carl Sagan uses to support his explanation.

T he phrase "flying saucer" was coined when I was in high school. The newspapers were full of stories about ships from beyond, in the skies of Earth. It seemed pretty believable to me.

Many people seemed to see flying saucers: sober pillars of the community, police officers, commercial airplane pilots, military personnel. And—apart from a few harumphs and giggles—I couldn't find any counterarguments. How could all these eyewitnesses be mistaken?

What's more, the saucers had been picked up on radar, and pictures had been taken of them. You could see the photos in newspapers and glossy magazines. There were even reports about crashed flying saucers and little alien bodies with perfect teeth stiffly languishing in Air Force freezers.

In college, in the early 1950s, I began to learn a little about how science works—the secrets of its great success: how rigorous the standards of evidence must be if we are really to know something is true; how many false starts and dead ends have plagued human thinking; how our biases can color our interpretation of the evidence; how belief systems widely held and supported by the political, religious and academic hierarchies often turn out to be not just slightly in error but grotesquely wrong.

Everything hinges on the matter of evidence. On so important a question as UFOs, the evidence must be airtight. The more we want it to be true, the more careful we have to be. No witness's say-so is good enough. People make mistakes. People play practical jokes. People stretch the truth for money, attention, or fame. People occasionally misunderstand what they're seeing. People sometimes even see things that aren't there.

Essentially all the UFO cases were anecdotes—something asserted. Most people honestly reported what they saw, but what they saw were often natural—if unfamiliar—phenomena. Some UFO sightings turned out to be unconventional aircraft; conventional aircraft with unusual lighting patterns; high-altitude balloons; luminescent insects; planets seen under unusual atmospheric conditions; optical mirages and loomings; lenticular clouds; ball lightning; sun dogs; meteors, including green fireballs; and artificial satellites, nose cones, and rocket boosters spectacularly reentering the atmosphere. (There are so many artificial satellites up there that they're always making garish displays somewhere in the world. Two or three decay every day in the Earth's atmosphere, the flaming debris often visible to the naked eye.) Just conceivably, a few might be small comets dissipating in the upper air. At least some radar reports were due to anomalous propagation—radio waves traveling curved paths due to atmospheric temperature inversions. You could have simultaneous visual and radar sightings without there being any "there" there.

There was the suspicion that the field attracted rogues and charlatans. Many UFO photos turned out to be fakes—small models hanging by thin threads, often photographed in a double exposure. A UFO seen by thousands of people at a football game turned out to be a college fraternity prank—a piece of cardboard, some candles, and a thin plastic bag that dry cleaning comes in, all cobbled together to make a rudimentary hot-air balloon.

How modest our expectations are about aliens—and how shoddy the standards of evidence that many of us are willing to accept—is demonstrated in the saga of the "crop circles."

Farmers or passersby would discover pictograms impressed upon fields of wheat, oats, barley, or rapeseed. Beginning with simple circles, first reported in southern England in the middle 1970s, the phenomenon progressed year by year. By the late 1980s and early 1990s, countrysides were graced by immense geometrical figures, some the size of football fields, imprinted on cereal grain before the harvest—circles tangent to circles or connected by an axis, parallel lines drooping off, "insectoids." Some of the patterns showed a central circle surrounded by four symmetrically placed smaller circles—clearly, it was concluded, caused by a flying saucer and its four landing pods.

A hoax? Impossible, almost everyone said. There were hundreds of cases. It was done sometimes in only an hour or two in the dead of night and on such a large scale. No footprints of pranksters leading toward or away from the pictograms could be found. Besides, what possible motive could there be for a hoax?

People with some scientific training examined sites, spun arguments, instituted whole journals devoted to the subject. Were the figures caused by strange whirlwinds called "columnar vortices," or even stranger ones called "ring vortices"? What about ball lightning?

But meteorological or electrical explanations became more strained, especially as the crop figures became more complex. Plainly, they were the work of UFOs, the aliens communicating to us in a geometrical language. Or perhaps it was the Devil, or the long-suffering Earth complaining about the depredations visited upon it by the hand of Man.

New Age tourists came in droves. All-night vigils were undertaken by enthusiasts equipped with audio recorders and infrared vision scopes. Print and electronic media from all over the world tracked the intrepid "cerealogists." Best-selling books on extraterrestrial crop-distorters were purchased by a breathless and admiring public. True, no saucer was actually seen settling down on the wheat, no geometrical figure was filmed in the course of being generated. But dowsers authenticated their alien origin, and channelers made contact with the entities responsible. "Orgone energy" was detected within the circles.

Questions were asked in the British Parliament. The royal family called in for special consultation Lord Solly Zuckerman, former principal scientific adviser to the Ministry of Defence. Ghosts were said to be involved, also the Knights Templar of Malta and other secret societies. The Ministry of Defence was covering up the matter. A few inept and inelegant circles were judged to be attempts by the military to throw the public off the track. The tabloid press had a field day. The *Daily Mirror* hired a farmer and his son to make five circles in hope of tempting a rival London tabloid, the *Daily Express,* into reporting the story. The *Express,* in this case at least, was not taken in.

"Cerealogical" organizations grew and splintered. Competing groups sent each other intimidating doggerel. Accusations were made of incompetence or worse. The number of crop "circles" rose into the thousands. The phenomenon spread to the United States, Canada, Bulgaria, Hungary, Japan, the Netherlands. The pictograms, especially the more complex of them, began to be cited increasingly in arguments for alien visitation. Strained connections were drawn to the "face" on Mars. One scientist of my acquaintance wrote to me that extremely sophisticated mathematics was hidden in these figures; they could only be the result of a superior intelligence. In fact, one matter on which almost all of the contending cerealogists agreed was that the later crop figures were much too complex and elegant to be due to mere human intervention, much less to some ragged and irresponsible hoaxers. Extraterrestrial intelligence was apparent at a glance.

In 1991, Doug Bower and Dave Chorley, two blokes from Southampton, announced that they had been making crop figures for fifteen years. They dreamed it up over stout one evening in their regular pub, The Percy Hobbs. They had been amused by UFO reports and thought it might be fun to spoof the UFO gullibles. At first, they flattened the wheat with the heavy steel bar that Bower used as a security device on the back door of his picture-framing shop. Later on, they used planks and ropes. Their first efforts took only a few minutes. But, being inveterate pranksters as well as serious artists, the challenge began to grow on them. Gradually, they designed and executed more and more demanding figures.

At first, no one seemed to notice. There were no media reports. Their artforms were neglected by the tribe of UFOlogists. They were on the verge of abandoning crop circles to move on to some other, more emotionally rewarding, hoax when, suddenly, crop circles caught on.

Bower and Chorley were delighted, especially when scientists and others began to announce their considered judgment that no merely human intelligence could be responsible.

Carefully, they planned more elaborate nocturnal excursions, sometimes following meticulous diagrams they had prepared in watercolors. They closely tracked their interpreters. When a local meteorologist deduced a kind of whirlwind because all of the crops were deflected downward in a clockwise circle, they confounded him by making a new figure with an exterior ring flattened counterclockwise.

Soon other crop figures appeared in southern England and elsewhere. Copycat hoaxers had appeared. Bower and Chorley carved out a responsive message in wheat: "WE ARE NOT ALONE." But some took this to be a genuine extraterrestrial message (although it would have been better had it read "YOU ARE NOT ALONE"). Doug and Dave began signing their art works with two Ds; even this was attributed to a mysterious alien purpose.

Bower's nocturnal disappearances aroused the suspicions of his wife, Ilene. Only with great difficulty—Ilene accompanied Dave and Doug one night and then joined the credulous in admiring their handiwork the next day—was she convinced that his absences were, in the marital sense, innocent.

Eventually, Bower and Chorley tired of the increasingly elaborate prank. While in excellent physical condition, they were both in their 60s now and a little old for nocturnal commando operations in the field of unknown, and often unsympathetic, farmers. They may have been annoyed at the fame and fortune accrued by those who merely photographed their art and announced aliens to be the artists. And they worried that, if they delayed much longer, no statement of theirs would be believed.

So they confessed. They demonstrated before reporters how they made even the most elaborate insectoid patterns. You might think that never again would it be argued that a sustained hoax over many years is impossible, and never again would we hear that no one could possibly be motivated to deceive the gullible into thinking that aliens exist. But the media paid brief attention. Cerealogists urged them to go easy—after all, they were depriving many of the pleasure of imagining wondrous happenings.

Since then, other crop-circle hoaxers have kept at it. As always, the confession of the hoax is greatly overshadowed by the sustained initial excitement. Many have heard of the pictograms in cereal grains and their alleged UFO connection, but they draw a blank when the names of Bower and Chorley—and the very idea that the whole business may be a hoax—are raised.

After Reading

Word Connections

1. "Many people seemed to see flying saucers: sober pillars of the community, police officers, commercial airline pilots, military personnel."

   What does the phrase *sober pillars of the community* mean?

   _____

   _____

   _____

2. What is a *cerealogist*?

   _____

   _____

3. "You might think that never again would it be argued that a sustained hoax over many years is impossible." Define *sustained*.

   _____

   _____

Connecting Meaning

1. What facts does Sagan give to explain UFO sightings?

_____

_____

_____

_____

_____

2. Does Sagan believe that crop circles are real or a hoax? State the evidence he gives to support his opinion.

_____

_____

_____

_____

_____

3. Do you believe in crop circles and aliens? Support your opinion.

_____

_____

_____

Selection 2

Source of Mysterious Skyfalls Unknown

RANDALL FLOYD

Before Reading

Before you read "Source of Mysterious Skyfalls Unknown," predict the topic, scan the story, and think about the reality of things falling from the sky. Have you ever heard or read about strange things dropping to the earth? Relate what you know to the information given.

Words to Preview

frayed	*(adj.)* worn away or into shreds	
substantiate	*(v.)* to support with proof or evidence	
speculation	*(n.)* a conclusion or opinion reached by incomplete evidence	
inundate	*(v.)* to overwhelm	
consumption	*(n.)* the act of eating or drinking	

During Reading   As you read "Source of Mysterious Skyfalls Unknown," continue to predict and visualize the ideas and monitor your comprehension. What is a skyfall and how is it explained?

L ate one summer night in 1954, Hewlett Hodges of Sylacauga, Alabama, was lying on her sofa listening to the radio when a large metallic ball crashed through the roof, bounced .off a table, and struck her leg.

The startled woman said the object, which weighed about ten pounds, was "hot and smoking" when it finally came to rest in a corner of her living room.

Except for some frayed nerves and a bruised leg, the elderly woman was unhurt. Mrs. Hodges had just become the first person in modern times to be struck by a meteorite.

Unverified accounts of individuals being hit by falling stars exist in nearly every country, but scientists say the odds of being hit by a meteorite are one in ten billion. Historically speaking, there is only one report, unsubstantiated, of a person being killed by a hurtling object from space—an unfortunate Italian monk in 1650.

That seems remarkable considering that millions of meteorites swarm into the Earth's atmosphere every day. Fortunately for humans, very few reach the ground. Nearly all, traveling at speeds fifty times faster than a high-powered rifle bullet, disintegrate into powder long before impact.

Occasionally, huge objects crash to earth with devastating consequences. Scientists believe Meteor Crater near Winslow, Arizona, was caused by such an impact thousands of years ago, while others contend that a colossal stone from space slammed into Siberia in 1908 and caused widespread destruction.

Such terrifying skyfalls have formed the plot for many science-fiction books and movies, including *Deep Impact* and *Armageddon*.

But meteorites are not the only celestial objects to arouse concern and speculation among earthlings. Down through the ages, stories of other spectacular skyfalls have thrilled and terrified more than a few witnesses.

In many parts of the world, frogs and toads have fallen numerous times and in monstrous numbers. So have worms, mice, snakes, bite-sized bits of meat, beans, blood, spiders, squirrels, fish, hot stones, and even cats and dogs.

Such phenomena have often been attributed to freak whirlwinds, storms, and other natural occurrences. But not always. All too often mysterious skyfalls occur whenever there are no high winds, no storm, no other natural explanation.

Such was the case in 1877, when thousands of snakes fell from a clear sky over Memphis, Tennessee. At first, investigators blamed the skyfall on winds kicked up by a hurricane off the coast, but they later dismissed the idea.

No one knew why the snakes—and nothing else—had been dropped on the city in such abundance.

Equally strange was a shower of warm stones that fell outside the offices of the *Charleston News & Observer* in Charleston, South Carolina, on September 4, 1886. The shower of stones, which struck twice within a five-hour period, shattered windows and pulverized the pavement outside the newspaper building.

Several times during the winter of 1891, residents of Valley Bend, West Virginia, found millions of unidentified white worms covering the snow. Where had the squirming creatures come from? Some witnesses swore they saw them falling from the sky.

The late nineteenth century was full of other bizarre reports of objects falling from the sky. On November 21, 1898, spider webs and spiders by the thousands dropped on Montgomery, Alabama. Some of the webs were described as several inches in diameter. The week before Christmas that same year, hundreds of frogs and toads reportedly fell on Alexandria, Virginia.

The twentieth century brought fresh reports of skyfalls. In June 1901, hundreds of small catfish, trout, and perch suddenly rained down on a cotton field belonging to Charles Raley of South Carolina.

On October 23, 1947, the town of Marksville, Louisiana, was inundated by fish—largemouth bass, sunfish, hickory shad, and minnows. The fish were described as "absolutely fresh and fit for human consumption." According to a local newspaper, the town threw a big fish fry that lasted all week.

In Shreveport, Louisiana, construction workers on July 12, 1961, had to take shelter when green peaches rained down on them from a thick cloud. No whirlwinds, tornadoes, or other high winds were reported in the area at the time. One possible explanation: an airplane flying overhead somehow lost a cargo of peaches.

After Reading

Word Connections

1. Create a concept of definition map for *phenomenon*.

   Diagram:

2. What does *armageddon* mean? Why could it be chosen for the title of a movie about skyfalls?

_____

_____

_____

_____

Connecting Meaning

1. Name at least three observable facts given in this story to substantiate skyfalls.

_____

_____

_____

_____

2. What was one opinion about the cause of green peaches raining on construction workers?

_____

_____

3. What does the author believe is the source of mysterious skyfalls?

_____

_____

4. How would you explain some of these skyfalls?

_____

_____

_____

Selection 3

Spontaneous Human Combustion (SHC)

ROBERT TODD CARROLL

Before Reading

Before you read "Spontaneous Human Combustion (SHC)," predict the topic, scan the story, and think about the mystery of SHC. Have you ever heard or read about SHC? Relate what you know to the information given.

Words to Preview	combustion	*(n.)* the process of burning
	ludicrous	*(adj.)* laughable because of obvious absurdity
	preposterous	*(adj.)* ridiculous
	skeptic	*(n.)* one who doubts or questions
	perplexed	*(adj.)* confused
	scornful	*(adj.)* treated with contempt
	attest	*(v.)* to supply or give evidence of
	implode	*(v.)* to collapse inward violently

During Reading   As you read "Spontaneous Human Combustion (SHC)," continue to predict and visualize the ideas and monitor your comprehension. Can spontaneous human combustion really happen?

The process of a human body catching fire as a result of heat generated by internal chemical action.

Many people have felt as if they were about to explode or that their bellies were on fire, but so far there are no accounts of anyone suddenly bursting into flames due to a case of spontaneous combustion originating within the body. It is true that many people have suddenly exploded or suddenly burst into flames, but these cases are all traceable to unfriendly fire from without. The very idea of a living animal, human or otherwise, igniting from spontaneous combustion in the belly or anywhere else in the body is ludicrous and preposterous. Perhaps that explains why stories of spontaneous human combustion abound in books about "mysteries."

To be fair to mystery lovers everywhere, it should be noted that spontaneous human combustion is almost exclusively reserved for corpses. Very few of the reports mention living persons as victims of such a wicked trick of nature. One tale from the seventeenth century claims a German man self-ignited due to his having drunk a lot of brandy. My guess would be that if drinking a lot of brandy caused self-combustion, there would be a lot more cases to study than this isolated report from Germany.

Skeptics do not think there are any good documented cases of **SHC,** although we admit that there are stories that claim that at least a couple hundred human beings or human corpses have spontaneously combusted. Many of the stories of corpses that have been perplexed by partially ignited bodies near unburnt rugs or furniture have been related by police investigators. "What else could it be?" they ask. Indeed, what else? Well, how about self-ignition due to dropping a lit cigarette, or ignition due to another person putting the match to a person or place. Many of the allegedly spontaneously combusted corpses are of elderly people who may have been murdered and torched by their killers or who ignited themselves accidentally.

The physical possibilities of spontaneous human combustion are remote. Not only is the body mostly water, but aside from fat tissue and methane gas, there isn't much that burns readily in a human body. To cremate a human body requires enormous amounts of heat over a long period of time. To get a chemical reaction in a human body that would lead to ignition would require some doing. The ignition point of human fat might be low, but to get the fire going would probably require an external source. If the deceased had recently eaten an enormous amount of hay that was infested with bacteria, enough heat might be generated to ignite the hay, but not much besides the gut and intestines would probably burn. Or, if the deceased had been eating the newspaper and had drunk some oil and was left to rot for a couple of weeks in a well-heated room, his gut might ignite.

I imagine that the reason some of these burnt bodies appear so strange has more to do with the difficulty of burning a human corpse than with spontaneous combustion. That a fire should burn some things and not others, that it should appear to have started from inside the body, or that there be no other evidence of foul play besides a smoldering corpse doesn't imply that the most reasonable explanation is spontaneous human combustion.

There may be many things we can't explain because we don't have enough information. In such cases, it does not seem beneficial to speculate unless there is some substance to our speculation. Has anyone tried to get a corpse to combust spontaneously? Are there any coroners out there who have seen this happen? If so, where are their reports? Is there a universal conspiracy of coroners to hide from the public this vital information? You'd think that if human corpses spontaneously combusted at least one coroner somewhere on the planet would have seen one. Why do corpses spontaneously combust only for police officers, especially British bobbys?

There are a few other curious things about spontaneous human combustion that should be considered. Fire burns at over 200 degrees F. The human body, when alive, is usually under 100 degrees F. A corpse would tend to cool off to room temperature. If a living being ever spontaneously combusted, the warning signs would be phenomenal: a 212-degree F. burning sensation! If a corpse self-ignited, it would be hard to keep it burning unless the room were very, very hot. In fact, the room would have to be nearly on fire itself to keep the corpse ignited. Once a fire has started, it will be self-supporting only if the temperature created by the combustion of the burning substance is as high or higher than its ignition point. A cool body in a cool room would be unlikely to do much more than smolder a little bit if it did self-ignite.

Nevertheless, we should not be scornful of those who fear that their fate might include **SHC** at some future date. The other night on TV, I saw a hypnotherapist who could probably cure this phobia in eighteen minutes or less. And for those cops who think **SHC** might be the best explanation for the next charred corpse they come upon, they can consult psychic detectives who will reveal the truth to them just by looking at a picture of the scene. People helping people: that's what pseudomysteries and psychics are for!

Furthermore, I can attest that there was a time in my life when I thought for sure my gut was igniting and I was going to die from internal combustion. Telling me such a thing was impossible would have done no good to persuade me otherwise. All rational argument is lost on one in deep pain. I hallucinated and had visions of imploding blue flames. Fortunately, a surgeon removed my gall bladder, and ever since I have noticed a decreased fear of **SHC.**

After Reading

Word Connections

1. What is a *skeptic*?

_____

_____

2. What is the British term used to refer to a police officer?

_____

Connecting Meaning

1. Does the author believe in spontaneous human combustion?

_____

_____

2. What facts does the author give to support his opinion about SHC?

_____

_____

_____

3. Do you agree or disagree with the author? Why?

_____

_____

_____

Portfolio Activities

Integrating Ideas

Do you believe in any paranormal phenomena? Why or why not? Have you or someone you know had any experience with paranormal activities? How would you explain this experience? Reflect on these ideas in writing or class discussion.

Extending Concepts

Choose a paranormal activity to investigate. Present and support opposing viewpoints on the existence or causes of ESP, ghosts, out-of-body experiences, near-death experiences, UFOs, psychics, or any other area of interest.

Collaborative Activity

Analyze several articles from supermarket tabloids. Share examples of verifiable facts, unsubstantiated reports, and informed and uninformed opinions.

Additional Portfolio Suggestion

What have you discovered about yourself as a reader? What have you read this semester that had the greatest impact on your life? Why? How have you grown or changed as a reader? Give evidence to support your opinion about your change or growth.

■ ■ ■ ■ Chapter Summary Graphic Organizer

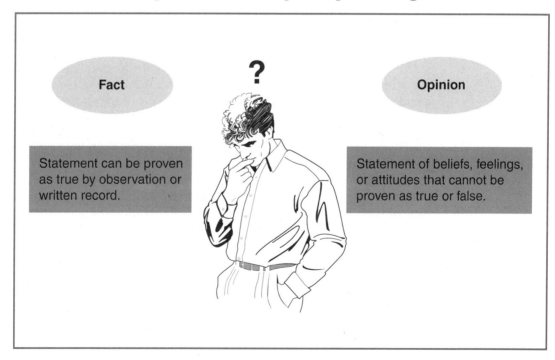

Fact

Statement can be proven as true by observation or written record.

?

Opinion

Statement of beliefs, feelings, or attitudes that cannot be proven as true or false.

14

Inference

Theme of Readings: *Advertising*

Advertising is the "wonder" in Wonder Bread.

JEF I. RICHARDS

▪ ▪ ▪ ▪ Advertising

Just as an author communicates to the reader through writing, a business communicates to the consumer through advertising. Consumers are exposed to hundreds of ads each day through television, radio, newspapers, magazines, and the Internet. It is estimated that the average consumer will spend a year and a half of his or her lifetime watching television commercials. Entertaining, slick, and persuasive, advertising continues to be somewhat of a mystery because many consumers believe it does not work on them. Yet businesses continue to use advertising, and it has been proven that ads do have an effect on people's buying patterns.

In order to gain the attention of the consumer, advertising provides general information given through words, pictures, people, and graphics. Often only minimal information is given. The consumer must therefore use clues to infer a complete message. He or she takes in the information and message and decides if that particular product or service is something to buy. Personal knowledge, experience, need, and the possession of enough money also influence the decision, of course.

Because of its prevalence, advertising has an impact on almost every aspect of our social, political, and economic life. It is important for us, as consumers, to be able to make valid inferences and to judge advertisements and the information in them as sound or misleading.

Chapter Objective

After completing this chapter you will be able to use given facts, details, and opinions to make an inference.

■ ■ ■ ■ Focus on Inference

Writers do not always place everything they want you to know on the printed page. Often writers will give you information so that you can "read between the lines" and interpret or infer what they are telling you. Inferences are educated guesses, conclusions, or judgments that you make when you read. These guesses are not made randomly. You must carefully examine the facts, details, and opinions given. You also need to use your own knowledge and experience to form judgments about the information. You may not be sure that your inference is correct. However, if you use information, knowledge, and experience, you will be able to support your inference.

Nowhere is the use of inference so evident as in advertising. Advertisements use words, pictures, or symbols to create a message for the viewer. For example, an advertisement sponsored by a food company shows a person smiling as he or she takes a bite of food. The smile in the ad indicates that the person enjoys the activity. Your experience shows that to enjoy eating, the food must be tasty. You infer or conclude that the food is tasty.

As you infer, you must remember not to go beyond the evidence or clues given. Inferences must be based on information, not on wild guesses. For example, from the advertisement previously described, you could not infer that the person is smiling while eating because the food reminds that person of home cooking. No clues were given in the ad to infer this information.

Look carefully at the advertisement on the following page.

You can infer from this advertisement that driving a Chrysler Concorde is so smooth and pleasurable that you forget your everyday chores. You lose yourself in the design and performance of the vehicle. The ad wants you to infer that, because of these factors, you should purchase this car.

To get you to come to this conclusion, headlines, pictures, and text are used. The headlines, as printed above the picture of the car, suggest the car will distract you from unexciting, routine errands. The blurred background of the picture helps you imagine the vehicle in your own world and imagine the smooth ride you will get in this car. Finally, the text below the picture, says " . . . you're lost in the stability . . ." This material gives you clues about the sound engineering qualities of the car and how they will affect you, the driver. Further information and prices can be obtained easily from the advertisement, if you conclude this car may be the one you wish to purchase. Together all elements of the ad almost want to hypnotize you into a state of desire for this car.

Sometimes you forget the milk.
Sometimes you forget the bread.
Sometimes you forget the store altogether.

With every corner you're lost in the stability of the Concorde LXi's cab-forward

architecture and low-speed traction control, not to mention the sound of its 225

hp V6. For more information, call 1.800.CHRYSLER or visit www.chryslercars.com.

The new 1999 Chrysler Concorde. LX starting at $22,190. LXi as shown, $26,010.*

ENGINEERED TO BE GREAT CARS

CHRYSLER CONCORDE

*Base MSRPs include destination, exclude tax.

Critical readers make inferences as they interpret the author's message. Just as with advertisements, the reader bases conclusions on information provided, as well as on experience and knowledge, to form valid and supported inferences about all types of readings.

■ ■ ■ ■ Short Exercises: *Inference*

Examine each advertisement carefully, and answer the questions that follow.

1. What organization sponsored the advertisement on page 270?

   _____

   What would you infer from the photo and headline?

   _____

   _____

   _____

   _____

   _____

   How does the text explain the message of the organization?

   _____

   _____

   _____

   _____

   _____

2. What company sponsored the advertisement on page 271? What service does this company provide?

   _____

   _____

   _____

   What message can you infer about the 800 phone number?

   _____

   _____

   _____

   _____

Denzel Washington

Put this card in the hands of a child and there'll
be no room for a gun. A needle. Or a knife.

It's only a piece of paper, but that
little membership card has helped
keep millions of kids off drugs, out of
gangs and in school. To learn how
you can help the Boys & Girls Clubs,
call: **1 - 8 0 0 - 8 5 4 - C l u b .**

BOYS & GIRLS CLUBS
OF AMERICA

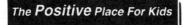

The *Positive* Place For Kids

1·800·32·SMART
of you
to ask our experts to please,
please explain the difference between
financing and leasing
a new GM car or truck.
They know and actually like to
talk about it. (amazing!) Hey, who else
to call but
GMAC
FINANCIAL SERVICES
?
http://www.gmacfs.com
CHEVROLET · PONTIAC · GMC · BUICK · OLDSMOBILE · CADILLAC
©1997 GMAC All Rights Reserved

What is the message inferred by this ad?

_____

_____

_____

_____

What does the handwritten text add to the message?

_____

_____

_____

_____

3. What company sponsored the advertisement on page 273?

_____

What message do you infer from this ad?

_____

_____

_____

_____

What clues are used to draw the conclusion about the message of the ad?

_____

_____

_____

_____

4. What company sponsored the advertisement on page 274?

_____

What do you infer as the message of this advertisement? Support your answer.

_____

_____

_____

_____

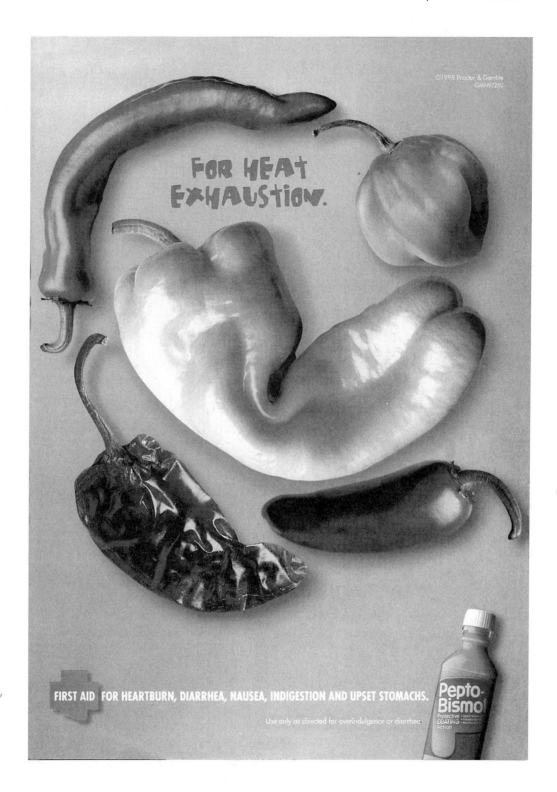

■ ■ ■ ■   Reading Selections

Selection 1   ## Simple Solutions

PATRICK G. HAYES

Before Reading   Before you read, "Simple Solutions," predict the topic, scan the ad, and think about health insurance. Are you and your family covered by some type of health insurance? What do you think about the cost? Relate your opinion about health insurance to those presented in this advertisement.

Words to Preview
premiums   *(n.)* amount paid for an insurance policy
foster   *(v.)* to develop or encourage
grievous   *(adj.)* serious

During Reading   As you read the ad, "Simple Solutions," continue to predict and visualize the ideas and monitor your comprehension. What does the author imply about health insurance?

Sometimes our nation's social problems seem so overwhelming that we fear we can never solve them. It's tempting just to give up. But the rising number of uninsured Americans—more than 43.4 million—is one problem Congress *can* help to solve. Right now.

The challenge is to develop targeted solutions that reach specific people. For example, more than 83 percent of Americans who lack health insurance either have jobs themselves or have spouses or parents who work. Although these uninsured people work, their incomes are too low to afford insurance premiums. This problem is greatest among the smallest businesses, where 35 percent of employees are uninsured. To address the situation, our nation needs to find ways to help small companies offer insurance. Congress *can* make this happen.

First, the government should provide tax credits for low-income workers in small firms. In addition, Congress should allow the self-employed—along with other people who purchase health insurance outside an employer group—to deduct the full cost of health-insurance premiums from their income taxes.

Finally, lawmakers must resist the many proposed public policy schemes that will increase the cost of health care. These proposals will only make the problems of the uninsured worse.

The government faces a choice: foster solutions today or aggravate an already grievous social problem for tomorrow. Let's urge our lawmakers to make the right decision.

For more information about the Blues, call 1-800-244-BLUE or visit www. bluecares.com.

Mr. Hays is President and CEO of the national Blue Cross and Blue Shield Association.

This advertisement is sponsored by the Blue Cross and Blue Shield Association, an association of independent Blue Cross and Blue Shield Plans.

After Reading

Word Connections

1. "Lawmakers must resist the many proposed public policy schemes . . . " What is the author implying by choosing the word *schemes* in this sentence?

_____

_____

_____

Connecting Meaning

1. What company sponsored the advertisement, "Simple Solutions"? Why is this important to know?

_____

_____

_____

2. State one of the facts mentioned in this advertisement.

_____

_____

3. What is the author's opinion of health insurance?

_____

_____

4. What does the author imply about the health insurance issue?

_____

_____

_____

_____

_____

5. Do you agree or disagree with the author's solution for the problem? Why?

_____

_____

_____

_____

Selection 2

What a Difference a Year Makes

OFFICE OF NATIONAL DRUG CONTROL POLICY
AND PARTNERSHIP FOR A DRUG-FREE AMERICA

Before Reading

Before you read "What a Difference a Year Makes," on page 278, predict the topic, scan the ad, and think about the drug problem in America. Do you feel the use of illegal drugs is on the increase? Relate how you feel about the drug problem to the information presented in the advertisement.

During Reading

As you read the ad, "What a Difference a Year Makes," continue to predict and visualize the ideas and monitor your comprehension. What is the ad saying about the drug problem?

After Reading

Word Connections

1. What are the multiple meanings of *roach* presented in the ad?

_____

_____

_____

2. List and define the multiple meanings of five additional words.

_____

_____

_____

_____

_____

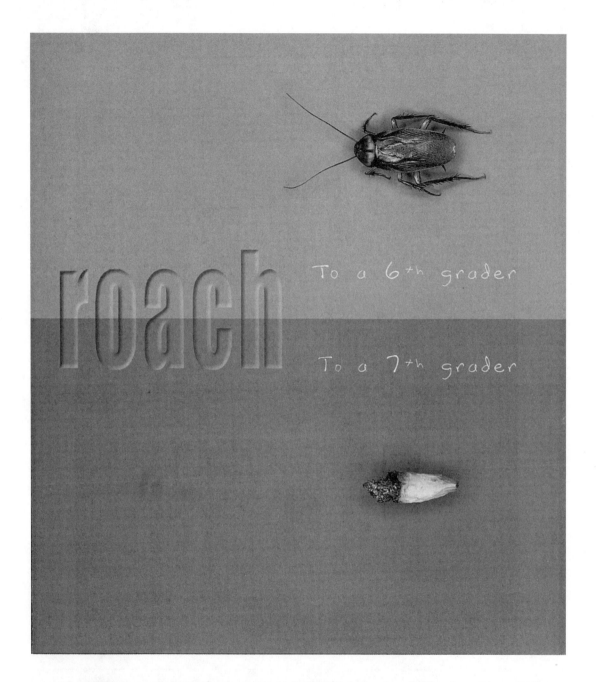

What a difference a year makes. In 6th grade, approximately 1 in 13 kids has tried marijuana. By 7th grade, approximately 1 in 5. Be sure your kids know you don't want them to use drugs. For helpful ways of keeping them drug-free, call 800.788.2800 or visit our Web sites: theantidrug.com and drugfreeamerica.org

Office of National Drug Control Policy | Partnership for a Drug-Free America®

Connecting Meaning

1. What organizations sponsored this advertisement? What service do they provide?

   _____

   _____

   _____

2. Are there any facts presented in this advertisement? If so, identify one.

   _____

   _____

3. How does this advertisement contrast the children in the sixth grade with those in the seventh grade in America?

   _____

   _____

   _____

4. What message can be inferred from this advertisement?

   _____

   _____

   _____

Selection 3

Denver, Colorado: June 3, 1998
MUTUAL OF AMERICA

Before Reading   Before you read "Denver, Colorado: June 3, 1998," predict the topic, scan the ad, and think about the career of firefighting. Do you think firefighters are everyday heroes? Relate what you know to the information given.

Words to Preview   **backdraft**   *(n.)* situation when a fire flashes
undue   *(adj.)* excessive

During Reading   As you read the ad, "Denver, Colorado: June 3, 1998," continue to predict and visualize the ideas and monitor your comprehension. What public service careers protect and serve your community?

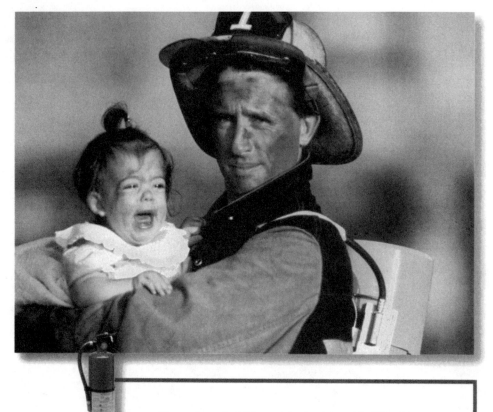

The walls are hot. The smoke, impenetrable. Was that someone behind that door...or just a backdraft that'll blow through the hall?

Denver, Colorado June 3, 1998 4:03 p.m.

You who protect and serve are everyday heroes. So we're more than committed to offering pension and retirement programs to protect you and your families.

Our commitment burns bright: to help provide those who work in the public service a future based on sound growth, not undue risk. That's the Spirit of America.

MUTUAL OF AMERICA

320 PARK AVE., NEW YORK, NY 10022 • 1 800 468 3785

Mutual of America Life Insurance Company is a Registered Broker/Dealer.

After Reading

Word Connections

1. What does the phrase *sound growth* mean?

_____

2. How would you define the *Spirit of America* as mentioned in this advertisement?

_____

_____

Connecting Meaning

1. Are there any facts presented in this advertisement? If yes, identify one.

_____

_____

_____

2. What does this advertisement imply about firefighters?

_____

_____

3. What message is Mutual of America sending to the consumer?

_____

_____

4. Why do you think the company chose to focus on those who protect and serve the community?

_____

_____

_____

■ ■ ■ ■ **Portfolio Activities**

Integrating Ideas

Do you think advertisements influence your purchase of a product or service? What should you be aware of when reading advertisements? How does an understanding of inferences help you with reading both advertisements and other selections? Reflect on these ideas in writing or class discussion.

Extending Concepts

Using an advertisement from a magazine or newspaper, write the given facts, details, and opinions that provide clues to the implied message of the ad.

Collaborative Activity

Create your own advertisement for a product or service that is either real or imaginary. Use the medium of your choice: print, tape, video, or live demonstration.

Additional Portfolio Activity

A parody uses comedy or ridicule to imitate an artistic work such as a piece of writing, a song, or an advertisement. You can often find examples of parodies of advertisements on the Internet or on television. Choose an advertisement and create your own parody of it.

▪ ▪ ▪ ▪ Chapter Summary Graphic Organizer

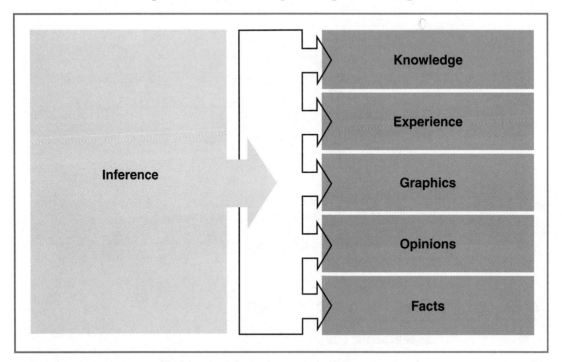

Review

Unit 5
Reading Critically

In this unit, you improved your ability to read critically by looking beyond the printed word for information given, sources used, and evidence provided to find the truth. You learned to distinguish a fact from an opinion and to draw a conclusion from inferences made.

A fact is a statement that can be proven as true by observation or written records. Statements of opinion give a person's feelings, attitudes, or beliefs and can not be proven true or false. An informed opinion is based on knowledge or experience with a subject and provides supporting details. An uninformed opinion lacks the knowledge, experience, or details to support it.

An inference is an educated guess based on facts and opinions presented. Not everything the author wants you to understand is always directly stated. You need to read between the lines to make an inference about the author's unstated points.

Having the ability to distinguish between fact and opinion and to infer information helps you to read critically and effectively.

■ ■ ■ ■ Unit Review Graphic Organizer

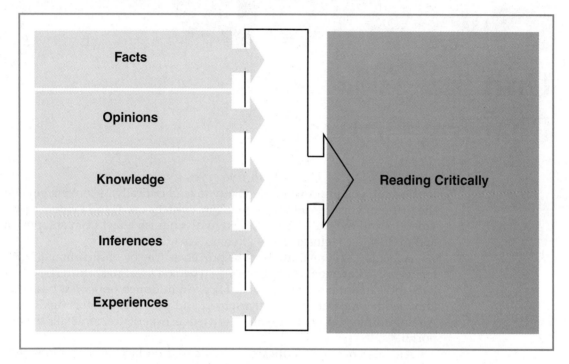

Portfolio Suggestion

Analyze an editorial. How does the writer support opinions and inferences? Do you agree or disagree with the writer's conclusions? Support your opinion.

Parts of Speech

The parts of speech are:

- **Adjective**

  Abbreviation: *adj.*

  An adjective describes a noun: I have *four red* cats.

- **Adverb**

  Abbreviation: *adv.*

  An adverb describes a verb: John swam *slowly* around the lake.

- **Conjunction**

  Abbreviation: *conj.*

  A conjunction is a word used to join words or groups of words: Money *and* power are often seen as markers of success.

- **Interjection**

  Abbreviation: *interj.*

  An interjection is a word or phrase that expresses strong feelings: *Wow!* That's great.

- **Noun**

  Abbreviation: *n.*

  A noun is a person, place, thing, or idea: *Mary* has a *friend* who lives in *New York City*.

- **Preposition**

  Abbreviation: *prep.*

  A preposition is a word that combines with a noun or pronoun to form a phrase: The student deposited his money *into* a savings account.

- **Pronoun**

  Abbreviation: *pron.*

  A pronoun is a word used in place of a noun: *She* is coming home tomorrow.

- **Verb**

  Abbreviation: *v.*

  A verb is a word or group of words that express action or state of being: Yesterday it *rained* all day.

B

Literacy Autobiography

The following questions[*] have been developed to help you write your literacy autobiography. Please understand that this is a list of questions to stimulate your thinking about your own literacy development. You do not have to respond to each question and restrict your thinking. Be creative as you record your literacy experiences.

- What are your earliest recollections of reading and writing?
- Were you read to as a child?
- Before you were able to read, did you pretend to read books? Can you remember the first time you read a book?
- Can you recall your early writing attempts (scribbling, labeling drawings, etc.)
- Was a newspaper delivered to your home? Do you recall seeing others read the newspaper? Did you read the newspaper?
- Did you subscribe to children's magazines? Did your parents or siblings have magazine subscriptions?
- Can you remember any indications that reading and writing were valued in the environment in which you grew up?
- Can you detail your first memories of reading and writing instruction?
- Can you recall reading for pleasure in elementary school?
- Did you ever use a public library? For what reason?
- Do you feel that you've ever read a book that has made a difference in your life?

[*]Adapted from M. McLaughlin and M. Vogt, *Portfolios in Teacher Education*, Newark, DE: International Reading Assn., 1996.

- Were you a reader in your elementary, junior high, and/or high school years? Did you read because it was required and/or for your own pleasure?
- What is your all-time favorite children's book? Novel? Nonfiction work?
- What contributions have your reading and writing abilities made to your life?
- What are you currently reading? Writing?

C

Reader Response Journal

Responding to literature in a variety of ways helps you to think critically about what you read, to construct meaning from literature, and to connect writing and reading. A reader response journal is an important way of evaluating your understanding of what you read and gives you an opportunity to respond to literature.

In your journal, you are encouraged to go beyond just writing a simple summary of what you have read. Some possible responses are to

- make comparisons and predictions,
- give opinions about the literature and the author,
- discuss an author's writing style,
- generate new interpretations or points of view,
- answer open-ended questions, or
- explain how you can relate to the characters through experiences or other readings.

You may ask yourself questions such as

- What was worth remembering?
- What was disappointing or confusing?
- What was interesting or thought provoking?
- What, if anything, did you object to?

You may include any other thoughts about your reading.

For each entry include your name, the title and author of the reading, and the pages of the reading that are covered by this entry.

D

Concept of Definition
Map Format*

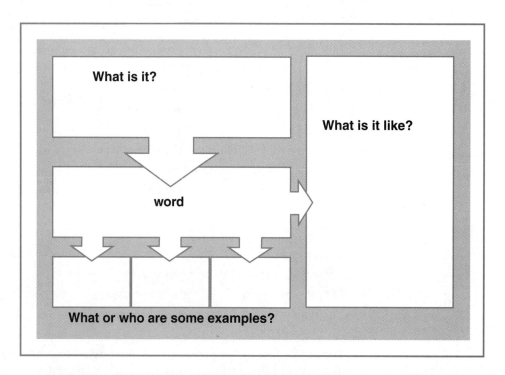

Source: Robert Schwartz and Taffy Raphael. "Concept of Definition: A Key to Improving Student's Vocabulary," *The Reading Teacher*. 39 November 1985.

E

Word Parts

Common Prefixes

Prefix	Meaning	Example
a-	on, toward	aboard
ab-	away, from	abduct
ante-	before	antedate
anti-	against	anti-aircraft
bi-	two	bicycle
circum-	around, about	circumscribe
com-/col-/con-	together, with, joint	committee/collect/ contact
contra-	against, opposite	contraband
counter-	contrary	counterclockwise
de-	reverse, remove	dethrone
dis-	reversal	disapprove
equi-	equal	equilateral
ex-	out of, former	exit/ex-wife
extra-	outside, beyond	extraordinary
hyper-	over, above, beyond	hyperventilate
in-/il-/ir-/im-	not	inactive/illegal/ irresponsible/ immature
inter-	between, among	interoffice
intra-	within	intramural
intro-	in, inward, inside	introvert
mal-	bad, wrongly	malformed
micro-	small	microsurgery
mis-	wrongly	misconduct
mono-	one, single	monorail
multi-	many	multilevel
non-	not	nonfat
post-	after	postoperative

(continued)

(continued)

Prefix	Meaning	Example
pre-	before	prerequisite
re-	again, back	recall
retro-	backward	retrorocket
semi-	half	semisweet
sub-	under	subfreezing
super-	above, over	superimpose
trans-	across, on the other side	transportation
tri-	three	tricycle
un-	not	uncommon

Source: Mary A. DeVries, *The Complete Word Book*, Englewood Cliffs, NJ: Prentice-Hall, 1991.

Common Roots

Root	Meaning	Example
-aud-	hear	auditory
-bene-	good, well	beneficial
-bibl-	book	bibliography
-bio-	life	biology
-cap-	take, seize	capacity
-capit-	head	capital
-cede-	to go	precede
-chron(o)-	time	chronometer
-cred-	believe	credible
-cur-	run	concurrent
-dict-	tell, say	contradict
-duc-/-duct-	lead	conduct
-equi-	equal	equivalent
-fact-/-fac-	make, do	factory
-fid-	trust	confide
-geo-	earth	geography
-graph-	write	autograph
-hetero-	different	heterosexual
-log-/-logo-/-logy-	study, thought	sociology
-mit-/-miss-	send	dismiss, submit
-mort-	death	mortal
-neuro-	nerve	neurotic
-path-	feeling	apathy
-poli-	city	cosmopolitan
-port-	carry	portable
-pos-	place, put	dispose
-reg-	rule	regal
-rupt-	break	erupt
-scop-	see	telescope
-scrib-/-script-	write	prescription
-sect-	cut	intersection
-sen-/-sent-	feel	sensitive, resentment
-spec-/-spic-/-spect-	look	spectator, specimen
-stru-	build	structure
-tele-	far	television
-tend-/-tens-	stretch	attend
-ten-/-tent-	hold	tenant, detention
-terr-/-terre-	land, earth	terrain
-tort-	twist	distort
-tract-	draw, drag	attraction
-vac-	empty	vacant
-ven-/-vent-	come	invention
-vert-/-vers-	turn	revert
-vis-/-vid-	see	vision, evident
-voc-/-vok-	call	advocate, evoke

Source: A. Waldhorn and A. Zeiger, *Word Mastery Made Simple*, New York: Made Simple Books, 1957, and J. Shepherd, *College Vocabulary Skills*, Boston: Houghton Mifflin, 1995.

Common Suffixes

Suffix	Meaning	Example	Part of Speech
-able	capable of	manageable	adjective
-an	belonging to	American	noun
-ance	state of, action	resistance	noun
-ant	causing, being	participant	noun
-ation	state, condition of	information	noun
-eer	one concerned with	auctioneer	noun
-ence	state of	independence	noun
-ent	state of	resident	noun
-er	performer of action	teacher	noun
-fy	form, make	magnify	verb
-hood	condition	brotherhood	noun
-ible	capable of	divisible	adjective
-ic	pertaining to	heroic	adjective
-ion	act, process	union	noun
-ism	system	symbolism	noun
-ist	agent, doer	chemist	noun
-ity	condition, degree	community	noun
-ive	tending toward	active	adjective
-ize	cause to be	maximize	verb
-ly	like	friendly	adverb
-ment	act, process	government	noun
-ness	state, quality	neatness	noun
-or	performer of action	instructor	noun
-ous	characterized by	joyous	adjective
-ship	condition, state	friendship	noun
-tion	act, process	irritation	noun
-ty	state of, condition	loyalty	noun
-ward	direction	homeward	adjective/ adverb
-y	full of	foamy	adjective

Source: Mary A. DeVries, *The Complete Word Book,* Englewood Cliffs, NJ: Prentice-Hall, 1991.

F

Reading Log

A reading log is an excellent place to collect information so that you can learn more about your attitude, habits, and preferences in reading. Keep track of your reading for the period of time specified by your instructor. (See the accompanying charts.) When you have completed your chart, think about yourself as a reader. Use the following questions to guide you. Write what you learned about yourself.

1. When you look over your reading log, what do you notice about yourself as a reader? What do you like to read? How much do you read?
2. Overall, how would you rate the books you have been reading? Are they easy or difficult for you? Explain.
3. What is your favorite genre? What is your favorite book?
4. Who is your favorite author? Why?
5. Think about yourself as a reader. How would you describe yourself as a reader?
6. What would make you a better reader?

Adapted from Sheila W. Valencia, *Literacy Portfolios in Action*, New York: Harcourt Brace, 1998.

Reading Log

Date
Title
Author
Pages
Comments

Date
Title
Author
Pages
Comments

Date
Title
Author
Pages
Comments

Date
Title
Author
Pages
Comments

Date
Title
Author
Pages
Comments

Date
Title
Author
Pages
Comments

Reading Log

Date
Title
Author
Pages
Comments

Date
Title
Author
Pages
Comments

Date
Title
Author
Pages
Comments

Date
Title
Author
Pages
Comments

Date
Title
Author
Pages
Comments

Date
Title
Author
Pages
Comments

Limited Answer Key

This limited answer key provides answers to short exercises and questions in the first reading selection in each chapter.

Chapter 1: Before Reading

Short Exercises: *Before Reading* **Strategies**   Answers will vary for all exercises.

Readings   Answers will vary.

Chapter 2: During Reading

Short Exercises: *During Reading* **Strategies**   Answers will vary for all exercises.

Readings   Answers will vary.

Chapter 3: After Reading

Answer Key

Short Exercises: *After Reading* **Strategies**

1. There is no good reason to wait to tell people you love how much you love them. Now is the time to tell them. You'll receive more love as a result.
2. We don't live forever. We could wait until it's too late.
3. You will find your day more peaceful if every morning you think of someone to love. It helps to keep you focused on the positive.
4. The author pictures someone to whom he will wish a day filled with love.
5. If you put more emphasis on giving love and less emphasis on receiving love, you'll find you have plenty of love in your life.

6. You can be a source of greater love by extending loving thoughts to all, even those people you feel do not deserve it.

7. Practicing random acts of kindness is an effective way of experiencing the joy of giving without expecting anything in return. It reminds you of the important aspects of life—service, kindness, and love.

8. The greatest reason to practice random acts of kindness is to bring greater contentment to your life.

Readings

Selection One: "Fear of Failure" by Dave Barry

1. The author was afraid that his attempts to speak to or date a girl would be disastrous.

2. Phil Grant was the author's friend who had the ability to talk to girls. Eric should call him because it's so hard to make the first move and sometimes you need a friend, like Phil Grant, to help you.

3. The author's mother drove them to the movies. He didn't really see the movie because he was so nervous. His arm became numb from placing it on the back of Judy's seat for two hours.

Chapter 4: Vocabulary Strategies
Answer Key

Short Exercises: Context Clues

1. domestic (work as household help)
2. humiliating treatment, degrading act
3. very important or significant
4. give in
5. presented
6. excessive and unfair
7. unlawful
8. regarded with devotion
9. easy
10. teachings

Short Exercises: Word Parts

1. one who studies the causes of diseases in populations (epidemics)
2. bringing about
3. substances in the blood that work against disease
4. more than one nation

5. study of the effect of the mind and brain on the immune system
6. to go above
7. believability
8. many applied sciences
9. ability to be seen
10. wide

Short Exercises: Concept of Definition Maps   Answers may vary. Possible answers follow.

1. What is it like? demonstrating

   Who is an example? Rachel Carson, Ralph Nader

2. What is it? a person who organizes, operates, and assumes the risk of a business

   What is it like? the owner of a new business; someone with an idea for making money in a new venture; success or failure at business

   Who or what are some examples? Donald Trump, Ben of Ben and Jerry's Ice Cream, Steven Dell of Dell Computers

3. What is it? successful accomplishment

   What is it like? working hard to finish; using all your skills; persevering; keeping at it

   What or who are some examples? a college degree, climbing a mountain, receiving an award in your field

4. What is it? widely known for an exceedingly bad reputation

   What is it like? a criminal, a cruel dictator, a tyrant

   Who or what are some examples? Adolf Hitler, Al Capone, Pol Pot

5. What is it? displaying courage

   What is it like? ignoring your pain to help another; doing something you never thought you could do; rising above your fear

   Who or what are some examples? a fireman rescuing someone from a burning building, jumping into the water to save a struggling swimmer, fighting a battle for rights

Short Exercise: Word Maps   Answers will vary.
Possible inclusions:

1. -logy, the study of: dermatology, the study of skin and skin related issues; toxicology, the study of toxic materials; biology, the study of living things
2. -tele, distance: telegraph, telescope, telephone, telephoto
3. -port, carry: portable, portage, porter, portfolio, support

4. -graph, write: autograph, telegraph, monograph, grapheme
5. -duc/-duct, lead: induce, induction, educate, duct, inductee

Readings

Selection One: "John Glenn: Man with a Mission" by William R. Newcott

After Reading

Word Connections

1. sunlight slanting through the window
2. "Sub-" means below or under.

   Word map possibilities: submarine, subcompact, subway, subculture, subnormal, subscript
3. involving vessels of the heart and blood

Connecting Meaning

1. John Glenn was the president of Royal Crown International and was elected senator from Ohio four times.
2. Changes to the human body in space are similar to aging. What are the differences between younger and older people in space? Would the body react differently with age?
3. Answers may vary. Possible answer: Glenn always wanted to go back into space after his initial flight.

Chapter 5: Topics and Main Ideas

Answer Key

Short Exercises: Topics and Stated Main Ideas

1. Topic: phobias, real fears

   Main idea: A phobia is a real fear, but it is a reaction that is out of proportion to a specific situation or thing.
2. Topic: a crowd's fear

   Main idea: Intelligent leadership could have kept the crowd's fear under control and prevented many deaths.
3. Topic: the look and sound of fear

   Main idea: This is the physical face of fear.
4. Topic: animal fears

   Main idea: Other animals respond to the environment with different senses and may experience varying amounts of fear because of your presence.

5. Topic: reducing fear

   Main idea: Sometimes a phobia can be extinguished by having another person demonstrate that a feared situation or object is not harmful.

6. Topic: irrational, involuntary terror

   Main idea: Irrational, involuntary terrors are this country's most prevalent mental-health problem, afflicting more than twenty-three million Americans.

7. Topic: drugs for phobics

   Main idea: Antianxiety and depression drugs such as Xanex and Prozac can prove useful in treating phobias, but many therapists say their use should be limited and not form the basis for treatment.

8. Topic: dental phobia

   Main idea: Fear of dentists is a common phobia.

9. Topic: technophobia

   Main idea: Technophobia—fear of technology—is another common problem, and one that's growing.

10. Topic: turkey phobia

    Main idea: Turkey phobia is a serious condition based on excessive worry over not being able to cook the bird correctly.

Readings

Selection One: "Virtual Therapy" *Psychology Today*

Word Connections

1. heights
2. Both have to do with making a person feel better.
3. What is it? to achieve an understanding of something through the senses

   What is it like? how you see a situation; your view; sensing something

   What or who are some examples? first impressions; your idea of the situation, getting the nonverbal message
4. Answers will vary.

Connecting Meaning

1. Virtual therapy is just the thing to help acrophobes overcome their fear of heights.
2. Patients wear a special helmet to experience the virtual world. They explore the virtual bridge in forty-minute sessions, beginning in a cafe and walking toward a raised wooden plank.

3. Reduced fear of heights has been shown by cleaning roof gutters, driving across bridges, or climbing mountains.

Chapter 6: Unstated Main Ideas

Answer Key

Short Exercises: Unstated Main Ideas

1. Topic: risk-taking sports
   Main idea: The popularity of risk-taking sports is growing.
2. Topic: bungee jumping
   Main idea: Bungee jumping is a risky activity.
3. Topic: types of risk
   Main idea: Each person's idea of risk is different.
4. Topic: tornadoes
   Main idea: Although dangerous, Texas tornadoes attract photographers, scientists, and filmmakers.
5. Topic: types of risk
   Main idea: Over the years, the types of risks have changed.
6. Topic: Roger Stoneburger
   Main idea: Stoneburger's risk-taking hobbies have become his career as a stunt man.
7. Topic: extreme sports or risky activities
   Main idea: Interest in extreme sports has risen due to media attention.
8. Topic: jumping from a dam
   Main idea: Chance McGuire survived a dangerous jump off a dam.
9. Topic: America
   Main idea: Risk taking is part of America's history.
10. Topic: Vicki Hendricks
    Main idea: Vicki Hendricks's hobbies involve dangerous activities.

Readings

Selection One: "Mud and Guts" by Robert La Franco   Before and during reading responses will vary.

After Reading

Word Connections

1. pushing the limits of what you can do
2. Possible answers: What is it? good feelings between friends

What is it like? getting along easily; having fun together; feeling comfortable with friends

What or who are some examples? a college roommate, a group of people who have been friends for a long time; club members

3. hidden or concealed

Connecting Meaning

1. Extreme sports are popular. Many individuals are taking vacations that involve a certain amount of risk.
2. Michael Ellis describes the risks of off-road biking in the desert and the risk of owning a business.
3. Some reasons given why people take vacations that involve risk are that there is no war to be fought, they like to gamble, or risk taking is an American quality.

Chapter 7: Supporting Details

Answer Key

Short Exercises: Supporting Details

1. Main idea: Fear was a tool for survival through the fight or flight response.

   Major detail: A threatening situation causes an adrenaline rush.

   Minor detail: Adrenaline causes man to run faster, jump higher, see better, think faster.

   Major detail: Fight or flight response causes unnecessary body functions to stop.

   Minor detail: Digestion stopped, and the immune system shut down.

2. Topic: fight or flight

   Main idea: Humans still have the fight or flight response.

   Major detail: In response to a threat, the body activates its fight or flight response.

   Major detail: Since you can't fight or flee, there is a physical reaction.

   Minor detail: Your heart races, your blood pressure rises, and your palms sweat.

3. Topic: fear in the workplace

   Main idea: Fear in the workplace can be used to the manager's advantage.

   Major detail: The manager sets clear expectations and definite consequences.

Minor detail: The employee must maintain a sales quota.

Minor detail: If the quota is not met, the sales territory is reduced.

4. Main idea: Films and novels capitalize on fear as entertainment.

Major detail: Stephen King is a successful writer of horror fiction.

Minor detail: He wrote *The Shining, Cujo,* and *Firestarter.*

Major detail: Horror films have been successful.

Minor detail: *The Haunting* and *Friday the Thirteenth* were successful.

5. Topic: fear

Main idea: Fear is an internal motivator.

Major detail: The fear of not being accepted causes people to act differently.

Minor detail: A particular brand of jeans or sneakers may be purchased.

Major detail: Fear of being unsuccessful in their career drives people.

Minor detail: They work long hours or take on extra responsibilities.

6. Topic: roller coasters and haunted houses

Main idea: Fear can be a profitable business.

Major detail: Fearful attractions drive up season's admissions to amusement parks.

Minor details: Word of mouth publicity attracts new customers. It also draws repeat customers.

7. Topic: horror films

Main idea: Watching horror films may be healthy for teenagers.

Major detail: Teenagers experience safe "escapes."

Minor detail: Screaming and laughing are accepted and encouraged.

8. Topic: virtual reality

Main idea: Virtual reality is used for treatment of phobias.

Major detail: An online shrink leads phobics through a virtual reality environment.

Minor details: Phobics experience fear safely.

Fear of flying and heights are treated this way.

Readings

Selection One: "Gift of Fear" by Gavin DeBecker

After Reading

Word Connections

1. overly anxious

2. Possible answers: What is it? insight, knowing or sensing without conscious thought

What is it like? a feeling, a hunch, an impression or suspicion

What or who are some examples? a feeling of impending danger, a mother sensing something is wrong with her child, knowing someone is right for the job

Connecting Meaning

1. Fear of being harmed by someone walking toward us on the street is one example of a fear that is not a signal of real danger.

2. Rule 1: The fact that you fear something is solid evidence that it is not happening. For example, if you stand near the edge of a cliff, you fear getting too close. If you get too close, you then fear falling.

   Rule 2: What you fear is rarely what you think you fear—it is what you link to fear. For example, the fear of someone walking toward us is linked with the fear of being harmed by that person.

Chapter 8: Chronological Order and Listing Patterns

Answer Key

Short Exercises: Chronological Order and Listing Pattern

1. Main idea: DeLuca's accomplishments over the past thirty years have placed him at the top of a company that has annual sales over three billion dollars.

   Signals: ages (ten-years-old, seventeen-years-old) and dates (1982, 1997)

   Details: Ten-years-old, DeLuca was picking up two-cent bottles.

   Seventeen-years-old, DeLuca opened Pete's Super Submarine Sandwiches.

   In 1982, he owned 200 stores.

   In 1997, there were over 12,500 Subway stores.

   Pattern: Chronological

2. Main idea: Robert L. Johnson changed the face of the cable industry by creating Black Entertainment Television.

   Signals: 1980, since then, now

   Details: Johnson is chairman and CEO of BET Holdings, Inc. He oversees four major cable channels.

   Pattern: Chronological

3. Main idea: There are important guidelines to remember if you work out of your home.

   Signals: bullets

   Details: Maintain a presence in your main office.

   Treat where you work as a real office.

Get dressed for work. Be consistent with your hours.

Pattern: Listing

4. Main idea: Two trends in the past decade have led to internships for liberal arts majors.

   Signals: first, second

   Details: Tuition costs have risen, and families want to know there's a job at the end of college.

   Internships are attractive to employers.

   Pattern: Listing

5. Main idea: Debbi Fields has achieved great success through her worldwide chain of cookies and baked goods stores.

   Signals: 1977, 1990, today

   Details: A young mother with no experience opened Mrs. Fields Cookie store.

   > The company began franchising in 1990.

   > Today she has 650 domestic locations and 65 international locations.

   Pattern: Chronological

Reading

Selection One: "For Liberal Arts Majors Only: The Road to Career Success" by Robin Ryan

Word Connections

1. A magnet company is a large company that attracts tens of thousands of resumes. Examples are Microsoft, Nike, American Airlines, Nordstrom, Coors, MTV.

2. Possible answers: What is it? an informal system where people with common interests assist each other

   What is it like? making connections, sharing contacts, sharing information

   What or who are some examples? calling a friend for a job, chat room discussions of college course content, attending a golf outing with business associates

Connecting Meaning

1. Liberal arts graduates often do not know their career options; through exploration they will discover their talents and opportunities.

2. The listing of examples such as the job searches of Dave, Allison, Sam, and Peggy are signals.

3. There is a world of opportunity you may not have considered.

   You need to look for the hot opportunities.

   Learn the job-hunting process.

4. Listing

5. Dave focused on his strong writing, editing, and computer skills to land a job as an editorial assistant.

   Sam landed a job as a grocery distributor because of his organizational and customer-relations skills.

Chapter 9: Definition and Illustration/Example Patterns

Answer Key

Short Exercises: Definition and Illustration/Example Patterns

1. Main idea: Prozac is the most widely prescribed antidepressant in America.

   Signals: is, has been

   Details: Prozac is approved for the treatment of depression, obsessive compulsive disorder, bulimia, panic disorder, and other conditions.

   Pattern: Definition

2. Main idea: You can reduce your fat intake at breakfast by making a few simple substitutions.

   Signals: for instance, other

   Details: Replace pork bacon with turkey bacon, use one-percent milk, try egg substitutes, use low-fat spreads instead of butter, and eat fat-free pound cake instead of pastries.

   Pattern: Illustration/Example

3. Main idea: Anorexia nervosa is an illness that affects mainly adolescent girls and features weight loss and change in behavior.

   Signals: is, are

   Details: Weight loss may be severe and life threatening.

   Personality changes include increasing seriousness, introversion, and obsessions.

   Pattern: Definition

4. Main idea: Bulimia is an eating disorder in which a person binge eats, then uses self-induced vomiting, diuretics, laxatives, fasting, or excessive exercising to prevent weight gain.

   Signals: is, defines as

   Details: Symptoms include recurrent episodes of binge eating, feelings of lack of control, overeating, regular vomiting, use of laxatives and diuretics, strict dieting, and excessive exercising. Self-evaluation is unduly influenced by weight.

   Pattern: Definition

5. Main idea: Herbal remedies have become a popular alternative to conventional prescription medicine.

Signals: for example

Details: Kava is used for anxiety, ginkgo biloba for cognitive benefits, valerian root for insomnia, and St. John's wort for mild depression. Ginger and chamomile are used to ease stomach upset.

Pattern: Illustration/Example

Readings

Selection One: "Forever Frazzled?" by Maya Bolton

After Reading

Word Connections

1. triggered
2. credited, attributed to
3. a current debate with active, intense, and opposing views that are far apart

Connecting Meaning

1. The author has ADD, which can occur, or first be diagnosed, in adults.
2. The two types are predominantly hyperactive and predominantly inattentive.
3. The author was often absentminded. She'd forget a phone call that had been interrupted, keys, notebooks. She procrastinated and had difficulty editing.
4. The author used a pseudonym for this story because she feared that others, particularly her coworkers, might consider her a shirker, someone who wants an excuse for flaky behavior.

Chapter 10: Comparison and Contrast Patterns
Answer Key

Short Exercises: Comparison and Contrast Patterns

1. Main idea: Freedom of speech on the Internet may be subject to restrictions by some governments.
   Signals: similarly
   Details: China requires registration of users of the Internet and e-mail. In the United Kingdom, state secrets and personal attacks are off-limits.
   Pattern: Comparison
2. Main Idea: Books by V.C. Andrews were removed from Georgia school libraries.
   Signals: similarities, same

Details: All four books by the same author were removed for "filthiness of material."

Pattern: Comparison

3. Main idea: Reasons behind censorship differ.

Signals: however, differ

Details: Presley was considered sexually suggestive.

The Beatles had possibly offensive religious beliefs.

Behavior on the KISS video would be dangerous for children to imitate.

Pattern: Contrast

4. Main idea: Stealth censorship, the unofficial censoring of a book collection, results in fewer books available for the public to read.

Signals: compare, yet, instead, just as

Details: Both types of censorship result in fewer books to read and affect the book world.

Different from official censoring, books quietly disappear from a library shelf, purchases are cautious, and manuscripts are rejected.

Pattern: Compare and contrast

5. Main idea: *Huckleberry Finn* is regarded as an American classic work of fiction. Yet it has been banned, removed from classrooms, and challenged by censors.

Signals: none; sense of the reading

Details: T.S. Eliot and Hemingway praised the book. It provided a theme for a James Joyce book. In contrast, it was removed from various places in 1885, 1905, and 1969. In 1989, Alex Haley defended it against would-be censors in Tennessee.

Pattern: Contrast

Readings

Selection One: "Free Speech: Lyrics, Liberty, and License" by Sam Brownback

After Reading

Word Connections

1. prestige coming from being huge and powerful
2. excessively violent
3. Answers will vary.

Connecting Meaning

1. There are many forms of free speech; some are offensive. These offensive forms should be protected but thoroughly criticized. Vigorous

criticism of the perverse, hateful, and violent is the best action to protect free speech in society.

2. Less time is spent doing homework, reading, or talking to Mom or Dad than listening to music.

3. Offensive lyrics or speech can be censored or criticized. The senator feels that the criticism is the best action to take in a free society.

4. Answers will vary.

Chapter 11: Cause and Effect Pattern

Short Exercises: Cause and Effect Pattern

1. Main idea: Ronny Zamora claims too much television viewing caused him to commit murder.

   Signals: reason

   Details: Zamora became accustomed to violence.

   He suffered "television intoxication."

2. Main idea: A study investigates the relationship of watching violent cartoons to violent behavior.

   Signals: causes, due to

   Details: Watchers of violent cartoons (Woody Woodpecker) hit other children, break toys, and are more destructive during playtime than watchers of less violent cartoons (Red Hen, for example).

3. Main idea: A study shows that those who watched more violent television were more aggressive even into adulthood.

   Signals: none; sense of the reading

   Details: 1960: The more violent the television they watched, the more aggressive the eight-year-olds were in school.

   1971: The same children, now 19, were more likely to get in trouble with the law.

   1982: Those who watched the most violent TV as children inflicted more violent punishments of their children, were convicted of more serious crimes, and were more aggressive with spouses.

4. Main idea: The 1990 Television Violence Act resulted from Senator Simon's campaign to reduce violence on shows that children might be watching.

   Signals: cause, result

   Details: Simon saw a gory film on TV.

   He was upset that there was nothing to prevent a child from seeing this.

   He urged the passage of a law reducing gore on television.

5. Main idea: There are several reasons for the prevalence of violence on television news.

    Signals: reasons

    Details: Fires and shootings are cheaper to cover.

    Violent news generates higher ratings. Market researchers set standards.

Readings

Selection One: "Does TV Affect Your Psyche?" by Jay Kist

After Reading

Word Connections

1. disappearing little by little
2. Possible answers: What is it? a person who serves as a model for behavior

    What is it like? wanting to be like someone, looking up to someone, following that person's values

    What or who are some examples? a parent or guardian, a teacher, a hero

Connecting Meaning

1. Television often neglects to show the real-life consequences of violence and makes violence seem like a quick and easy solution to real-life problems. Watching television violence encourages violent behavior among young people.
2. Major networks have to compete with cable TV, which offers more violent programming.
3. Those who watched music videos and TV movies more frequently took greater risks (e.g., smoking, sexual activity, stealing, cheating).
4. Answers will vary.

Chapter 12: Problem and Solution Pattern
Answer Key

Short Exercises: Problem and Solution Pattern

1. Main idea: Credit card issuers are sneaking more and more charges into monthly bills. Debtors need to watch for these charges.

    Signals: none

Details: Walter Dodge was automatically charged for a warranty he didn't want.

After some hassle, the charge was removed.

Luckily, the charge was easy to spot.

2. Main idea: Keith's story underscores the importance of knowing what bankruptcy is and how to file properly.

Signals: none

Details: Keith thought bankruptcy was his only option.

Now he is barred from any line of credit for four years.

He could have cut a payment deal. He had other options.

Readings

Selection One: "In Debt All the Way Up to Their Nose Rings" by Joshua Wolf Shenk

After Reading

Word Connections

1. No added responsibilities or actions are necessary.
2. caring about how someone or something appears to others
   Examples will vary.
3. Answers will vary.

Connecting Meaning

1. Generation X is accumulating a great deal of debt, mostly through credit cards. There seems to be little desire to live within their means.
2. Between 1990 and 1995, the average outstanding debt for those under twenty-five grew.
   Sixty-five percent of college students have credit cards.
   Of debtors seeking professional help, more than half are between eighteen and thirty-two.
   Student loan debt is increasing.
   Credit cards are used for more than necessities.
3. No solution is offered by the author. Student solutions will vary.
4. Students are choosing higher-paying careers so they have the ability to reduce debt rather than pursuing their first interests.

Chapter 13: Fact and Opinion

Answer Key

Short Exercises: Fact and Opinion

1. Montz believes in ghosts.

   Facts: He lives in New Orleans. His business, "Hauntings Today," has "ghost" tours, a newsletter, and a group of specialists who investigate ghosts.

2. Facts: Three calm rabbits became agitated. They started hopping wildly in their cages right before a 5.2 earthquake hit.

   Opinion: The Chinese and Japanese believe animal sightings are useful and have made them a part of an earthquake warning system.

3. Some so-called remedies are the venom of snakes, honey, liver, or wrapping in manure or peppermint oil.

   Opinion: These "cures" are quackery and have caused tragedy by people turning away from traditional cures.

4. Facts: The short time of contact between the feet and coals, the feet being moist, and a layer of insulating ash are factors that decrease the number of burns and injuries.

   Opinion: Other people explain firewalking by the power of faith; the power of the mind; and the power of positive thinking.

5. Facts: A footprint, measuring ten by six inches, was found on Mom Ray Mountain. It was wider than any human foot and had longer toes.

   Opinion: It could be a legendary creature, known as "Wildman," an ape, or a human ancestor hiding in the Asian forest.

Readings

Selection One: "Crop Circles and Aliens: What's the Evidence?" by Carl Sagan

After Reading

Word Connections

1. reliable, upstanding members of the community

2. someone who studies crop circles

3. to keep in existence

Connecting Meaning

1. UFOs turned out to be natural phenomena, such as aircraft with unusual lighting, high-altitude balloons, optical mirages, ball lighting, and meteors, to name a few.

2. Sagan believes they are a hoax. In 1991, two men from England confessed they had created the circles—first as a prank, then as serious art. The men signed their initials on their art. They were able to demonstrate making the circles. Copycat hoaxers even appeared.

3. Answers will vary.

Chapter 14: Inference

Answer Key

Short Exercises: Inference

1. Boys and Girls Clubs of America sponsored the ad.

    You could infer being a member of the club has positive benefits for young people.

    The text explains what the clubs have kept young people away from, for example, violence and drugs.

2. GMAC sponsored the ad and provides financial services.

    You can infer that if you use the 800 number, you are making a smart move.

    The message is that GMAC experts know best about financing and leasing a General Motors car or truck.

    The handwritten text personalizes the message.

3. Procter & Gamble (Pepto-Bismol) sponsored the ad.

    The message is that Pepto-Bismol will help soothe stomach upset after hot, spicy foods like peppers.

    The text, "heat exhaustion," indicates the hot, spicy nature of the food. The first aid symbol indicates Pepto-Bismol will help.

4. Mattel sponsored the ad.

    Answers will vary. This ad could elicit a wide variety of responses. Possible response: Barbie's message is that young girls should believe in themselves.

Readings

Selection One: "Simple Solutions" by Patrick G. Hays

After Reading

Word Connections

The word schemes imply that what is proposed is not exactly what is meant. Schemes may be unrealistic or devious.

Connecting Meaning

1. Blue Cross and Blue Shield sponsored the ad. Their business is health insurance.
2. More than 43.4 million Americans are uninsured.
3. Health insurance is a problem for Americans.
4. If you follow the plan presented (tax credits for low-income workers, Congress allowing the self-employed to deduct premiums from income taxes, lawmakers resisting increasing health-insurance costs), then the problem will improve.
5. Answers will vary.

Acknowledgments

Chapter 1 Page 8, "Brick by Brick" by Bill Shore. Reprinted with permission from the November 1999 Reader's Digest. From *The Cathedral Within* by Bill Shore. Copyright © 1999 by William Shore. Reprinted by permission of Random House, Inc.; page 11, "Parents Are Strange Animals . . . Aren't They?" by Ray Morris. Reprinted by permission from Ray Morris; page 13, "Four Generations," by Joyce Maynard. Copyright © 1979 by Joyce Maynard. Originally appeared in *The New York Times* magazine, April 12, 1979. Reprinted by permission of Brandt & Brandt Literary Agents, Inc.

Chapter 2 Page 23, "Real Friends" by Catherine Weiskopf. From *Current Health 2*, February 1998, v24, n6, p. 16(2). Special permission granted. *Current Health 2*® copyright 1999, published by Weekly Reader Corporation. All rights reserved; page 25, "Facing the Limitations of Long-Distance Friendships Can Be Downright Traumatic" by Catherine Walsh. Copyright © 1998 by American Press, Inc. Reprinted by permission; page 27, "Can Men and Women Just Be Friends?" From *Jet*, August 18, 1997, v92, n13, p. 12(3). Reprinted by permission from Johnson Publishing Company.

Chapter 3 Page 32, From *Living, Loving & Learning* by Leo F. Buscaglia, Ph.D., edited by Steven Short. Published by Ballantine Books. Copyright © 1982 by Leo F. Buscaglia, Inc.; page 33, Reprinted from *Don't Sweat the Small Stuff . . . And It's All Small Stuff* by Richard Carlson, Ph.D. Copyright © 1997, Richard Carlson, Ph.D. Published by Hyperion Books; page 36, "Fear of Failure" by Dave Barry (originally titled "Breaking the Ice" in the *Fort Worth Star-Telegram*, February 16, 1992). From *Dave Barry Is Not Making This Up* by Dave Barry. Copyright © 1994 by Dave Barry. Reprinted by permission of Crown Publishers, a division of Random House, Inc.; page 39, Excerpt, as attached, from "Y Not Love?" by Helen Stapinski. Reprinted from *American Demographics* magazine, February 1999. Copyright 1999. Courtesy of Intertex Publishing Corp., Stamford, Connecticut. All Rights Reserved; page 41, *True Love*, by Patricia Jensen, pp. 66–70 from *True Love: Stories Told To And By Robert Fulghum*. Copyright © 1997 by Robert Fulghum. Reprinted by permission of HarperCollins Publishers, Inc.

Chapter 4 Page 61, Excerpted from "John Glenn: Man With a Mission" by William R. Newcott. From *National Geographic*, June 1999 (v195, n6). Reprinted by permission from the National Geographic Society; page 66, "Oprah Winfrey" from *American Heroes: Their Lives, Their Values, The Beliefs* by Dr. Robert B. Pamplin, Jr. and Gary K. Eisler. Thorndike Press, 1995. Copyright © 1995 by The Pamplin Entertainment Corporation. Reprinted by permission of The Gale Group; page 70, From *The Greatest Generation* by Tom Brokaw. Copyright © 1998 by Tom Brokaw. Reprinted by permission of Random House, Inc.

Chapter 5 Page 83, From *Fears and Phobias*, by Margaret O. Hyde, published by McGraw-Hill. Copyright © 1977 by Margaret O. Hyde. Reprinted by permission from the author; page 83, Excerpted from "Who's Afraid of the Big Bad Phobia?" by Stephen Rae, which appeared in *Cosmopolitan*, September 1994, v217 n3 p218(4). Reprinted by permission from Stephen Rae; page 86, "Virtual Therapy" from *Psychology Today*, November–December 1994, v27 n6 p20(2). REPRINTED WITH PERMISSION FROM PSYCHOLOGY TODAY MAGAZINE, Copyright © 1994 Sussex Publishers, Inc.; page 89, Excerpt titled "Red Flag" from "5 Who Conquered Fear" by Cathy Perlmutter. From *Prevention*, July 1992, v44 n7 p57 (16). Reprinted by permission of *Prevention* Magazine. Copyright 1992 Rodale Inc. All rights reserved; page 93, "Help! I think I'm Dying" by Dr. Abbot Granoff. From the Introduction to Dr. Granoff's book, *Help! I Think I'm Dying! Panic Attacks and Phobias* ISBN #0-938423-04-5. Reprinted by permission from Dr. Abbot Granoff.

Chapter 6 Page 104, "Mud and Guts" by Robert La Franco. From *Forbes* February 9, 1998, v161, n3, p168(3). Reprinted by Permission of Forbes Magazine. © 1998 Forbes; page 107, "On Her Own Terms" by Nancy Prichard. From *Women's Sports and Fitness*, Nov–Dec 1995, v17 n8 p41(3). Reprinted by permission from Nancy Prichard; page 111, "Riders on the Storm: Tornado Chasers Seek the Birthplace of an Elusive Monster" by Howard B. Bluestein. From *The Sciences Magazine*, March–April 1995, v35 n2 p26(5). This article is reprinted by permission of *The Sciences* and is from the March/April 1995 issue. Individual subscriptions are $28 per year. Write to: The Sciences, 2 East 63rd Street, New York, NY 10021.

Chapter 7 Page 125, from *The Gift of Fear: Survival Signals That Protect Us From Violence* by Gavin de Becker. Copyright © 1997 by Gavin de Becker. By permission of Little, Brown and Company, Inc.; page 129, "Everything

You Always Wanted to Know About Fear (but Were Afraid to Ask)" by David Cornfield, as published on website: http://www.arvotek.net/soulwork. David Cornfield B.A., LL.B., M.T., is a psychotherapist, career counselor, business coach, trainer, organizational consultant and author, based in Toronto, Canada, who specializes in helping individuals and organizations find greater meaning through their work. For more information, visit his web site at www.soulmaking.com; page 133, "Courage & Fear" by Christine Bruun. Reprinted by permission from Christine Bruun.

Chapter 8 Page 142, excerpted from *The Career Fitness Program: Exercising Your Options*, Fourth Edition, by Diane Sukienik, William Bendat, and Lisa Raufman. Copyright © 1995 by Prentice-Hall, Inc.; page 145, "Advice From the Top and How To Get There" by Brian Caruso. From *Employment Review*, August 1997 issue. Copyright © 1997 by Employment Review. All rights reserved.; page 146, excerpt titled "Tips for Working at Home" from article titled "Conference Calls in Your Pajamas: The Pros and Cons of Working from Home" by Bradley Richardson. Copyright 1999 – TMP Interactive, Inc. All Rights Reserved. You may not copy, reproduce or distribute this article without the prior written permission of TMP Interactive. This article first appeared on Monster.com, the leading online global network for careers. To see other career-related articles, visit www.monster.com; page 146, from "Working for Credit: How to Make the Most of a Semester-Long Internship" by Jo Ann Tooley. From *U.S. News & World Report*, November 17, 1997. Copyright © 1997 by U.S. News & World Report; page 147, page from Mrs. Fields Cookies website (http://www.mrsfields.com/the_story/story-bottom.html.). Reprinted by permission from Mrs. Fields Famous Brands; page 148, "The Road to Career Success" by Robyn Ryan. Reprinted from *Job Choices in Business: 1998*, with permission of the National Association of Colleges and Employers, copyright holder; page 151, "Fastest Growing Occupations, 1992–2005" from *Occupational Outlook Quarterly* published by the U.S. Department of Labor; page 154, "Making a Job Search Plan" by Bob Adams. Reprinted from *The Complete Resume & Job Search Handbook for College Students* © 1999, Adams Media Corporation. Published by Adams Media Corporation; page 159, From *In Step With Life and Work*, by Stephen Warren. Reprinted by permission from Stephen Warren.

Chapter 9 Page 165, from "Eating Disorders: Anorexia and Bulimia Nervosa" from *Ask NOAH About: Mental Health* website http://noah.cuny.edu/wellconn/eatdisorders/html; page 166, "Antibiotics to X-rays: Century's Mind-Boggling Medical Milestones" from Associated Press, March 29, 1999. Reprinted by permission from Associated Press; page 167, from "Information on Prozac" from *Helsinki* website. http://www.psych. helsinki.fi/

janne/mood/prozac; page 168, "Satisfying, Low-Fat Breakfasts" by Tom Ney. From *Ask Chef Ney*. © by Women.com Networks; page 169, from "A Brief Introduction to Anorexia Nervosa" by Dr. Peter Rowan from The Priory Hospital website. http://www.priory-hospital.co.uk.htm.anorex.htm; page 169, "Fact Sheet: Bulimia Nervosa." From "Eating Disorders: Anorexia and Bulimia Nervosa" from *Ask NOAH About: Mental Health* website. http://noah.cuny.edu/wellconn/eatdisorders/html; page 170, "A List of Common Herbal Medications" by Kitturah B. Schomberg-Klaiss, D.O. From website: http://www.geocities.com/HotSprings/Villa/2617/herbal.htm. © by Yahoo, Inc. Reprinted by permission from Kitturah B. Schomberg-Klaiss, D.O.; page 171, "Forever Frazzled?" by Maya Bolton. Reprinted with permission from HEALTH, © 1998; page 175, "Understanding Obsessive-Compulsive Disorder" by Catherine Weiskopf. From *Current Health 2*, November 1998 issue, p. 19(1). Current Health®, Copyright © 1998 by Weekly Reader Corporation. All rights reserved; page 179, "An Armful of Agony: Treatment Options for Self-Mutilators" by Claudia Kalb. From *Newsweek*, November 9, 1998. © 1998 Newsweek, Inc. All rights reserved. Reprinted by permission.

Chapter 10 Page 186, from "Censorship and the Internet" by Craig Atkinson. From http://home.golden.net/craig/censor/essay/html; page 189, "MTV Censors KISS Video" by Marcus Errico, August 21, 1996. Used by permission from E! Online, http://www.eonline.com; page 189, Adapted from "What Johnny Can't Read: Censorship in American Libraries" by Suzanne Fisher Staples. From http://scholar.lib.vt.edu/ejournals/ALAN/winter96/pubCONN.html, April 13, 1999; page 190, "The Bonfire of the Liberties: Censorship of the Humanities" by Frances Leonard. Reprinted by permission from Frances Leonard, Director, Texas Humanities Resource Center; page 191, Excerpted from "Free Speech: Lyrics, Liberty and License" by Senator Sam Brownback; page 195, "Textbooks and Fairy Tales: The Value of Classic Myths" by Barbara Keeler. From *Los Angeles Times* January 14, 1990. Copyright, 1990, *Los Angeles Times*. Reprinted by permission; page 200, edited version (as attached) of "Stuff a Gag in the V-Chip" by Art Hilgart. From *The Humanist*, September–October 1997 issue, v57 n5 p3(1). Reprinted by permission of the author. Art Hilgart teaches at Western Michigan University and Kalamazoo College and produces the public radio program, "Broadway Revisited."

Chapter 11 Page 206, "The Man Who Counts the Killins" by Scott Stossel. From *The Atlantic Monthly*, May 1997. Reprinted by permission from Scott Stossel; page 210, "Does TV Affect Your Psyche" by Jay Kist. From *Current Health 2*, December 1996, v23 n4 p18(3). Special permission granted, *Current Health 2*® copyright © 1996, published by Weekly Reader Corporation. All rights reserved; page 213, "Roofies: Horror Drug of the 90s" by Judy Monroe. From *Current Health 2*, September 1997 issue, v24 n1 p24(3). Current Health®, Copyright © 1997 by Weekly Reader Corporation. All rights reserved.

Chapter 12   Page 217, selection titled "They Each Had a Gun" (as edited). From *Gun Control: Public Safety and the Right to Bear Arms* by Ted Gottfried. Copyright © 1993 by Ted Gottfried. Published by The Millbrook Press. Reprinted by permission from Ted Gottfried; page 225 (top), excerpted from "Card Tricks" by Carrie Coolidge. From FORBES, November 15, 1999, p. 288; page 225 (bottom), The first four paragraphs plus the first line from the fifth paragraph from "10 Things You Should Know Before Filing Bankruptcy" by Kelly Beamon. From *Black Enterprise*, March 1997, v27 n8 p9(4). Copyright 1997. Reprinted with permission of BLACK ENTERPRISE Magazine, New York, NY; page 227, "In Debt All the Way Up to Their Nose Rings" by Joshua Wolf Shenk. From *U.S. News & World Report*, June 9, 1997, v122 n22 p38 (2). Copyright, June 9, 1997, U.S. News & World Report. Visit us at our Web site at www.usnews.com for additional information; page 232, "Downsize Your Debt: Is Credit Card Debt Cramping Your Cash Flow? By Raising Your Prosperity Consciousness, You Can Ease the Money Squeeze and Get On The Path to Financial Freedom" by Glinda Bridgeforth. From *Essence Magazine*, September 1996, v27 n5 p91 (4). Reprinted by permission from Glinda Bridgeforth, author of the upcoming book, *Girl, Get Your Money Straight*, to be published by Broadway Books in January 2001; page 237, "Choose a Debt Consolidator Carefully" by Valerie Lynn Gray. From *Black Enterprise*, May 1997, v27 n10, p13(2). Copyright © 1997. Reprinted with permission from BLACK ENTERPRISE Magazine, New York, NY.

Chapter 13   Page 249, excerpted from "Looking for New Haunts: Larry Montz, Ghostbuster" by George Gurtner. From *New Orleans Magazine*, October 1996, v31 n1 p115(2); page 250, excerpted from "Etho-Geological Forecasting: Unusual Animal Behavior and Earthquake Prediction" by David Jay Brown. From website: http://www.levity.com/mavericks/quake.htm; page 250, "A Little Skepticism Would Be Healthy" by Al Seckel and Pat Linse, http://www.klab.caltech.edu. Reprinted by permission from Al Seckel; page 252, "Cryptozoologists try to separate strange fact from science fiction" by Leslie Alan Horvitz. From *Insight On The News*, January 27, 1997, v13 n3 p44 (2). Reprinted with permission from *Insight*. Copyright 1997 News World Communications, Inc. All rights reserved; page 253, "Crop Circles and Aliens: What's the Evidence" by Carl Sagan. From *Parade Magazine*, Sunday, December 3, 1995. Copyright © 1995 by Carl Sagan. Originally published in *Parade Magazine*. Reprinted with permission of the Estate of Carl Sagan and from PARADE Magazine; page 258, "Source of Mysterious Skyfalls Unknown" by Randall Floyd. From *The Augusta Chronicle* July 4, 1999. Reprinted by permission from Randall Floyd; page 261, "Spontaneous Human Combustion" from *The Skeptic's Dictionary* by Robert T. Carroll. Reprinted by permission from Robert Todd Carroll, Ph.D.

Chapter 14   Page 268, Chrysler advertisement, as attached. Reprinted by permission from Daimler Chrysler Corporation; page 270, Advertisement featuring Denzel Washington. Reprinted by permission from the Boys & Girls Club of America, National Headquarters, Atlanta, Georgia; page 271, Advertisement, as attached. Used with permission of General Motors Corporation; page 273, Pepto-Bismal advertisement, as attached. © The Procter and Gamble Company. Used by Permission; page 274, "Barbie" advertisement, as attached. Barbie© ad courtesy of Mattel, Inc.; page 275, "Simple Solutions" by Patrick G. Hays. Blue Cross Blue Shield advertisement. Reprinted by permission from BlueCross BlueShield Association; page 278, "Roach" advertisement. Reprinted by permission from the Partnership for a Drug-Free America. ®; page 280, Mutual of America advertisement, as attached. Reprinted by permission from Mutual of America.

Appendix   Page 292, 294, "Common Suffixes." From *The Complete Word Book: The Practical Guide to Anything and Everything You Need to Know About Words and How to Use Them* by Mary A. DeVries. Copyright 1991 by Mary A. DeVries. Published by Prentice Hall Business & Professional Division; page 293, "Common Roots" taken from *Word Mastery Made Simple* by A. Waldhorn and A. Zeiger and *College Vocabulary Skills* by James Shepherd.

Index